On the Road to Kandahar

By the Same Author

Al-Qaeda: Casting a Shadow of Terror (*published in a revised edition as* Al-Qaeda: The True Story of Radical Islam)

On the Road to Kandahar

Travels through Conflict in the Islamic World

JASON BURKE

Sandra,
with best wishes,
hope to see you
somewhere hot and
dusty soon,

Jason

ALLEN LANE
an imprint of
PENGUIN BOOKS

ALLEN LANE

Published by the Penguin Group
Penguin Books Ltd, 80 Strand, London WC2R 0RL, England
Penguin Group (USA) Inc., 375 Hudson Street, New York, New York 10014, USA
Penguin Group (Canada), 90 Eglinton Avenue East, Suite 700, Toronto, Ontario, Canada M4P 2Y3
(a division of Pearson Penguin Canada Inc.)
Penguin Ireland, 25 St Stephen's Green, Dublin 2, Ireland (a division of Penguin Books Ltd)
Penguin Group (Australia), 250 Camberwell Road,
Camberwell, Victoria 3124, Australia (a division of Pearson Australia Group Pty Ltd)
Penguin Books India Pvt Ltd, 11 Community Centre,
Panchsheel Park, New Delhi – 110 017, India
Penguin Group (NZ), cnr Airborne and Rosedale Roads, Albany,
Auckland 1310, New Zealand (a division of Pearson New Zealand Ltd)
Penguin Books (South Africa) (Pty) Ltd, 24 Sturdee Avenue,
Rosebank, Johannesburg 2196, South Africa

Penguin Books Ltd, Registered Offices: 80 Strand, London WC2R 0RL, England

www.penguin.com

First published 2006
1

Copyright © Jason Burke, 2006

The moral right of the author has been asserted

Set in Monotype Bembo
Typeset by Rowland Phototypesetting Ltd, Bury St Edmunds, Suffolk
Printed in Great Britain by Clays Ltd, St Ives plc

A CIP catalogue record for this book is available from the British Library

HARDBACK
ISBN-13: 978–0–713–99896–2
ISBN-10: 0–713–99896–2

TRADE PAPERBACK
ISBN-13: 978–0–713–99947–1
ISBN-10: 0–713–99947–0

For my parents

and for the victims of the bombings
in London on 7 July 2005

'I have always dreamed,' he mouthed, fiercely, 'of a band of men absolute in their resolve to discard all scruples in the choice of means, strong enough to give themselves frankly the name of destroyers, and free from that taint of resigned pessimism that rots the earth. No pity for anything on earth, including themselves, and death enlisted for good and all in the service of humanity — that's what I would have liked to see.'

Joseph Conrad, *The Secret Agent*

'I have been called a sentimentalist. It's true. I was a journalist because, when I got up in the morning and read the paper, there were pieces of news in it that angered me. I wanted to express my anger as clearly as possible, but I was unable to do much more than that. I certainly didn't have a theory, much less a comprehensive ideology. I didn't want to go beyond the limits of what I was sure of. So I was considered unconstructive, irresolute, and a petty moderate. Still, I don't think I am ready to compromise on what makes me angry.'

Albert Camus

Contents

List of Maps   xi

Introduction: I Was a Teenage Guerrilla   1

1 The Shrine and the Fire   21

2 Afghan Summer   41

3 Afghan Autumn   58

4 The House of Wisdom   78

5 The First Boy Was Shot at Around Three O'clock   95

6 A Short War in the Hindu Kush   116

7 Afghan Winter   129

8 Aftermath   140

9 Back to Kurdistan   156

10 Secrets and Lies   172

11 The Magical Misery Tour   189

12 The Debacle   206

13 Miss Sixty   224

14 A Centre of Gravity   243

Conclusion: London and Pakistan   265

A Guide to Further Reading   283
Glossary   287
Acknowledgements   293
Index   295

Maps

1 Afghanistan and Pakistan   xii
2 Iraq   xv
3 The Islamic World   xvi

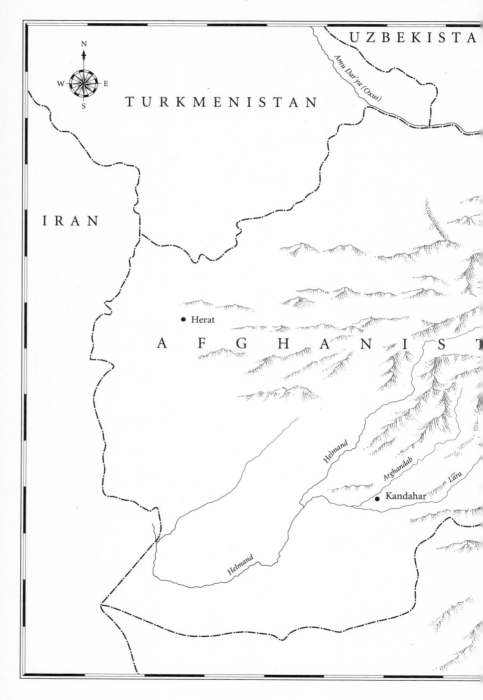

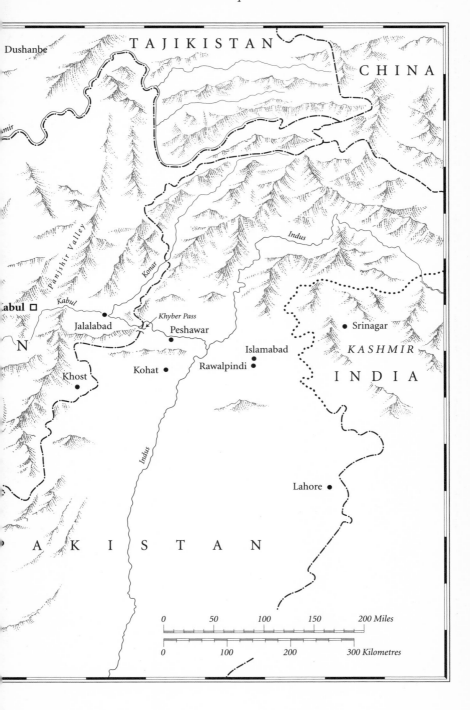

Dushanbe

TAJIKISTAN

CHINA

Indus

Panjshir Valley

Konar

Kabul

Kabul □

Jalalabad

Khyber Pass

Peshawar

Srinagar

Islamabad

KASHMIR

N

Khost

Kohat

Rawalpindi

INDIA

Indus

Lahore

PAKISTAN

| 0 | 50 | 100 | 150 | 200 Miles |

| 0 | 100 | 200 | 300 Kilometres |

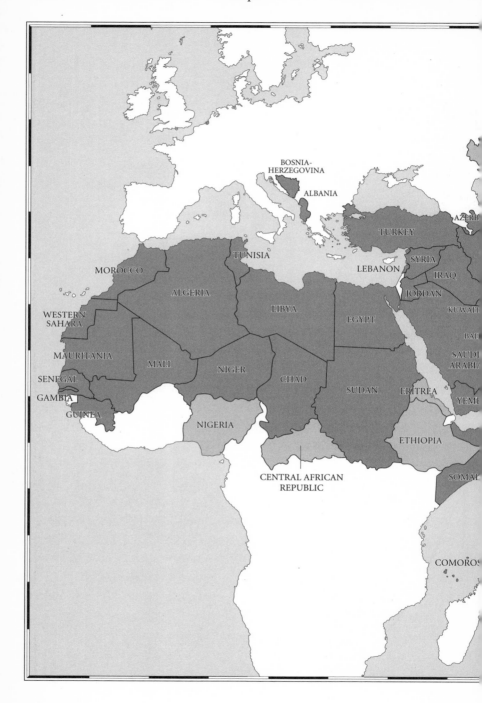

Majority Muslim

Strong Muslim presence
but not a majority

Introduction: I Was a Teenage Guerrilla

We buried the letter at the bottom of one of our bags and left the next morning, travelling west in a local bus on a bad road that led across high hills with slopes of pines broken by slabs of grey rock. Where there was shadow there were strands of dirty snow and, with the chill that came with evening, it was clear why so many refugees had died in the mountains when they had fled earlier in the year. We stopped overnight in a small village set on the lip of a deep gorge and stayed in a roadside hostel where we slept on the floor and were woken several times by gunfire. In the morning we ate thin yoghurt with warm bread and drank tea the colour of polished copper from small glasses and watched impassive local villagers lead heavily equipped troops through their fields and up into the higher hills. There was a 'big operation' underway against the guerrillas, we were told. By the afternoon we were out of the mountains and on a straightening road down to the plains. There we were to give the letter to a man in the refugee camp in the desert outside the frontier town where several thousand families lived on United Nations aid. We found the man, who opened the letter, read it and told us that the best way to cross the border was simply to take a taxi. It would cost about $10 and take less than an hour. We were very disappointed.

Sometimes, when drunk or desperate to impress, I tell people I fought as a teenage guerrilla. It's not entirely true. I wasn't a teenager, I was 21. And, though I did carry a gun, I didn't fight. In fact, on the few occasions shooting started, I hid in a ditch.

It was the summer of 1991. Saddam Hussein's ill-judged attempt to seize Kuwait and its oil had ended in swift and predictable defeat by an American-led military coalition a few months previously. In the war's aftermath, the Shia Muslim population of the south of Iraq rebelled, swiftly followed by the Kurds living in the north.

Both believed that they would be supported by the allies. But the allies had stood by while Saddam's tanks and helicopters dealt first with the Shias and then pushed the Kurds back into their historic mountain strongholds in a series of bloody battles which prompted more than a million refugees to head to the Turkish and Iranian borders. In all, at least a hundred thousand died.

To start with there was little that distinguished my trip, with a friend from university called Iain, from that of any other pair of second-year undergraduates backpacking round Europe. We hitched across Turkey, drank too much Efes beer and were delayed for some time in a cheap hotel in Cappadocia by two Danish girls. But on reaching Van, a city in the east of the country, the half-formed plan that neither of us had really discussed, though we both knew existed, began to emerge. We started, relatively carefully, contacting people who we thought might be able to help us meet the PKK, the local Kurdish Marxist guerrillas, then seven years into an insurgency in the mountains of southeastern Turkey. In fact, to have met them would have been very dangerous and we were gently persuaded of this by a carpet salesman in Van's main bazaar, who pointed out that the group had a habit of taking Western tourists hostage. He suggested an alternative: crossing the border into Iraq. There, in the north, the Kurds were on the brink of setting up a genuine independent state. This was more or less what we had hoped to do anyway.

He told us that we would have to travel to Hakkari, a rough and ready town 100 or so miles away, go to the Hotel Umit, ask for 'Achmed' and say that 'Apple' had sent us. We took the bus, found the old hotel not far from the centre of town and told Achmed about Apple. If the melodrama amused him, Achmed showed no sign of it. Within an hour we had been handed the sealed letter in a mouldy hotel room by two taciturn men who neither removed their overcoats nor sat down during the hour we spent with them. In the square outside Turkish troops jumped down from trucks and fanned out through streets full of market stalls, goats and old jeeps. From there, with our letter safely stowed, we headed through the mountains and down to the plains, the refugee camp and the border.

I had never been in a refugee camp before. It was noon and the sun came straight down and the dust blew hard across the open spaces between the tents. A crowd of women and children with an astonishing variety of containers jostled around a water tanker. I asked Iain if the lemon juice I had squeezed into my hair was making it blond and me more like the sun-bleached combat veteran I hoped to resemble. He said no. Because there was no post and telephones were too expensive several refugees gave us letters to deliver to friends and family which I promptly left in the taxi that took us to the border with Iraq the next morning. En route we passed an American base with long lines of armoured vehicles in neat ranks. At the border there were Kurdish soldiers, looking impossibly romantic in their beards, chequered headdresses, traditional baggy trousers, wide cummerbund-style belts and square tunic tops. A ragged banner slung over a portrait of Saddam Hussein that had been shot to pieces told us that we had entered Iraqi Kurdistan.

I would like to be able to say that I had a consuming interest in the Kurds and had wanted to be part of their struggle for a long time. I can't, however. I ended up with the peshmerga, or 'those who face death', as the Kurdish irregular soldiers are known, for a variety of reasons, none particularly noble but all fairly common to young men. I went to Iraq because I did not want to go backpacking in Thailand again or work in a supermarket ware-house all summer as I had done the year before, because I had just split up with my first serious girlfriend and wanted to make a point, and, perhaps most of all, because I hoped for some good stories to tell in the college bar. As I had wanted to be a journalist since I was 15 and had watched the pictures of the air assault on Iraq and the 'hundred-hour war' that succeeded it on a small black and white TV in the rented house I shared with five other students through the previous winter, I could dress up what was basically a post-adolescent adventure as a rather extreme form of work experience. During the spring I had read and re-read the biography of Don McCullin, the great British war photographer whose iconic black and white images and troubled personal life seemed to me to be tragic, romantic, compassionate and harsh in equal measure.

I bought a lot of film, took two very old cameras and a couple of lenses and a notebook and decided that Iraq was where I would make my name.

By the time Iain and I arrived there, in July, the military situation had almost stablized. The fighting in the south of the country was long over. In the north, the Western troops who had guarded a 'safe haven' inside Iraqi territory, warding off Iraqi air or ground attacks, had just pulled back on to Turkish territory. Their immediate task, which was humanitarian rather than military, had been completed. With aircraft stationed in Turkey providing a 'protective umbrella' over what was to become the Kurdish enclave in the foothills and plains of the mountains along Iraq's northern border, the Gulf War appeared to be effectively over. In fact the withdrawal of the allied troops, a few days before Iain and I arrived in the country, had been marked by a series of sharp engagements which threatened to shatter the tentative truce that had been established between Kurdish forces and the Iraqis over previous weeks. We knew nothing of any of this, having barely read the newspapers or listened to the radio as we made our way through Turkey. Somehow we did not think it necessary to keep up with exactly what was happening. In fact, we were almost completely ignorant of all but the roughest outline of the history of northern Iraq, its people, their cultures or society. We had read the newspapers, or at least a few of them, during the spring and seen the pictures of the Kurdish exodus from northern Iraq in the first weeks of the uprising but little more. Nor did we know anything much about Iraq or indeed the Islamic world more generally. We were also almost entirely ignorant of Islam but, in the tradition of Western travellers to the region, we did not think that would present much of a problem.

We learned to shoot on a hill outside Dohuk, a city thirty miles south of the border with Turkey. A family of refugees standing in the apricot glow of the evening light in front of their makeshift shack watched us without much emotion. Jets left a lattice of vapour trails high in the clear sky above us but we could not tell if they were Iraqi or allied planes. We were shown how to fire on automatic and on single shot, how to aim when prone and crouching, and were firmly told never to fire from the hip or when standing upright. We were shown how to switch magazines and slide back the stiff bolt to bring a round up into the chamber and how to take the gun apart, clean it and reassemble it. The session ended with a quick reminder to look out for mines and with 'the naming of the parts' in both major Kurdish dialects, English and, for the sake of variation, German, Turkish, Farsi and Arabic. For a very short period I knew the word for 'safety catch' and 'firing pin' in about six languages.

The unit was led by Firyad Barzani, a relative of Masud Barzani, the leader of the Kurdish Democratic Party or KDP, the larger of the two major factions in northern Iraq. Firyad, who was in his early thirties, had been introduced to us the day before when we had presented ourselves at the local KDP office as volunteers. He cut a dapper figure in his sharply pressed tunic and trousers, open-necked shirt and cummerbund with its seven interlocking links, neat, swift stride and handgun holstered on his hip. He was pleased with the training, particularly when we actually hit one of the targets set up for us. That evening, as we ate dinner in the abandoned schoolhouse that was serving as a temporary base, Firyad tried to teach us the Kurdish national anthem. The words, almost a parody of a nationalist guerrilla army's marching songs, were difficult to take seriously.

'Nobody should say the Kurds are dead because the Kurds are alive,' the anthem ran. 'Our banner shall never be lowered, Our homeland is our faith and religion, We are the heroes of revolution and the colour red, Just look how bloodstained our history is, The Kurdish people are gallantly standing to attention, Ready to decorate their living crown with blood. The Kurdish youth is ever present and ready to sacrifice their lives.'

It was not just the language of the national anthem that made us smile. The peshmerga fulfilled almost every quality of the stereotypical guerrilla. They were astonishingly impressive men, but comical too. They marched for miles with impossible loads on little food, they voiced the most astounding platitudes about 'the struggle' and 'the soil', they rarely bothered cleaning their weapons which, wrapped in their red chequered headscarves, they used, as all self-respecting irregular fighters should, as pillows. This amused us, possibly more than it should have done. We laughed openly at one peshmerga, a huge man with long drooping moustaches and a mass of bullet belts wrapped around his enormous chest armed with a light machine gun and an AK47 and a long bayonet. For their part, the peshmerga were hospitable and open. They were interested in us, happy that students from so far away should come and be a part of their struggle. But our lives were a mystery to them. Most of the peshmerga were farmers or manual labourers in peacetime and had little concept of the world beyond their villages, let alone overseas.

Firyad led our group south and east, following the high roads in the foothills of the mountains away from the Iraqi troops on the plains. We had no map and, as Saddam had banned any local cartography, none was available. As a result Iain and I had almost no idea where we were. There had been little in the way of excitement, just some more target practice and a martial arts demonstration and a parade on a mountain pass for a group of the KDP's senior commanders. The lack of action did not bother us. Simply being in Iraq, waking at dawn for breakfasts of yoghurt and flatbread, the broken Kurdish we were trying to learn, the constant presence of the weapons around us, the veterans' stories of combat and forced marches and air raids, the photographs and notes that I hoped would somehow make my name as a journalist, was enough. Most of the men had been wounded at least once. Mustafa, a tall, bespectacled, highly educated and serious man, a middle-ranking political official whom we called 'the commissar', pulled up his shirt one evening to show us the neat entry wound on his belly and the massively scarred exit wound on his back, as big as a hand, caused by the two bullets that had struck him several years before. Neither Iain nor I had any great wish to be blooded in combat.

July had turned to August by the time we reached the Lesser Zab river. It was late in the afternoon and the dust had dropped with the heat and we crossed the river on a giant raft packed with men and trucks and material. Brown scrubby hills, deforested by centuries of war and overgrazing, lay along the northern skyline. To the south the flat expanse of Lake Dokan shone greasily in the sun like fish scales. A dirt road coiled around a sharp crag and led up to a plateau beyond, several miles square. The plateau was almost entirely covered in rubble – the remains of Qala Diza, a town of 70,000 people that had been completely destroyed by Iraqi army engineers in a three-week-long operation the year before. There was no reason for making the detour to the site of the town but Firyad had, not unreasonably, wanted to show us, the day-trippers, exactly what had happened there. Until then little had been said by the peshmerga about the violence done to the Kurds over the preceding few years and I had little idea about the reality of what had happened to them.

Yet the scene at Qala Diza was peaceful. Among the grey ruins children ran and played, off-duty peshmerga walked with arms full of watermelon and AK47s over their shoulders, women in white headscarves and bright red traditional dresses embroidered with sequins, beads and embroidery cooked on open fires as the men sat on lumps of broken masonry and smoked hand-rolled cigarettes. Someone had painted 'Why?' on one of the huge cracked slabs of concrete, the remnants of roofs, which lay across much of the landscape. The Iraqi army engineers had left the trees standing and the high poplars and cedars rose from among the piles of rubble alongside stands of tangled and rusted reinforcing rods. In an angle formed by two of the collapsed roofs, Qala Diza's pharmacist had set up a makeshift clinic, piling his small cache of medical supplies in a corner and laying a single thin mattress on the bare earth. Qala Diza had no sanitation system, a single well and, inevitably, widespread gastro-enteric illness, particularly among the young. The pharmacist, astonishingly neat in a clean white short-sleeved shirt and traditional baggy trousers, was worried about cholera. He had salvaged a battered stand for an intravenous drip which stood next to the single mattress, though there was no bottle, tube or solutions to go with it. Near by a young girl in a bright red dress swept the dirt in front of the pile of stones that had once been her two-storey house and smiled when I took her picture.

A few days later we visited the eastern town of Halabjah where 5,000 people had died in a chemical weapons attack three years earlier. The town had been flattened four months after being gassed. A swarm of dirty, ragged children mobbed our pick-up truck when they saw Iain and me sitting in the back, even though we were surrounded by armaments. They thought we had come to hand out food. I remember an old man standing in the rubble wearing a black chequered kaffiyeh and a dry smile. 'Tell your people about us,' he said to me. 'Tell your people what happened here.' In the end I told the *Daily Mail*, which spiked the story, and my local paper, which published it and paid me £50.

While our unit had been based near Qala Diza, fierce fighting had broken out again in Suleimaniyah, fifty miles away. In several days of running street battles the peshmerga, who had briefly held the city in late March and early April, had won back control of it from Saddam's troops. When we arrived there was still incessant gunfire, though the main combat was over. The first move by our group, which varied between a dozen and thirty men, was to set down our weapons in a park, borrow bats and a ball from a nearby house and engage in an impromptu table tennis tournament on two concrete tables that stood, incongruously intact, among the rubble. A mile or so away we could hear what sounded like a fairly intense firefight.

In retrospect I can see why we were kept out of any real combat. First, most of the ongoing fighting was being done by peshmerga from the Patriotic Union of Kurdistan, the rival group to the KDP. At the time I was unaware of the intense competition between the two parties. Second, Firyad's orders were clearly to use us, two young enthusiasts from the West supposedly transported by our admiration for the Kurds, as a mobile peshmerga propaganda unit. This explained, at least in part, why we had been dragged round so many different front lines and had met so many troops. His job was to expose us to enough danger to give us some credibility in the eyes of the fighters but, above all, to keep us alive. Third, it must have been abundantly clear to everybody that if we had got

caught up in any genuine fighting, we would have been a total
liability. On my first evening in Suleimaniyah, unused to the local
moonshine, I had left our group drinking to find a quiet corner in
which to throw up. I had staggered down a street and was leaning
against a wall when someone started shooting and, like dogs bark-
ing at night, gunmen all over the city seemed to join in. It was
pitch black and the unit, Iain and all the weapons were hundreds
of yards away. As the firefight continued around me I knelt,
oblivious, on a pavement, bile in my throat, palms on my thighs,
wanting only that everyone should go away so I could empty my
stomach in peace. On the odd occasion that we did fire our
weapons, the noise generated by a Kalashnikov on fully automatic
was such that we were deafened for days. The thought of actually
having to reload while actually under fire, fumbling for a new clip
with sweating hands, was terrifying. It was very clear that a happy
and comfortable middle-class upbringing in a leafy part of north
London close to Hampstead Heath, with a trip to Hendon library
with my father every three weeks and physical activity limited to
soccer at school and the odd hiking trip, did not make for natural
soldiering ability. Nor was Iain, who came from a small village in
Gloucestershire, much better off.

We made an odd pair. When we were photographed with our
peshmerga unit, Iain, 6' 4" and easily the tallest, always stood at
the back, his blond hair under a chequered scarf. I, shorter and
darker, stood or knelt near the front, my arms around men of a
similar build either side of me, rifle over my shoulder. Neither of
us was particularly confident, with all the usual insecurities of a
21-year-old male, but where I compensated by working on my
steely gaze, worldly cynicism and what I hoped was a brooding, if
somewhat slender, muscularity, Iain smiled incessantly; where I
affected detachment and professionalism, gun in one hand, camera
in the other, Iain projected a whimsical eccentricity. Together, we
felt, we made a good team. And we were both full of curiosity,
excitement, nervous energy and humour. Thankfully, we were
also sufficiently mature to realize the completely artificial nature
of the roles we were playing. We were both vastly amused when

we were able to buy postcards bearing the legend 'Greetings from Iraq' and find someone travelling to Turkey who was able to send them home for us. One went to the college bar, another to the girl who had dumped me a few months before.

The final capture of Suleimaniyah by the Kurds changed the whole dynamic on the ground, putting the Iraqis on the defensive. Over the previous weeks the peshmerga and Saddam's troops, largely conscripts, had avoided fighting each other. Now the de facto truces that rival local commanders had established with each other throughout Kurdistan began to break down. Driving down one road near the city, our unit was suddenly caught up in a huge Iraqi armoured column. The soldiers were so stunned to see a single pick-up full of peshmerga suddenly in their midst that they did nothing and we were able to escape unharmed. But at a nearby checkpoint, manned by Iraqi soldiers who had let us pass unhindered in the past, we ran into more trouble. Firyad and his men had to struggle hard to get us through and for a short time it looked as if they might not actually prevail. Suddenly acutely aware of our lack of Iraqi visas and very conscious of what might happen if things went wrong, Iain and I agreed it was time to head home. Getting ourselves kidnapped was not part of our plan.

It happened like this. We were in the border town of Zakho, looking to get back to Turkey and talking to a group of men sitting outside a shop. One of their friends was driving across the border and halfway to Istanbul, they said. It was about 7 p.m. He'd give us a lift in a couple of hours, they said. With hindsight the whole thing stank. No one was driving anywhere in northern Iraq after sunset at the time, least of all across the border and into Turkey. But we were students and the prospect of a free ride was very tempting. So we drank warm Coke and waited. After an hour the men suggested some dinner at a hotel near by. We politely declined. They insisted. We still said no. They showed us, very amiably, their slick-looking handguns, quite unlike any other weaponry we had seen in northern Iraq, and hinted heavily that we should get in their car, an old black Mercedes. We did not seem to have a great deal of choice. We got in and were driven to a hotel on the outskirts of Zakho, and put in a bedroom. The sun was setting outside and we could see the lights coming on in the city through a window with a thick wire grille over it. We were both very frightened. The men came back to check on us periodically and each time they made sure we saw their guns. But they were drinking and on each occasion they returned they were more inebriated. It was nearly midnight when one of them drunkenly left the door to the room unlocked. We carefully opened it and stepped into a long, narrow corridor, lit as harshly as a hospital. We crept along it, found a side door that was also unlocked, slipped through it, went round the back of the hotel, through a stand of pine trees and, walking swiftly and then running, headed down a long slope to a bridge that led over a river and into twisting back streets.

What followed was either farce or film noir or both. Our escape had been quickly noticed and we soon realized that a car was tracking us through the streets. Caught once in the open, we saw it was the big, black Mercedes. We would run down one street, double back and then head down another. Then we would see its headlights sliding along a wall ahead of us and we would flatten ourselves into a doorway. The lights would flicker past us and the car would move on. We would head down a different alley, only to find the headlights swinging round in front of us again. This went on for some time. I don't remember seeing anyone else on the streets at all. Nor do I remember any fear, just a lot of adrenaline, a fierce determination to avoid the Mercedes and whatever it contained, combined with a sense that the whole situation was too ludicrous, too cinematic, to be in any way dangerous. Finally, with a magnificent sense of the dramatic, we were pinioned by headlights against a wall in a blind alley. We had nowhere to run. But this time it wasn't the Mercedes. It was a landcruiser full of peshmerga.

I did not think about the faith of the Kurds until much later. Their religion had not been obvious to me. The slogans of the guerrillas, their nationalist and revolutionary rhetoric, had obscured the less obvious signs of what was actually a profound, if tolerant and moderate, faith. Had I asked, all the Kurds would have stated with pride that they were Muslims. Had I looked, I would have seen the amulets that many of the peshmerga from the rural areas wore round their necks. Had I listened a little closer and understood a little more, I would have known that saying inshallah, or God willing, was not simply 'fatalistic' but a manifestation of a culture in which religion is very present. I did not notice the religion because the Kurds did not look like the Muslims I had imagined. They were not fanatical, they did not wear white robes along with their kaffiyehs, they were open and engaging and literate and worldly; in short, they were everything I hoped I was. As a result, almost unconsciously, I had decided that they were not Muslims at all.

Since that summer in Iraq, I have spent many years travelling, living and working in the Islamic world, from Morocco to south-west China, from Uzbekistan to Malaysia. I have spent years living in Pakistan and Afghanistan, at least a year in Iraq, have eaten noodles with Thai Muslims and couscous with Algerian muja-hideen, drunk tea with Berbers in the Atlas Mountains and coffee with the Acehnese, argued with hardline Taliban mullahs, mystic Sufi teachers, Pakistani holy men who doubled as feudal landlords and corrupt Palestinian politicians. I have drunk beer with Iraqi poets and whisky with Indian bankers, Mecca Cola with Kashmiri militants and tea with (aspirant or failed) suicide bombers of various nationalities, and I can now see that the trip to Kurdistan was the beginning of a long process of learning, the lesson of which has been that the term 'the Islamic world' does not describe a uniform monolith where odd creatures called Muslims live their lives according to an arcane and reactionary religion but a huge, varied and dynamic spiritual, cultural and political entity that defies defi-nition geographically, ethnically or racially. Experience has also taught me to be aware, not only of my own preconceptions, but of all generalizations.

Some of the Muslims I have met did indeed believe that the Koran, the Muslim holy book, was a genuine blueprint for society that can and should be realized on earth. Others loved and admired the prophet Mohammed and his teachings but understood the impossibility of implementing them in the modern world. Some were without genuine 'faith', but were sustained by and proud of the shared cultural and historical heritage of Islam. Few even performed all of the five fundamental acts, none too onerous, that define a Muslim as laid down at the faith's start 1,300 years ago: praying five times a day, performing the pilgrimage to Mecca (the hajj), giving alms, fasting during Ramadan, the holy month, and bearing witness that 'there is no God but Allah and Mohammed is his prophet'. Fewer still sought the expansion of their religion across the world. A very large number felt defensive, worried about the impact of what they saw as an aggressive and belligerent 'West' on their cultures and societies. But an equally large proportion, indeed often the same people, were attracted and inspired by 'the West' too. Few were drawn to violence. 'Islam', I slowly came to realize, is a label that can be applied to many things and adequately describes none of them.

The 1990s saw 'Islam' slowly creeping up the global agenda. At the beginning of the decade, in the aftermath of the collapse of communism, it had been questions of nationalism and ethnic identity, especially in the Balkans and the former Soviet states that had dominated debate. There were also arguments about 'post-conflict intervention', peacekeeping, nation building and similar issues that had surfaced as the international community, individually and collectively, sought ways of structuring, influencing and living in the new post-Cold War world order. Political scientists spoke of the end of History, not in the sense of an end to events, but as a way of explaining the triumph of American or Western liberal democracy and the societies that had produced it. The new push to globalization and the interconnectivity allowed by liberalized capital markets and advances in communications technology seemed only to confirm the planetary dominance of the package of ideas, economic theories, moral and ethical norms and culture by which, broadly speaking, 'the West' defines itself.

Yet towards the end of the decade it became clear that there were many who were deeply suspicious of the dominance of this

one, fairly particular, version of modernity and 'progress'. Some
saw it as an extension of a process of Western imperialism that had
been underway for several centuries. Many hoped to construct an
alternative that might more closely match their interests, cultures
and societies. There was the anti-globalization movement and,
drawing on far more profound social and intellectual roots, there
was religion. The dawn of a new millennium (at least according
to the Christian calendar) saw a resurgence of religious funda-
mentalism, the belief that the only true, just and godly way to structure a society is based on the actual implementation of a rigorous,
literal and usually highly selective reading of holy texts. In India,
Hindu fundamentalists were at the height of their power; in America
their Christian counterparts were more influential than they had
been for decades. Radical Jewish fundamentalists held the balance
of power in Israel despite their small, though growing, numbers.
Then, of course, the 9/11 attacks brought Islamic fundamentalists,
who had been major players on a regional stage for thirty years or
more, to global notice in a horrible and spectacular way.

Since then there has been a huge amount written and said about
Islam in general and Islamic militancy in particular. When I returned from covering the war in Afghanistan of autumn 2001, I was
shocked to find that the nature of the causes of the 9/11 attacks had
been badly misunderstood. For a whole variety of reasons, ranging
from the mendacity of various governments through to long-
standing social and cultural preconceptions about the nature of
violent religious and political action, the September 11 attacks
were being attributed to a shadowy, tightly structured radical militant group called al-Qaeda, led by a terrorist mastermind named
Osama bin Laden. This group, it was widely said, was responsible
for violence all over the world. Dozens of long-running mili-
tancies, with profound roots in social, economic, cultural and
religious factors in the Islamic world and beyond, were simply
being dismissed as the work of one crazy Saudi dissident and a few
of his acolytes. I was sufficiently angered by the intellectual laziness
of such analyses and sufficiently concerned by their potential consequences to write my first book, which was published in early

summer 2003 and examined the structure of contemporary Islamic militancy while exploring some of its ideological and historical roots. Al-Qaeda, I said, was an idea, not an organization.

One of the main problems that faced me when writing that book was a lack of accurate terms for the phenomenon I was describing. As a result I devoted a considerable proportion of its 300-odd pages to showing how the word 'al-Qaeda' was misunderstood and wrongly applied. This problem of terminology still exists. The vocabulary to describe the new situation we find ourselves in and the threat we face is still evolving. We often speak of 'the Islamic world' and 'the West' without really thinking about what we mean. The terms imply some kind of absolute division between the two, a division that no one who pauses to consider the sheer diversity of languages, cuisines, economic linkages, the population composition, diplomatic connections and political systems that lace our complex modern world together can genuinely think exists. I too have used 'the Islamic world' and 'the West' repeatedly, not least because no other convenient labels exist. However, I hope that, in this book's pages, it will become obvious how much people share across the world and how factors such as gender, age, music, sport, even spirituality and formal religious belief, make any attempt at division of the world into two or more distinct 'civilizational blocs' arbitrary and ridiculous.

But the misconception of al-Qaeda was only part of the problem. There was also a wave of appallingly misinformed statements on Islam or 'the Islamic world' in general. The huge variety of practice, belief and observation in Muslim-dominated societies, so much of it fused with local cultures and conditions, so textured and so complex, was reduced, in much of the debate among non-Muslims, to a single stereotype that was based on a vision of the most conservative, the most rigorous and the most belligerent interpretation of the faith. A single thread of a huge and rich tapestry had been drawn out and declared representative of the whole. All major religions have resources within them that can be exploited for different uses, belligerent or pacific, tolerant or intolerant, yet it was a minority strand within a minority strand, epitomized by Osama bin Laden and his fellow extremists, men who mined Islam for all that was most inflexible, violent and bitter, that stood for the faith in the dark days following the atrocity of the attacks on New York and Washington. Nor was it just radical right-wingers or religious conservatives in America who felt that there was an existential battle underway between good and evil, right and wrong, truth and falsehood. Several colleagues and friends of mine made little effort to disguise their view that Islam was a backward religion and that 'Muslims' were a clear and present danger to all the basic values of liberal democracy. This too shocked, concerned and angered me. It also saddened me greatly.

Perhaps the most depressing characteristic of the clash-of–civilizations argument, which would be ironically amusing if it were not so dangerous, is the coincidence in views and ideas of its proponents both in the Islamic world and in the West. In the West newspaper columnists talk about 'the Islamic world' as a monolith, Muslim conservatives make similar statements about 'the American-led West'. There is talk of 'the Arab' or 'the Islamic' mindset on one side, Western, Christian or Jewish 'mind' on the other. In the West, American senators talk of bombing Mecca as a reprisal for attacks on the USA while in Saudi Arabia and elsewhere radicals talk of bombing America as a reprisal for attacks in Palestine, Chechnya, Kashmir, Iraq and Afghanistan. And all of them believe they belong to a discrete religiously defined group that must battle violently in a Hobbesian competition for the earth's scarce moral, intellectual and physical resources and that they are engaged in a last-ditch, gloves-off, no–holds–barred battle against a fanatical and irrational enemy which is aggressive, belligerent and intent on expansion until all alternative cultures, societies and belief systems are eradicated. All deploy a range of spurious historical and cultural references to justify what are fundamentally prejudiced and ignorant views and all twist actuality to fit their ideas.

These debates and issues are raised many times, in a variety of ways, in the pages that follow. There are other elements too that recur again and again. There are many examples of the different ways in which the resources within Islam are deployed, possibly consciously, possibly unconsciously, by individuals looking for consolation, empowerment or a means to unite, radicalize and mobilize others. There are many episodes that examine the complex process by which radical ideas gain purchase among a broader population, the two-way relationship between the propagandist and the propagandized and the critical role spectacular public violence can play. Another key theme is the role of myth – the deliberate or accidental distortion of historical fact – in determining how individuals see their world and how leaders make decisions that have extraordinarily significant consequences. One of my first lessons in the way history could be pillaged and then deployed to become a critical part of the mindset of individuals, communities and nations had come in Kurdistan where Kurdish officials regularly cited Salah al-Din, the Kurdish-born warrior-king who liberated Jerusalem from the Crusaders in 1187, as a Kurdish nationalist. Yet Saladin had fought for himself, Islam and the Arabs, and had shown no interest in his Kurdish identity at all. When, later, I began to study the statements of Islamic militants, who also attempted to appropriate the life and deeds of the ecumenical and religiously tolerant Salah al-Din, I saw again how history could be made to serve the ends and means of men.

Back at the time of the first Gulf War, there was also plenty to make me aware of the similar exploitation, through exaggeration, outright suppression or selective amnesia, of more contemporary events. In the run-up to the conflict there had been a huge amount of publicity about the chemical weapons strike at Halabjah. In 1990 the US-led allies, after years of denying Saddam's culpability in human rights abuses, suddenly began discovering evidence of the Iraqi dictator's evil nature and the horror of the regime they had previously backed. And as they changed tack so did their ideological enemies. Many on the left eulogized Saddam as a David standing against an American-led global capitalist Goliath, often even drawing, with no appreciable awareness of the irony, on the same erroneous sources used by the right during the 1980s. It was the best training I could have received for a career in journalism.

For a long time I saw such rhetoric as harmless. But in recent years it has become evident that ideologically charged analysis has consequences which affect the lives of billions in a very direct way. The time it took for people and policymakers to understand the truth about al-Qaeda was a critical delay that significantly hindered the struggle against terrorism. Many of the reasons behind the decision to go to war in Iraq in 2003, a war that was drastically counterproductive in terms of the overall strategy to counter modern Islamic militancy, can be traced to the failure to understand the true nature of the phenomenon of modern Muslim radicalism. Much of the terrible mishandling of the subsequent occupation can be attributed to the triumph of ideology over an open and unprejudiced assessment of the facts.

As a working journalist, I have been deeply involved in the process of the representation of the 'Islamic world' and cannot pretend to be blameless. No one, of course, can fully appreciate all sides of the issue and I do not claim to be able to. My view has been personal and often from the ground. It is usually true that the closer you get to something, particularly war, the less you know. But on the other hand direct experience can be invaluable for judging what actually happened and, perhaps as importantly, what others think of what happened. You hear what they say; you see, sometimes, what they see. Splitting my time between the West and the Islamic world over the last decade or so has shown me how the same events, contemporary or historic, can be viewed in a wide variety of ways or, in the case of those who believe in a clash of civilizations, in a tragically similar fashion.

This book is not meant to be a comprehensive history and analysis of the myriad factors that have determined the course of radical Islam and the response of the world to it in recent years. Attempts to reduce a phenomenon such as Islamic militancy, with so many varied manifestations all based in specific local and political and historical contexts, to a single overarching theory are bound to fail anyway. Nor do simplistic analyses of the response to the threat by governments and populations around the globe help much either. We live in an astonishingly complex world and easy, simple answers do not necessarily help us make sense of it.

When I first drafted this introduction, in the spring of 2005, I wrote that I had enjoyed the privilege of a front-row seat for many of the most astonishing, epoch-making events of the last few years and that I was deeply grateful for the opportunity to see what I had seen. I wrote that I was profoundly aware that I had only ever been part of the audience and that I knew that I was watching real people with real emotions and real lives who, unlike me, could not flip their notebooks shut, say thank you and go home at the end of the working day to a safe, developed, democratic home. The book, I wrote, was primarily about them. But then, on 7 July 2005 four suicide bombers killed more than fifty people in London, my own city, on the transport system that I have used for my entire life, narrowly missing a number of my friends and family. I too found myself spending terrible hours ringing my sister's silent mobile phone before hearing that she was safe. And then I realized that the book I was writing was not about 'them' at all, but, in this global era, of globalized cities and globalized faiths and globalized militant movements, it was about us.

We did not see the black Mercedes again. The Kurdish fighters drove us through the deserted back streets of Zakho and dropped us at a cheap hostel where we slept on the roof on rope beds. At dawn we did what we should have done the night before and got a taxi north, back to the border, back through the checkpoints and back into Turkey where we spent a week on the beach and then headed home to the UK. I finished my degree, went backpacking in India and spent five years reporting local and then domestic British news. But the time I had spent in Iraq had had a profound effect on me and in the early spring of 1998 I resigned from the national newspaper I was working for and headed to Pakistan.

1. The Shrine and the Fire

Just behind my apartment in Islamabad was a plot of land covered in mimosa trees, wild cannabis and scrubby, prickly bushes. It was a graveyard and though no one tended it or came to grieve at the dozen or so mounds of earth which lay among the rubbish under the trees, no one built on it either – though the potential for profitable development of such a prime piece of urban real estate was high. It had been there for a hundred years or more and the most modern and most secular of Pakistan's cities had grown up around it like grass growing around a stone. Though it was now surrounded by vast white villas built by the nouveau riche and broad tree-lined roads and embassies and big private schools, it sat among it all like a still, small reminder of the past.

To one side of the graveyard, you could see the house of Benazir Bhutto, the former prime minister. It had twelve-foot-high walls, rumoured to have been built in deliberate defiance of planning regulations. On the other side of the graveyard was the substantial embassy of North Korea, to whom, it was whispered, Pakistan sold blueprints for nuclear bombs. Watching the embassy, and Bhutto's house, and my apartment, were two plain-clothed intelligence agents who usually sat on the pavement in a patch of shade below a eucalyptus tree and read popular newspapers. I knew them quite well after a while and they smiled sheepishly when greeted. Occasionally, when my motorbike broke down, I asked them for a lift.

Half a mile away was the local market. In a concrete and glass complex built in the 1960s, kebab vendors shouted for custom and vegetable salesmen pushed overloaded bicycles through milling crowds. Most of the men wore shalwar kameez, the traditional ensemble of wide-cut trousers and long shirt that, despite the inroads made by Western clothing elsewhere in south Asia, was

still favoured throughout Pakistan. There were few women present, and most wore headscarves, though in one café favoured by
wealthier teenagers girls sat in jeans and T-shirts. In the central
square policemen leant their AK47s against the walls of the local
court and drank tea with their shackled prisoners squatting beside
them. The lawyers sat under awnings in their open-air offices and
dictated letters to clerks in shirtsleeves who tapped at ancient
typewriters with little piles of empty tea cups at their elbows.
Around them the modern buildings were rotting slowly. Their
exposed iron reinforcing rods were rusty and the bright sun picked
out the streaks of mould and the dirt smeared along their walls.

I was pleased to be there. Pakistan, with its mix of south Asian
chaos and Middle Eastern edge, its stunning landscapes and chaotic
politics, had always interested and attracted me. I had arrived with
no means of income but, on the basis that there were very few
reporters based in Islamabad, was confident I could earn a decent
living. I had about £1,000 in savings and the rent was paid on my
apartment in Islamabad for a month; my girlfriend, a photographer,
was coming out to join me and I was very happy.

Unlike when I made my trip to Kurdistan, I had done some
research before travelling and had learned something of the
chequered political history of the country I was to live in. I learned
about the blood-soaked birth of the state in the hideous communal
carnage caused by the partition of British dominion in south Asia
into Hindu-majority and Muslim-majority states in 1947. I learned
how the idea for Pakistan had originated in the fear that the
subcontinent's Muslims would be politically, culturally and socially
swamped by the demographic superiority of the Hindus once the
British left. I learned that the army had ruled the country for
over half of its existence, crippling the development of any real
democracy. Most recently, I had read, two political factions had
alternated in power. Both appeared either corrupt or incompetent
or both.

I still, however, knew little about Islam. I knew the name of the
religion meant peace or submission, and came from the same word
used in the Muslim greeting *salaam aleikum* or peace be with you.

I knew that the prophet Mohammed had lived in the seventh century CE, that he was human, not divine, and that he was considered to be the last of a series of messengers sent by God, or Allah, that included Jesus, Moses and Abraham. I was aware that, roughly speaking, 90 per cent of Muslims were Sunni and the rest were called Shia following a schism over the succession to the office of caliph, the leader of the Muslim community, after Mohammed's death. I knew that the call to prayer was the *adhan*, and that the muezzin was the man who delivered it. But that was about all. I had not even read the Koran. I saw Pakistan very much as an extension of India, though with slightly different-flavoured spiritual practices and food. Islam was neither a threat nor a particular attraction, simply part of the general local exoticism.

Within a week or so of my arrival in Islamabad, I heard about a festival, or *urs*, that was to be held at the shrine of Bari Imam, a local saint, on the outskirts of the city. Few of the Westerners I was mixing with seemed interested in such events, but I was freshly arrived and still avid for new sights and sensations. The road to the shrine wound through the diplomatic enclave, where most of the city's expatriates were corralled in neat homes behind barbed wire and whitewashed walls, and then on through pale gold wheat fields and scrubland. In a small lake, children were playing among semi-submerged cattle. Their parents stood a little way off in the dirt lanes outside single-storey homes made of old, narrow bricks, wooden planks, breezeblock and concrete. Smoke from cooking fires curled from gaps in the flat roofs of the houses, rising straight in the still evening air. The village was surrounded by woodland and backed by the line of steep forested hills that marked the northern limit of Islamabad. I could hear monkeys hooting in the trees.

I left my motorbike under a tree and started walking. The broad road up to the shrine was choked with pilgrims in long columns, ten abreast and often twenty or thirty deep. Each group had come from a different town or village and was led by musicians who played their drums and trumpets and men who carried huge flags in primary colours with silver and gold tinsel wrapped round the staff. Behind the bands and the flags, the pilgrims were carrying giant mock-ups of ships or mosques made out of coloured glass and shiny plastic tiles on platforms attached to long wooden beams that each ran across the shoulders of a dozen men. Everyone seemed very excited, laughing and joking and waving at the villagers and the children and me, inviting us all to join the procession.

Just before the shrine was a broad, grassy field which had stalls along its edges and was crowded with people. There were boys selling pappadums, 18-inch wide discs stacked a yard high, as big as cymbals. Others offered kebabs, cubes of stringy meat charred over narrow iron braziers, garlands of deep pink flowers, bracelets of tinsel or ridiculous foil hats. There were women hoping to henna hands in complex patterns of whorls and hatchings, tables full of portraits of Bari Imam, the dead saint, row after row of red, pink, green and gold glass bangles, and neat stacks of bright yellow halva puri sweets. A bearded strongman oiled his muscles while two assistants melodramatically manoeuvred his barbells, each consisting of a rusty iron bar with lumps of concrete at either end, into position in front of an expectant crowd.

The shrine itself was a small chamber, its walls entirely covered by tiny squares of mirrored glass, set in a simple whitewashed mosque in a sunken courtyard paved in marble. Several large and very old banyan trees overshadowed it, their roots curling down into the courtyard. A second wall formed a large compound in which hundreds of canopies and tents had been pitched by the pilgrims. Groups of men squatted around the cooking fires talking loudly in a range of unrecognizable local languages. Clusters of women in headscarves and bright dresses and trousers sat on woven straw mats, listening to a band playing thin reedy music. Goats were tethered to guy lines and banners inscribed with religious slogans in Urdu, the national language, were draped over the tents. Above it all were rows of the big, bright flags the pilgrims had carried from their home towns.

I wandered around, very pleased with myself for finding so much 'genuine' south Asian colour. I had hoped to supplement my income from written journalism by taking photographs for stock picture libraries in the UK and I knew that the images would sell well. Then I clearly heard someone say, 'All right, mate,' in a strong Yorkshire accent. I turned round but could not work out who had spoken. Then I heard the greeting again. Grinning at me was a tall young Pakistani man in a dark shalwar kameez.

He was a 22-year-old taxi driver who lived in Leeds and his name was Majid Khaliq. He knew he had been indistinguishable from the men around me and was smiling at my failure to spot him. He was 'British born and bred', he told me, too quickly. But he was also the son of Mohammed Khan who was the brother of Mohammed Nazir who was a farmer in the village of Handpur Kaloney, near Mirpur, and so was 'a Paki too,' as he put it. And it was from Handpur Kaloney – well over a hundred miles away – that he had walked with fifty of his 'brothers' from the village a few days earlier. He had never been to Pakistan before.

I asked him what a Leeds taxi driver was doing at the Bari Imam *urs*. He laughed. 'I just love it here,' he said. 'It's just fookin magic. It's like right good, innit. I walk round and I'm like proud and like it's just mental. Everywhere you look there's something mad going on. It's like . . . It makes me feel proud like.'

A group of pilgrims invited us to sit with them. All the pilgrims kept to their own areas. It was only because he was with me, Majid said, that the men from Peshawar, all from the ethnic Pashtun tribes that dominate the western third of Pakistan, would allow him, a Punjabi from the eastern plains, on to their patch. We walked round the compound, past whirling dancers, a large crowd of women brawling to get their hands on free rice, a number of preachers and a man with an enormous quantity of iron chains draped around his neck walking steadily round a fire with very wide eyes.

We walked up the low hill behind the campsite. Two young Pakistani men in smart white kurtas approached us and spoke only to me in poor English. They were university students, they said. They did not glance at Majid. From the hill we could see the busy encampment beneath us and behind it the hills darkening as the sun went down. A few fireworks popped and crackled above the smoking bonfires and the shrines, strung with multicoloured bulbs, around the campsite. Behind us, Islamabad's straight lines were picked out by the streetlights flicking on, sector by sector and the white neoclassical colonnades of the prime minister's residence could just be picked out in the gloom. Cars were streaming through its broad avenues and neon winked out at us.

When we went back to camp Majid and I watched the pilgrims dance around their model ships and temples to bless them with songs before illuminating them with candles and parading them through the compound. Then Majid told me, rather abruptly, that I should leave before it was fully dark. I sensed that there was something he didn't want me to see so I thanked him, said that he was right and I'd better get going. He seemed relieved. I walked a little way back up the hill and scanned the compound to see if I could spot him. I did, but only with difficulty. All the men in the encampment had formed lines. Majid was kneeling in the first rank facing the setting sun, his palms turned towards his chest in the first motions of prayer.

The outward ritual of religion in Pakistan was obvious. There were hundreds of festivals like that at Bari Imam's shrine all over Pakistan every year. There were the rows of men who prayed outside their offices at lunchtime and the sudden surge in traffic on the roads of Islamabad as the time for Friday prayers, the most important of the week, drew close. There were the pilgrims on their way to Mecca who crowded the airport, all already wearing their white cloth pilgrim's robes in recognition of Mohammed's basic message that all men were the same before God and the blessing, *bismillah al rahim al raham*, in the name of Allah the almighty, the all merciful, that taxi drivers uttered before pulling away from the kerb and newsreaders said before reading the news. There were the recorded prayers played after the safety briefing on every flight on Pakistan's national airline. But what was less clear to the outsider was the degree to which Islam articulated so much of daily life for a very large proportion of the population. I began to understand that their religion, like all successful faiths, *worked*, fulfilling essential functions on a personal, social and, sometimes, political level.

My own upbringing had been resolutely secular so, in a sense, I was learning as much about the role of any religion, not just that played by Islam. This growing comprehension of the sheer instrumentality and ritual of faith came slowly, as did all my understanding of what was going on around me. There was no sudden revelation, just a series of different details picked up from different scenes that eventually fitted together into a more general picture. This episodic, somewhat haphazard process, was not smooth. Like any journey, it had starts and stops, pauses and accelerations. I learned slowly, dismantling some existing prejudices, reconciling others with what I saw, or, relatively often, inadvertently replacing them with fresh ones.

One day I visited a *pir*, a Sufi saint. Again I had very little understanding of the Sufi strain of Islam, though I had enjoyed a performance of traditional Sufi music at a friend's house soon after arriving in Pakistan. Sufism had sprung up in the centuries after the death of the prophet Mohammed as a reaction against the increasing legalism of mainstream, orthodox Islam and was an almost mystic strand of the faith that emphasized personal spirituality rather than outward displays of religious observance. Sufism had rapidly spread, proving particularly popular in areas that were peripheral to the main Arab-dominated heartland of Islam, not least because it allowed an easy synthesis of local spiritual customs, including all sorts of saints, shrines and rituals, with the rigour of the new monotheistic religion. Much of what I had seen at Bari Imam had been a legacy of Sufi practice, I learned, including both the consumption of *bhang*, a milk drink laced with cannabis, and the asceticism of the man who had been draped in chains. The saint I went to see was the direct descendant of a greatly respected Sufi holy man.

Mian Shamshuddin lived in a tumbledown house in the eastern Pakistani city of Lahore and spent his mornings doing what his father and grandfather had done before him: sitting on a cushion on a rope bed tapping his supplicants on the head with a metal

spatula and mixing charms which had to be burned in a holy place
to be fully effective. The people sitting on the straw mats of his
simple whitewashed front room had come to him with toothaches,
marital problems, impotence, trouble at work, economic diffi-
culties, because they 'were once a good worker and now felt tired
and bored all the time'. Some said they, or people they knew,
were possessed or cursed. I watched Shamshuddin perform an
exorcism on a man who had recently been to India and had been
taken over by devils. It was a very tough exorcism, Shamshuddin
told me, because Indian spirits were very aggressive. 'I am a
patriotic *pir*,' he said, and smiled.

Watching the *pir* was instructive. He was a GP, consumer
helpline, counsellor and psychotherapist all in one. In a state as
poor and corrupt as Pakistan there was simply no one else to
perform such functions, or certainly not affordably, and people
naturally turned to popular religion as a result. Where the state
failed, religion itself or charitable religious networks filled the gaps.
Pirs did much more than merely heal the depressed or perplexed.
I later learned that the *pir* at the shrine of Bari Imam in Islamabad,
in addition to raising large sums of money to pay for free food for
the very poor, had just launched a campaign against opium and
heroin use in local villages. Narcotics were causing massive social
damage but the local police had been bought off by very wealthy,
and very heavily armed, drug dealers. The only man with the
power and will to act was the local living saint, who fought drug
use in the name of Islam. Yet I knew that popular religion, though
often a positive force, was not always so benign. I suspected there
must be resources within Islam, popular or otherwise, that could
be put to much darker uses. These too became apparent only
slowly.

A year after arriving in Pakistan I came across a single-paragraph
news story in a local paper describing the killing of a 'witch' in a
remote part of the Punjab. It described, with scant detail, how an
old mad woman called Muradam Mai had been murdered in Chak
100P, a village which, like thousands in the Punjab, was still known
by the number it had been given by the British administrators

eighty years previously. How Muradam Mai died was simple. Why she died was less straightforward.

From the small plane that flew me down to the town of Rahim Yar Khan I could see thousands of villages sitting like brick islands in a sea of wheat, cotton and sugar cane. To the east the crops blurred into the Cholistan desert, known locally as the walking sands; in every other direction the long thin fields continued as far as I could see. The rains had come at last and the plane, an old Fokker turbo-propped eighteen-seater, dipped and shook as we flew under the thick, dark clouds. Two days of downpour had turned the Punjab's rich, red dust to mud and the fields were spotted with rust-coloured pools reflecting the grey sky.

I found Muradam Mai's family easily enough, living in a small wood-and-brick house a mile or so from the village where she died. I sat on a rough bench outside the house with chickens and small children scrabbling in the mud around my feet and, in my basic Urdu, spoke to her son, a landless labourer. He told me, supplementing language with gesture, that his mother's troubles began when, two years previously, she had started behaving 'stupidly' and her moods swung rapidly from ranting anger to utter passivity and she began disappearing for weeks at a time. From inside the house he fetched a dirty card file full of documents. After a year of bizarre behaviour, a local doctor had apparently diagnosed his mother as 'paranoid schizophrenic' and referred her to a hospital in Lahore, 300 miles north. The referral, of course, was a joke. Her family could not even afford the bus fare, let alone medication, and her wanderings worsened.

At 8 o'clock one morning Muradam Mai was found sitting in Chak 100P's village shrine surrounded by burnt paper which the villagers said were pages from the shrine's Koran. A group of men then dragged her the half a mile from the shrine to the village square where they cut off her fingers and gouged out her eyes, probably with a stick. Two men then poured petrol over her and lit it. Other villagers stoked the flames with wood and dropped tyres filled with kerosene over her. By the time the police arrived, at around noon, Muradam Mai was very dead and a crowd of seventy gloating men stood around her corpse. 'She burned the Koran, so we burned her,' they told the first officer on the scene.

That officer was Maqsood Ahmed, the local police chief. He was very pleasant, offering me a chair and ordering tea and biscuits. He laid the file on Muradam Mai on his desk, passing me her identity card and medical records. As far he was concerned the reasons for the murder were clear. 'These people acted in a regrettable way but are strong Muslims,' he said. 'We have identified the suspects and they will be brought to book.'

The rain had lifted by the time I got to the village itself. Chak 100P was a collection of mud-and-brick huts surrounded by green fields, muddy pools full of fat, shiny-skinned cattle and relatively recently purchased tractors. There was a new concrete mosque in its centre. The village elders agreed that the case was straightforward. Chak 100P's headman, Ishfaq, said the woman died because the villagers 'love Islam', adding that men from other villages had since taunted them, saying they were not 'good Muslims' because they were unable to protect their own Koran. 'It was the younger ones who did it mainly,' Ishfaq said. 'Their religion is angrier than ours was at that age. But to burn the Koran is a terrible thing. I'm not saying what happened was good but such anger is difficult to contain.'

I spent several days in Chak 100P and spoke to scores of people connected with the case. They all accepted my questioning without any rancour, amused and flattered by a foreigner's interest. As I worked, a different picture of the death of Muradam Mai began to emerge. As well as being old and mentally ill and from the poorest, most marginalized elements of the village, she was also from the Seriaki ethnic minority, whose language and supposed 'difference' has often provoked suspicion among the major ethnic groups of Pakistan. In addition, when ill, she had taken to wandering through the village shouting incomprehensible words which many villagers believed were curses. Even if they were not, they told me, they would bring bad luck. Worse, Muradam Mai was a woman, breaking all the rules of convention to walk alone and unchaperoned in a conservative, male-dominated world.

Eventually I found a teacher in a nearby town who had driven out to the village when he had heard what had happened and picked up some of the paper that Muradam Mai had burned in the shrine. It was not from the Koran at all, he told me, but was the charred remains of paper charms given to Muradam Mai by a *pir* whom she had approached to cure her mental illness.

I wondered what sort of a role religion had played in the murder. Muradam Mai was hated, with the visceral loathing of the weakest and the oddest that all communities, no matter how developed, can summon. The village felt that she was 'wrong' and a threat and needed to be acted against. But for that hate to be acted on clearly required something more. By accusing Muradam Mai of burning the Koran, though they no doubt knew it was not true, the villagers, or at least those who joined the lynch mob, could convince themselves and their peers that it had been their duty to kill her. Religion had not been the cause of the violence but had certainly provided an excuse for it. It had legitimized what would otherwise have been an illegitimate act.

One evening in Chak 100P, when I was talking to the head of the village, a crowd gathered to watch and listen. I asked a few questions of the onlookers and then asked them if they had anything to ask me. There was a long pause, then one man stood up. 'Why does the West hate Islam?' he asked. I said that I did not think it did. 'Then why do Western clothes and sports-shoe manufacturers put holy Islamic on underwear?' he countered, citing an article in the local-language press that had apparently claimed that a random pattern of short and interlinked curling lines on a new line of men's underpants produced by a Western manufacturer was actually a disguised version of one of God's ninety-nine names. There was a murmur of approval from the other villagers. 'Why are Muslims oppressed in Kashmir by the Hindus who are the allies of the West?' asked a second man. 'Why are there so many rapes in the West?' said a third. Then the questions came more rapidly. Is it because the men cannot protect their women or because there is 'free love'? 'Why has the West got so rich when the Islamic world is so poor?' Why does the West want to humiliate Islam?'

Soon dozens of questions were being fired at me. I did my best to answer them sensibly and the villagers courteously listened to what I had to say. The situation was surreal. We were having an animated and apparently reasonable discussion just a stone's throw away from a dark stain in the red soil which marked where Muradam Mai had been burned. After an hour, all I could see of my interlocutors were the pale shapes of their shalwar kameez in the darkness and Ishfaq, the headman, brought a few candles out to light us. Eventually it started to rain again. The villagers went back to their homes and I drove away.

At the beginning of my time in Pakistan, I could not distinguish between the various forms of violence I encountered and I was astonished and appalled by much that I read, saw and reported. Then, after a year or so, I found myself becoming more habituated to the brutality that was so much a part of the life of the country and began to see its variety. I became something of a connoisseur of the grisly. The beatings given to suspects in police stations, the casual domestic violence, the boiling water poured over young wives whose dowries disappointed, the battles between villages or tribes that involved mortars and anti-aircraft guns, the serial killer and his thirty victims, the transsexual prostitutes who murdered their policemen clients, the feudal lords who whipped or battered their bonded labourers, the dacoits or bandits, the shadowy extra-judicial assassination squads – all were labelled and graded on my mental scale. Yet, though I became accustomed to its myriad forms, the extent of the violence continued to surprise me. When I went on a Pakistani army operation to destroy an opium crop high in the hills of the North-West Frontier, the tribesmen deployed light artillery to defend their fields. The army countered with two batteries of heavier artillery and tanks. Violence visited the most happy of occasions like an unwanted, uninvited guest. Celebratory automatic fire at weddings regularly killed people, including brides and grooms and proud parents. During the annual kite-flying festival, overexcited men ran out into the street to fire their AK47s into the air in celebration and accidentally shot scores of the children who had taken to the roofs to watch swooping, gliding splashes of colour in the sky. When a petrol tanker over-turned and the crowd that gathered with cups and saucepans to steal its load fell to fighting, someone started a fire that incinerated fifty people. Pakistan was a country where the strong bullied the weak and the weak bullied the weaker.

However, it was not violence that dominated lives but insecur-ity. Everyone in the country was worried about threats, potential and actual. So at a national level, though nobody could ever provide a reason why New Delhi might actually want to add 150 million truculent, poor and often illiterate Muslims to India's already fractious population, there was the perpetual fear of in-vasion from the east. Then there was the mutual insecurity of the various major ethnic communities, the feudal landowning classes, the new commercial and industrial classes and the bureaucracy. Even the army, in power for half of Pakistan's history and half a million strong, was always on the watch for threats to its own unassailable political, social and economic position. There was insecurity among the thousands of tribes and their leaders, all of whom were terrified that a rival might gain an advantage in the perpetual scramble for scarce supplies of electricity, government wheat or bureaucratic sinecures. Villages vied with other villages, families with other families. Politics was seen simply as a means to bolster a particular interest group's precarious position.

One of the reasons this took a while for me to grasp might have been that, having been raised on the post-Enlightenment optimism of the West with its faith in reason and progress, such endemic existential fear was alien to me. People in the West trust their technology, systems of checks and balances, welfare structures and, more or less, their leaders, to protect them. For the average citizen of Pakistan, as in any country where authority depends not on consent but on force and custom, there is no such safety net. There is only what native wit, luck and the patronage of someone with more influence or power or even greater literacy can provide. When a poor Christian friend of mine was being harassed by a bureaucrat, I sorted it out with one phone call to a minister. When

Muradam Mai in Chak 100P needed the police, they took three hours to come, despite their headquarters being a twenty-minute drive away. Jobs could disappear overnight, homes could be bulldozed just as quickly by wealthy developers who wanted land. Nor was there ever any warning of the many natural disasters – flood, drought and earthquake – that regularly struck. The result was a pervasive, and largely justified, sense that everything that anyone had was under threat. In such circumstances, it was unsurprising that many turned to the myriad resources of religion for consolation, support, justification or simply in a bid to make sense of the world around them.

The way popular folk religion managed to perform many of these functions had already become obvious to me. So too had the ways the resources inherent within the faith could legitimize violence. But the scenes I had witnessed at Bari Imam, with the *pir* and in Chak 100P had seen religion being deployed in relatively private roles, or at least within the confines of small groups and communities. I began to see that religion played several roles, often profoundly opaque, complex and contradictory ones, in the life of the nation too.

The issues surrounding the role Islam played in the vexed question of Pakistan's national identity was brought home to me when I watched the crowds celebrating Pakistan's successful testing, in response to India's earlier tests, of a nuclear device. They, and the nation's media and leaders, applauded the 'Islamic bomb'. As it is evidently impossible for any weapon to follow a religion, the application of the label interested me. The crowds, it seemed, were celebrating for three main reasons: one nationalistic, one religious and one that fused both nationalism and religion. First, the nuclear tests had shown that Pakistanis were the equal, more or less, of the old enemy, the far larger, far wealthier, far more powerful Indians. Second, the crowds exchanging sweets, throwing flowers in the air and marching through the streets were, as Muslims, proud that the ummah, as the global community of Muslims is known, now included a nation that possessed a nuclear strike capability. This was a cause for great celebration as it showed that it was not merely the Jews and the Christians who could master the technology and husband the resources necessary for such a project. A third reason for rejoicing was the fact that it was Pakistan among all the Muslim countries, even those that were more developed or had more oil or more important holy sites, that had been the first to 'go nuclear'. Within weeks of the tests, despite the subsequent sanctions that hamstrung the nation's economy, a series of monuments to commemorate Pakistan's great achievement were erected in the form of thirty-foot-high scale models of the mountains in the southwestern province of Baluchistan under which the devices had been tested. Made of translucent mud-coloured fibreglass, they were illuminated from within by powerful lamps and were astonishingly ugly.

For nationalistic Pakistanis, being a Muslim and being a patriot were inextricably linked. After I had been in Pakistan for about a year a small war broke out in Kashmir, the former principality that had been split after fighting between India and Pakistan between 1947 and 1949. The war had started when a force of Pakistani troops occupied a series of strategic heights inside Indian territory prompting massive infantry attacks and air raids to force them out. I flew up to the front line to spend some time with Pakistani soldiers holding one section of the frontier a few miles north of the main battle zone.

Major Nadeem, 35 years old with a small moustache and dark circles around his eyes, commanded a detachment of three British-made 5.5-inch Second World War howitzers dug in on a shelf of rock in a gorge at an altitude of 10,000 feet. The forward positions were much higher, among the rocks and scree slopes of the high ridges on the skyline, and from them the peaks of the high mountains of the Karakoram range were clearly visible to the north, a row of sharp triangles above the ochre tones of the lower hills. To the east were more tan-coloured dusty hills, indistinguishable from the others, where the Indians were.

When they fired their guns, the Pakistani soldiers shouted a question: *Yaum e takbeer?*, Who is the greatest?, and when the guns rocked back on their wheels with their muzzles flaring in the evening light they shouted the answer to their own question. *Allahu akbar.* God is the greatest. Nadeem had three books in his bunker: General Erwin Rommel's *War in Africa*, a biography of England cricketer Mike Brearley and the Koran.

I walked up to the bunkers on the crests of the hills above the gun battery. In the forward positions, a young captain greeted me enthusiastically despite being busy shelling a road where I could see an Indian jeep weaving to avoid the fire. The Indians predictably retaliated and we ducked into the caves where one part of his force were living. His men had cleared broken rock to make an area for cooking lentil curry and rice, a place for sleeping and a small area for prayer where a large rock painted white indicated the qibla, or direction of Mecca. It was cold and we were high enough for me to hear the sound of Indian shells spinning through the air beneath us on their way down into the valley.

The young captain told me his father had been taken prisoner by the Indians in one of the three wars India and Pakistan had fought. 'It gives me another reason to hate those Hindu bastards,' he said to me.

'Have you ever met an Indian?' I asked.

'No, have you?'

'Yes, many times. I've spent months in India,' I answered.

'What are they like?'

'Like you,' I said.

Over dinner that evening Colonel Nawaz Herl, the young captain's senior officer, shrugged wearily when I told him about the conversation. We were sitting in the unit's officers' mess, a large canvas tent pitched on a bend beside the river a mile or so back from the front line. Dinner was chicken tikka followed by sponge pudding and was served on regimental silver by soldiers wearing white gloves. During the main course Indian shells crashed down close enough to send lumps of shrapnel thumping into the walls. I did not have much of an appetite. Herl, a slim-shouldered man in his early forties with prominent teeth, a large nose, merry eyes and small bushy moustache, was feeling expansive. 'India and Pakistan have been fighting over Kashmir for fifty or more years and we have

still failed to sort it out,' he said. 'The fighting can't go on indefi-
nitely. There has to be some other way found to resolve the issue.'

He helped himself to some sponge pudding. 'Eating well is a
gift from God,' he said, smiling and beckoning to the soldier with
the custard.

I jumped as an Indian shell exploded not far away. 'And fighting?' I asked.

'That is the work of man,' he said, and winked.

The North-West Frontier Province of Pakistan was the land of
the Pashtuns, the tribal ethnic group which had been split between
Afghanistan and the Raj when the westernmost border of the
British dominions in south Asia had been set at the end of the
nineteenth century. The line drawn by the British bureaucrats had
remained as the western frontier of the new nation of Pakistan
when it was formed in 1947 but the tribes who lived along the
border did not care much for modern nation states of any description. 'We are Pashtuns first, Muslims second, Pakistanis third,' I
was repeatedly told when travelling up on the frontier. On the
Pakistani side of the border were the so-called Tribal Agencies,
another legacy of the Raj, where Islamabad's authority was legally
limited to the roads. It was rough country, harsh and ugly. Settlements tended to shun sites next to the rare rivers and streams in
favour of more easily defensible locations on the top of hills.
Villages typically comprised a series of walled compounds, or *qala*,
each including several buildings and sometimes dozens of inter-
related families. The outside walls of the compounds were sometimes joined, so larger villages resembled fiercer versions of Italian
hill towns. Inside, the houses varied from the rude and filthy to
the magnificently decorated, some equipped with vast deep-freezes
full of goat meat, widescreen televisions, satellite phones and air
conditioning, all bought with cash from smuggling, drugs, relatives
working in the Middle East or, as one old man proudly told me,
sons drawing social security in the UK.

The houses were fortified for a reason. The Pashtuns were
governed not by Islamabad, or even by Islam, but primarily by

their tribal code, *pashtunwali*. The code depended on a complex web of obligation, such as hospitality to a stranger or protection of a guest, and violence, decreeing that any perceived insult to the 'honour' of a man, a family or a tribe must be avenged at all cost. In a lawless borderland where adult males do not leave home without an automatic weapon, the code served a useful purpose. With potential escalation to lethal violence seconds away at any time, actual violence was limited.

I used to enjoy heading up to the frontier. Peshawar, the main city of the North-West Frontier Province (NWFP) was a noisy, dirty, edgy place with violence seemingly just below the surface. But, despite appearances, it was safe. Foreigners were not seen as enemies and I spent many evenings sitting in open-air restaurants or the homes of taxi drivers, merchants and tribal chiefs. All were contemptuous of Islamabad, the Punjabis whom they said domi-nated the Pakistani state and the borders that they knew they could cross at will. One of my better contacts in the NWFP was Javed Ibrahim Parachar, a tribal chief who, like many such men, was both an elder and a religious scholar. Both roles brought authority, respect and, if managed correctly, wealth. Parachar, who had managed things correctly, lived in the town of Kohat, a collection of whitewashed Pakistani army bases, rambling old alleyways, mosques and refugee camps set among a ring of dusty hills forty miles south of Peshawar. A narrow alley behind the bazaar led through to an open courtyard and his home, where dozens of passages linked scores of rooms with faded rugs on the floor and cushions along each wall. As well as being chief and scholar, Parachar was also a businessman, a farmer, a member of parliament, the vice-chancellor of an Islamic university and principal of a series of Islamic schools or medressas where several hundred young men, largely from poor families attracted by the free education, studied. He was 5' 7", 13 stone, chubby with a full beard, heavy eyelids and a row of small warts on the back of his neck. When I first met him he had pointed to the bullet holes in his white Toyota pick-up truck and laughed heartily. 'They shot 170 bullets into this car,' he said, chuckling, 'and six into me. But still they didn't kill me.

God protects me because I do good for His people and I am a good Muslim.' The ambush, I knew, had followed a series of murderous attacks on local Shia Muslims which Parachar was reported to have instigated, funded and organized.

But Parachar was most troubled, he told me repeatedly, not by the Shias and supposed heresy and division within Islam but by the 'moral corruption' that threatened his community. It was difficult to tell exactly what moral corruption meant but it appeared to include, more or less, any change that might alter the customs of traditional Pashtun society or at least those customs that Parachar was most keen on maintaining. These customs, Parachar had decided were also 'Islamic' customs. So for him modernization, Westernization, globalization and the extension of the powers of the central Pakistani state into tribal affairs were all fused into one great assault on all that was right and certain and Muslim. In his view, this moral corruption was a continuation of the assault on Islam that had characterized relations between Jews, Christians and Muslims since the prophet Mohammed had first preached the faith to the people of the Arabian peninsula 1,400 years ago. The spearheads of this attack were myriad, he said. There were the satellite dishes that had begun to arrive in the previous few years, the internet cafés that were opening everywhere, the foreign ways of dressing that were spreading, the Western music on the radio and the godless politicians in Islamabad. One of the greatest threats of all was the idea that women should be educated and able to work and should be free to choose their own husbands. And it was clear that if violence was necessary to maintain social order, then Parachar supported violence.

So when Lal Jamilla Mandokhel, a mentally ill 16-year-old girl from a local village was raped, Parachar backed the decision of the elders to have her shot dead by her own family – in front of the tribe – to punish her for bringing shame on them all. And when I asked him about the Pashtun girl from a nearby tribe who had eloped with a young boy from another ethnic group and been tracked and gunned down with her lover, Parachar simply shrugged and said that, wrong though the practice might seem to us in the West, it was his culture and his religion. 'This is justice,' he declared and ended the conversation.

Such violence to women, which was endemic in Pakistan, was one of the few things that made me genuinely angry during my stay in the country. I enjoyed living in Pakistan, and I liked most of the people I came across. Almost all were warm, courteous and interesting. I spent many hours in the offices of the Islamic militant groups, drinking tea and eating lemon sponge cake with pink icing while they told me the reasons for their jihad against the unbeliever. I did not feel threatened by them at all, partly because their rhetoric was never directly personal, partly because I thought that they would feel it dishonourable to have harmed me while I was their guest, partly because few showed much in the way of anti-Western sentiment and partly because it is difficult to imagine that anyone who is carrying a plate of multicoloured cake is dangerous. Their concern for events outside Pakistan seemed negligible. My own interest in the militants was somewhat abstract too. I saw them as part of the landscape, an element of the extraordinary, vital, exciting, visual and mental feast that was, for me, Pakistan. Sometimes they even struck me as almost comical. On one occasion, while I was camping with my girlfriend in the far north of the country, a group of heavily armed and bearded young men emerged from the trees around us and ringed our tent. But a quick conversation elicited companionable handshakes and a gift of some chocolate. The men were training for action in Afghanistan and Kashmir, they said proudly, before wishing us luck with the local trout fishing and disappearing back into the forest.

I also enjoyed Pakistan because it worked for me personally and professionally. It was not difficult to sell stories to editors in Britain about the country and I easily made a decent living. I missed London and, especially on a weekend when Islamabad was deathly quiet, pubs and clubs and music and friends, but the combination of intellectual stimulation, companionship and adrenaline offered by my new life more than compensated.

And then, of course, there was Afghanistan.

2. Afghan Summer

At about three o'clock on a Friday afternoon in August in Kabul I watched an execution and two amputations. I was sitting, along with several thousand other men and a few score children, on the concrete terraces of the city's stadium. Lessons from the Koran had been read aloud over the public address system as people sat and talked and bought nuts and small glasses of green tea from hawkers. Then the conversation had died away and everyone watched what was happening on the football pitch beyond the running track in front of us. Two men had been led into the pitch's centre circle and made to lie on their stomachs. Their arms were tied behind their backs and, for a few minutes, a team of white-coated surgeons huddled round them and then moved away. They had amputated a hand and a foot from each of the men tied up on the grass. Later, outside the stadium, I saw a Taliban soldier holding the severed hands above his head, blood from their wrists running down his own, to keep them away from some scruffy, laughing children who were jumping up around him to trying touch them.

Then a third man was made to squat in front of a goal. His hands too were tied behind his back. The crackling loudspeakers announced that he was a convicted murderer called Ghulam Hussein and that he was to be punished, according to the Islamic legal principle of compensation or revenge for the family, by the brother of his victim. There was a short pause and then a man took a Kalashnikov from one of the Taliban and held it out awkwardly in front of him, clearly unused to handling weapons. He held it away from his body like someone shaking rain off an umbrella and then pulled the trigger and six or eight rounds rattled out in a sharp burst. The condemned man, still on his haunches, span, toppled over, landed on his side, then strained his head upward looking at the sky. A roar went up from the crowd like when a boxer has a weakening opponent in a corner. Then another short burst rattled out and the man was dead. Fifteen minutes later two football teams emerged into the warm sunshine for the afternoon fixture.

It was the second day of my first trip to Kabul in 1998. The Taliban had been in control of the Afghan capital for two years and had already made themselves one of the most reviled regimes on the planet. The ultra-conservative 'Islamic militia' with their long beards, turbans, guns, draconian rules and regulations and, of course, their public executions were a great story. However, they were not the only reason I was sitting on the terraces watching someone being killed.

I had always wanted to visit Afghanistan. It was one of the reasons I had moved to the region in the first place. I had always been fascinated by the country and by its history, even if my impressions were based largely in myths and stereotypes. Though brought up in a cosmopolitan, urban environment very different from those parts of British society which still regret the passing of the Empire, my interest in southwest Asia undoubtedly owed a substantial amount to the romanticization of the region by success-ive generations of British writers, soldiers and diplomats. Though I was aware enough to realize that Churchill's or Kipling's depic-tions of Pashtuns as upright, noble warriors who fought a clean fight was mythologized nonsense that reflected the need to glamorize an enemy who actually won from time to time, I still found it difficult to see the North-West Frontier or Afghanistan clearly. And of course there was the classic contemporary Western traveller's desire to uncover the authentic, the untouched, the 'unspoilt' and the 'backward'.

So when, in the summer of 1998, I first travelled to Afghanistan, I was profoundly happy to find that it was everything that I hoped it would be. I flew in on a tiny United Nations jet which landed at an airstrip in the far northeast of the country on a runway made of steel plates that were slick with recent rain. Burned-out buildings and wrecked tanks lined either side and men with guns wearing *pakol*, the flat, round woollen hats so symbolic of the mujahideen, stood around in picturesque groups. I had flown in because there had been a terrible earthquake and for a week I travelled by helicopter and donkey through villages smeared down sides of hills, talking to old men standing on the rubble which covered their homes and families, sleeping in shepherds' huts or wherever my local donkey driver wanted to stop. The earthquake had hit perhaps the poorest part of the country, a region containing some of the most stunning scenery I had ever seen. One evening I sat on the roof of a makeshift clinic run by a team of British nurses. To the south were the white-topped mountains of the Hindu Kush and to the north were the plateaus and plains that led away and down to the Amu Darya or Oxus river, the border with Tajikistan and Uzbekistan. When I got stuck for a day or so in a mountain village when a helicopter broke down, I had spent the time reading, walking, making tea in a decorated, Chinese-made thermos flask with wild mint and rolling and smoking cigarettes. In the ten days I was there, I sent one story to a newspaper in Britain and earned around £200. It was everything I had wanted to do, and Afghanistan was everything I had wanted it to be.

A few days after witnessing the execution in Kabul, I went up to the front lines twenty-five miles north of the capital. After four years of campaigning about 80 per cent of the country was nominally under the control of, or at least theoretically loyal to, the Taliban. In most of Afghanistan there was no obvious 'front line' as such, more a fractured mosaic of allegiances that followed tribal, ethnic and cultural rather than physical landscapes. However, half an hour's drive north of Kabul, lines of trenches stretched either side of a shell-pocked deserted no-man's land. The positions split the Shomali plains, a bowl of fertile land ringed by hills that was once one of Afghanistan's most productive farming areas. Nearest Kabul were the Taliban. Facing them were the Northern Alliance, a rough agglomeration of factions from a variety of ethnic groups.

The only vehicle I could find for hire in Kabul was a white minivan driven by an old man called Fateh Mohammed who spoke to himself a lot. There was much talk of fanatical Arab fighters in the Taliban trenches but I saw none. In fact, to my great surprise, the most forward positions were occupied by a small detachment of fighters with distinctive round-faced central-Asian features. They were from the Hazara ethnic minority, a community of largely Shia Muslims known for their religious moderation who had often been persecuted by the largely Sunni Muslim Taliban. The Taliban were drawn largely from the Pashtun tribes from the east and south of the country who made up, just, a majority of the population and were usually seen as either a vehicle for ethnic chauvinism or a radical Sunni Muslim fundamentalist movement. This was very confusing; by rights, the Hazara should have been on the other side. But Mohammed Sher, the young commander in charge of the detachment, explained to me that he and his men were there because he was loyal to another commander, who was Hazara, who in turn followed the orders of a third commander, from the Tajik ethnic minority, who was loyal to a 'big commander', a Pashtun, who had decided to throw his lot in with the Taliban a year or so earlier. Each link of the chain, it appeared, involved the exchange of resources, mainly food, money and a degree of security in return for labour. The Hazara were there, I realized, because loyalty in Afghanistan is not always ethnic, religious or even tribal. It is usually to whoever is putting the dinner, in this case a thin soup with stale bread in it, on the table, and a good leader is one who changes sides at the right moment. Mohammed Sher told me that he and his men had left their homes in Maidan Shah, a town south of Kabul, a few weeks earlier to do a few months' stint on the front line and he hoped they would be back home in time to get the harvest in later in the summer.

As we spoke a tank dug in about thirty yards away fired, sending a shell screeching over our heads. The TV crew I had accompanied up to the front line had needed some images of actual combat and, though the tank's crew were slightly uneasy at engaging in any fighting in the middle of the day as they had come to an amicable agreement with the men in the trenches opposite to bombard each other in the morning and evening only, had been persuaded to let off a few rounds from the rusty old T62 for the cameras. I wondered, for a brief moment, about those for whom our outgoing was incoming.

Whoever they were, they were clearly irritated by having their lunch interrupted and retaliated with a mortar, sending the fighters into their bunkers and the journalists scrambling into vehicles. It was at this point that I discovered that the minibus I hired in Kabul had a faulty ignition. So I sat, concentrating very hard on not being scared, as Fateh Mohammed jabbered to himself, turned the key, jabbered some more, turned the key again, and again, and again, before finally he released the handbrake, dropped the clutch, and jump-started the vehicle by rolling us down the hill towards the enemy.

It was the first time that, as a journalist, I had been 'under fire' and I was pleased and excited and not entirely sure how to respond. Reporters, I had read, took drugs, drank lots, fought or had sex with inappropriate partners after such experiences. None of these things seemed very practical in Taliban-run Kabul. I went over to the Reuters office and played table tennis all afternoon and drank tea and thought about it. There was a nine o'clock curfew and I was back in my room in the semi-derelict Intercontinental Hotel shortly after sundown.

Every day in Kabul I found my ideas challenged and my perceptions shifting. I found that the TV images of smashed buildings that featured in every bulletin from the city had all been filmed in one specific area and that much of the rest of the capital, though battered, chipped, pocked by bullets, filthy and run down, was actually intact. Indeed Kabul, I was surprised to find out, had not only escaped serious damage in the ten-year war that had followed the Soviet invasion of 1979 but had actually done quite well out of the occupation. Many of the newer buildings I saw in the centre of the city, the parks and the modern housing around its northern edge had been built with Soviet aid money. Even the damage that I could see, such as the cracks in the hotel walls caused by a missile strike, were not the result of the war against the Soviets as I had imagined but had been sustained in the struggle between the various Afghan factions who battled for control of the country after Moscow's forces had pulled out. And it was clear that, though undoubtedly grim, the image of Kabul as a city cowed by poverty

and repression was false. There might have been only one functioning restaurant, two barely functioning hotels and no traffic
but there was still plenty of life. I was astonished to see files of
schoolchildren, boys and girls, walking through the streets on
their way to class, chattering happily or breaking away from their
teachers to play with toys such as a hoop and stick or a horse made
of nailed wood set on wheels taken from an old pram. The money
market was always crowded and noisy, not least because the
vagaries of the local currency meant speculation could be very
profitable. A wry humour kept many going, in spite of the depri-
vation and, in all but the high summer months, the cold. And then
there was the sheer, aesthetic beauty of the city itself, with its clear,
unpolluted mountain air, long rows of ash and sycamore trees,
empty roads, dusty parks, crumbling walls of medieval fortifications, even its battered buildings and brown hills that rose from
amongst the uneven rows of stacked, flat-roofed homes like the
backs of whales from amongst waves.

After several days in the city, filing features on 'life under the
Taliban', I decided to drive down to Kandahar, the spiritual and
administrative headquarters of the regime, to learn more about the
people who now ran Kabul. I had also been commissioned by one
newspaper to find out what I could about Osama bin Laden, the
Saudi-born 'terror mastermind' living in Afghanistan who was
being blamed for two massive bombs that had destroyed American
embassies in Dar-es-Salaam and Nairobi two weeks earlier. I knew
that bin Laden had a base about twenty miles outside Kandahar,
near the airport, and a contact in Pakistan had passed on details of
someone in the city who apparently could assist in arranging a
meeting with, if not with bin Laden himself, then one of his close
associates.

I hired a local taxi, a battered Toyota Corolla estate, from the
stands on the southeastern rim of Kabul and, with a Kabuli medical
student called Ahmed as a translator, drove out of the city under
the thin sky of the very early morning. The roads were empty but
for packs of dogs and the occasional man on a bicycle, swathed in
a blanket against the chill. The Taliban guards huddled round a

small fire at the city limit waved us through their checkpoint,
barely glancing into the car, and once past them we drove quickly
along a good road that dipped away off the plateau of Kabul and
down towards the south. From a ridge we saw the road ahead of
us, stripped of its surface by decades of erosion and use and as
white as a bone against the dust of the valley. The road, which ran
the length of the eastern flank of Afghanistan, had been built in
the early 1970s and not maintained since the Soviets left; jagged
sections of concrete protruded from potholes six feet wide and ribs
of tar and rusted iron jabbed out from drifts of gravel and dirt and
dust. Often, there was no trace of a surface at all and the road
became a rubble-filled trough. The driver of our taxi, anxious to
finish the journey and pick up another fare, drove as fast as he
could, accelerating hard, stamping on the brake on the rim of huge
craters, swinging the vehicle between obstacles, sending a plume
of fine dirt into the air behind us. Ahead of us other vehicles could
be seen doing the same, each with its passage marked by a boiling
cloud of dust. Sometimes they disappeared entirely into a particularly deep dip, leaving their dust trail bizarrely disembodied in the
air. Often our driver pulled off the road and took the car down
dry watercourses that ran parallel to it through the fields and the
desert on either side. It was an extremely uncomfortable ride and,
when the sun began to climb, also an extremely hot one.

Yet there was plenty to distract me. Subtle signs indicated the
change of climate and cultural influence as the miles went by. The
stands of slim ash and poplar that were so characteristic of the north
and east of the country thinned out and soon any trees at all were
something of a rarity as broad plains, scruffy with furze and hard,
spiny bushes, stretched away either side of the road. Past the city
of Ghazni, ninety miles south of Kabul, camels became a frequent
sight, moving with their odd, knock-kneed rocking motion across
the open ground. And the architecture of the villages changed too.
As wood became scarcer the flat roofs of the north were replaced
by the round, conical, mud and wattle roofs of the desert south.
On my right, the dry hills of Afghanistan's almost impenetrable
central core lay on the horizon. To the left were the mountain

ranges along the frontier with Pakistan, a jumble of huge slabs of rock, deep defiles, scree slopes and eroded plateaus all the colour of sawdust. Our driver was from one of the local Pashtun tribes and he, Ahmed and I discussed how the Americans would retaliate following the East African bomb blasts. The driver was concerned that they might bomb Afghanistan, and though I said that I did not think they would do anything so clumsy, Ahmed decided that teaching me the *shahadat*, the declaration of faith which, if uttered with genuine conviction, means that you are a Muslim, would be a good idea. *La illallla alillah Mohammed rasul illahah*, he repeated again and again, there is no God but Allah and Mohammed is his prophet, until I had memorized it. Partly he was fulfilling the duty of all Muslims, when they first meet a non-believer, to offer them their faith but also, more practically, was concerned about possible anti–Western riots in the event of a US strike. 'Mr Jason,' he had said earnestly, 'it won't stop them but it might slow them down for a while.'

We stopped for the night at a *chaikhanna*, a roadside inn, in the small town of Qalat, a strip of dusty shops selling dates, old jam imported from Iran and multicoloured blankets. A row of battered cars, trucks and jeeps were lined up outside in the dust. We ate bad boiled meat, salty stewed spinach and rice and flatbread and watermelon. The sun went down rapidly and it suddenly became cold. I slept on the *chaikanna*'s open raised terrace, preferring the fresh air and a view of the desert, the hills and the stars to the packed and stuffy interior. In the early morning, wrapped in a blanket and unnoticed, I watched as the entire population of the inn, staff and customers alike, filed out into the pale, low sunlight, formed several lines, threw down the blankets they had slept on and performed the morning prayer.

From Qalat there was still four or five hours' driving to Kandahar. An hour into the journey we broke down and, as the driver hitched back to the town to pick up another air filter, Ahmed continued his impromptu lesson in Islamic theology.

In the morning, I had seen one man, an old greybeard in a magnificent slate-grey turban shot through with golden filaments, sing out the call to prayer. I asked Ahmed what he had sung. The words, it turned out, were almost identical in sentiment to those of the *shahadat*: 'God is great, I bear witness that there is no god but Allah, I bear witness that Mohammed is his prophet. Come to prayer. Come to prosperity and health. God is great.' In the so-called pagan era before the coming of Islam, Ahmed told me as we sat in the rapidly shrinking shadow of the immobilized Corolla, the various fractious tribes of the Arabian peninsula had worshipped scores of different deities. This was why the call to prayer, the *adhan*, and the *shahadat*, stressed that Allah was the only God. One God meant unity, not *fitna*, or division, Ahmed went on, and the prophet Mohammed, 'peace be upon him', had been sent by Allah to bring the true faith once more to the world and to end the perpetual warring between the tribes by uniting them in peace. Mohammed's message was not intended to replace the religion brought by Moses, Abraham and Jesus to the Christians and the Jews, Ahmed said, but to correct the deviations from true practice that had developed over the years and also to provide a creed for the Arab people who had so far missed out. There was also a political element contained within the call to prayer and its injunction to monotheism, Ahmed told me. At the time of Mohammed's revelations Mecca, the prophet's home town, had been run by a group of rich tribes who owed their wealth to pilgrims coming to see the many different gods whose idols stood in the main temple. Destroying the idols, unifying all in one God, meant the end of their iniquitous and unjust rule.

One element that interested me was the stress laid on 'bearing witness' in the call to prayer. Along with what Ahmed told me about the way Mohammed was trying to reform his own society, it supported my own sense that Islam was a profoundly political religion. The frequent, quotidian testament of faith emphasized how the religion's public and demonstrative element was a critical part of the prophet's message. On a very small scale, I had seen in the morning how a disparate community of travellers could be, at least momentarily, unified in the ritual of prayer. And, as Ahmed had told me, there was no pre-set hierarchy that had determined the order in which the men had lined up in the dust. It was simply the oldest and most respected man who had stepped forward from the assembled few dozen people to lead the prayers. Islam, it appeared to me, was as much a social project as a path to internal spirituality. It was a religion in which action in the real world was an integral part of worship. Ahmed pointed out that the Koran, the compilation of the revelations that the prophet Mohammed received, was, in addition to being great poetry, a book of laws and ethical and moral guidance that provided a code of behaviour which, if followed by everyone in all aspects of their life, would ensure peace and justice for all.

'How do the Taliban fit into all of this?' I asked.

'They are very hard people,' Ahmed said. 'Very rigorous people. Not so educated people.' He explained quickly that the Taliban were not qualified religious scholars or ulema but mullahs, the equivalent of country parsons. 'They want to bring justice and peace but only their kind of justice and peace. They think everyone else is wrong and they are right and they find in our Holy Book and the words of the Holy Prophet, peace be upon him, what they want to find. You will see.'

The sun was almost directly overhead when the driver returned with the air filter and we did not reach Kandahar until mid-afternoon. It was not a prepossessing city. There was a cluster of concrete villas in the wealthier areas, a poorer old town full of winding alleys and tenements, the remnants of the city walls, several bazaars that seemed to be filled mainly with bad meat hanging on greasy hooks and cheap tin pots and pans. The only link with the outside world was a public telephone office with a single crackling line on which you could dial Pakistan but nowhere else. There was no way of calling Kabul and the Taliban apparently relied on radios to communicate. The city was dominated by the barren landscape all around. The dirt and sparse fields of the hinterland were bleached yellow and punctuated by vast and craggy rock outcrops that rose out of the horizontal with appalling suddenness. In the heat haze they looked like rows of tall-masted galleons on a dead flat sea. It was so hot that in the still furnace of the afternoon the air had a burned taste on the tongue.

I got a room at the United Nations run hostel in a residential area in the west of the town. Ahmed preferred to stay with relatives near by. I washed the dust out of my nostrils, hair and eyes, ate and then walked out of the hostel's iron-gated compound, down a short dirt road to where Mullah Omar, the reclusive one-eyed cleric who led the Taliban, lived in a high-walled compound with painted gateposts decorated with multicoloured tiles. The governor of Kandahar, Mullah Hassan Akhund, with whom I had arranged a meeting for later in the afternoon, lived next door.

The Taliban phenomenon had begun just outside Kandahar in the summer of 1994 when Omar, a veteran of the war against the Soviets, decided that the banditry, robbery and rape that was endemic in the area at the time had to stop. He rallied a group of villagers, attacked the encampment of the local warlord who had recently abducted and raped a young girl and hanged him from the barrel of a tank. Other local men had swiftly joined up and more recruits had come from amongst the tens of thousands of students in religious schools in Pakistan. These students, often Afghan refugees or their sons, were called Taliban, which meant seekers in Persian. And within two years of Omar's *coup de main* in Kandahar, the Taliban were running the country. Yet the movement owed its astonishingly rapid success to more than the simple fact that the people of Afghanistan were tired of war and banditry. Omar and his band of local vigilantes had started their campaign at a moment when the geopolitical stars were perfectly aligned in their favour. Pakistani generals saw the Taliban as useful proxies and sent them experts and weapons, men like Javed Parachar in the North-West Frontier Province saw them as a force against evil and sent massive reinforcements from their religious schools, devout merchants and princes in Saudi Arabia sent cases of cash and Washington stayed silent, distracted by the Balkans, leery of international affairs generally and not unhappy to see Afghanistan stabilized, even if it was by a bunch of hardline radicals.

Akhund, who had governed Kandahar for nearly four years, was known as a conservative with a fiery temper. Yet he was in a conciliatory mood, offering me sugared almonds and pomegranate on my arrival. It was pomegranate season, he said, and told me that once the Kandahari varieties of the fruit, renowned for their sweetness, had been exported all over the region. I asked him about the early days of the Taliban and their campaign and we talked about their aims. 'We are merely interested in bringing peace and security to our homeland,' he said. We discussed bin Laden. Tapping his wooden leg, the result of an injury sustained fighting the Soviets, against a table, the governor said there was no proof of the involvement of bin Laden, who was 'a guest in his country', in the attacks on the two embassies. After all, he added, the Taliban desired good relations with all nations. I asked him about the criticism of their treatment of women. He tapped his leg against the table again and answered tersely: 'It is the West who is making these criticisms. No one in my village makes these criticisms. Why is everybody always focusing on this question of women and not on the security we have brought? Before we came there was rape and violence everywhere in the country and now there is none.' As we left his assistant asked me if I thought the Americans would bomb Afghanistan. No, I answered again, there weren't any decent targets for them to hit, and I set off to buy some pomegranates in the bazaar. A few hours later, seventy-five US Tomahawk cruise missiles struck six 'terrorist training camps' in the hills that had lined the eastern horizon on the drive down from Kabul.

Suddenly, after only about four months in the region, I was in the middle of a major story. I was so excited I was shaking. I had very little idea of what I should do. Getting to the site of the missile strike, hundreds of miles away in very hostile country, was out of the question. I certainly could not see how I could do it safely. I filed a quick despatch to two London newspapers on a satellite phone from the United Nations compound and then waited to see what would happen. I thought about going for a walk through the city but decided against it. I thought about Ahmed's lessons and repeated the *shahadat* to myself. The compound had low walls and a single, bolted gate but the night seemed very quiet and there was no hint of trouble. Being in Kandahar, the heartland of the Taliban, was clearly either a very good thing or a very bad thing.

It turned out to be the former. Though there was considerable anger in much of Afghanistan – in Kabul an Italian soldier with the UN was shot dead and elsewhere UN offices were attacked – in Kandahar everything remained calm. Ahmed went to the main mosque for Friday prayers and reported that an angry crowd had been quietened by the governor's appeal to the Pashtun tradition of hospitality and the protection of guests. Had I been more experienced, I probably would have headed into the city and done some proper reporting but, as I had never been in such a situation before, I simply made a couple of short forays out into the streets around the UN hostel and decided that sticking with all the other foreigners was the best thing to do. Though the Pakistani border was a mere fifty miles away the UN team in Kandahar had been told by their office in Geneva that the roads were too dangerous to drive and that a plane was to be sent from Islamabad. The Taliban suggested that it would be safest to travel at prayer time when the people most likely to harm us would be otherwise occupied and so, after two days in the compound, we drove at speed through Kandahar's half-empty streets and through the checkpoints on the rim of the city and soon we saw the slim white lines of the UN plane through the haze over the desert. A Taliban helicopter gunship wheeled overhead as we boarded and took off. From Islamabad, I filed my story, which ran under the completely unwarranted headline 'How I escaped from the Taliban' and sold a picture of the back of the governor's house to a tabloid for £1,000 on the basis that it was bin Laden's base.

Within a month of returning to Pakistan I was back in Kandahar and this time was able to spend several weeks driving through the south and southwest of Afghanistan. I spoke to Shias in the western city of Herat who were being persecuted by the Taliban, to Taliban fighters themselves, to women who had been banned from schools or from offices, to merchants happy with the security that the Taliban had brought that allowed them to move their goods without fear of

banditry, to opium farmers, to clerics in the Sufi shrines, even to
a couple of Arab militants who were on their way to a training
camp in the east of the country. In Herat I walked through the
Great Mosque, where young boys sat in ranks around the central
court and the consonants of their murmured chanting of the Koran
hissed like a seashell through the 500-year-old arcades, and out
through the city to the plain where a cluster of huge minarets,
giant 150-foot columns of sandstone and blue glazed terracotta
tiles, rose from a plain strewn with rubbish and rubble. I bought
some small, sour apples from an old woman with tattooed hands
and asked her about life in Herat and the Taliban. She looked
about her carefully. 'Mushkil,' she said, using the Persian word for
difficult or hard, 'Mushkil, mushkil.'

I did not hate the Taliban the way some did in the West. Perhaps
that was due to the protection they had offered me. Perhaps, as a
man, I felt less viscerally about the restrictions they placed on
women. Perhaps, as with the extremists I met in Pakistan, they
simply seemed too distant, too exotic, too bizarre to be any kind
of a personal threat. Perhaps, having seen and met them, I was less
willing to accept that they were simply 'mad mullahs', as they were
rapidly dubbed, and dismissed, by many. One thing that few
realized was that the Taliban view of the world was extraordinarily
parochial. Some could not even point to Afghanistan on a world
map, others laughed uproariously at the idea that a man could walk
on the moon. When I asked one in jest if I could join his group
of religious police, he conferred with colleagues, agreed, then
asked if I was a Muslim, then, on hearing that I was not, apologized
for not being able to employ me immediately but promised that if
I came to the mosque with him in the morning he would convert
me and then all would be well. Few of the Taliban had even heard
of the various internationally infamous Islamic militants such as bin
Laden who were living in their country. And though some of the
senior Taliban, such as the governor of Kandahar, were imposing
men, many others were almost pathetic. They were often very
young and, though supposedly running government ministries,
they spent their days sitting on the floor beside a radio and a glass

of tea in the corners of the big rooms in the huge mouldering office blocks that had been constructed by the Soviets. In winter, some of them had a bar heater and sat with one or two secretaries, usually men even younger than they were, talking, reading the Koran and playing with prayer beads. I felt sorry for them. They were part of the tragedy that was Afghanistan, not its cause.

I spent hours talking to such men. These were the ideologues who formed the movement's core, not the foot soldiers who were sitting in the trenches because their commander had decided it was in their best interests or because the cleric in charge of their school had ordered them to join up en masse. They believed that the disasters that had befallen their country were due to a failure to implement the basic laws that had been laid down by Mohammed in the Koran – or at least their particular interpretation of those laws. Many of them had grown up in refugee camps and could barely remember life before the Soviet invasion. They imagined pre-conflict Afghanistan as a golden age when Islamic traditions, village customs and the tribal code of the Pashtuns ensured peace, prosperity and justice. It was a myth, of course, but it did not stop them hoping that they might be able to turn it into reality.

In fact, much of what the Taliban did and thought was underpinned by fear. Most of all they feared anything that was foreign or new. Given their experience of the last thirty years, it was not difficult to see why they associated 'modernity' with war and violence and chaos. One of the causes of the Taliban's profound misogyny was their linkage of women, particularly Kabuli, middle-class, educated, unveiled women, with modernity and thus threat. This meant that controlling women was central to bringing about their vision of a peaceful and ordered agrarian society. Women were, in the minds of men who had been kept from almost all but the most perfunctory contact with the opposite sex since their early teens, a different species. They were also the incarnation of temptation, the vehicle of 'moral corruption'. So the logic of enforcing the use of the burka in towns like Kabul was that it would protect men from being led astray and women from men who were weak. The Taliban wanted to realize their own imagined idea of a perfect society and, for the supposed good of everyone, were prepared to use force to do so.

And, though the Taliban did not see it themselves, it also became rapidly clear to me that they fell squarely within a long tradition of similar revivalist and reformist movements in Afghanistan. Each, as was the case elsewhere in the Islamic world, had been a reaction to a perceived threat or to a massive social upheaval. In the nineteenth century the threat had been from the British who sparked a jihad, or 'holy struggle', each time they invaded. In the first decades of the twentieth century it had been Afghan monarchs, full of ideas imported from Europe who, in attempting to impose new 'modern' ways of structuring society, had set the provinces ablaze with revolt. The Marxist regime that took power in the mid-1970s had provoked a rebellion when they tried to enforce measures to redistribute land, educate women and curtail the power of the clergy. And the resistance to the Soviets itself had been, in part, the traditional fight of the conservative Afghan provinces against a modernizing, centralizing, interfering power. In each case, the rallying flag had been Islam and the enemy had been 'modernity'. For many Afghans, the Soviet army, which had burned thousands of villages, destroyed irreplaceable centuries-old irrigation systems, killed hundreds of thousands and forced 5 million into exile, were the only representatives of the secular and supposedly progressive 'West' they had ever come into contact with. The graffiti on the wall outside the offices of the religious police in Kabul read: 'Throw reason to the dogs. It stinks of corruption'. Given the country's recent history, I could see why they felt as they did.

I could also see why the Taliban had originated in the desiccated, sun-struck, dirt-poor desert villages of Afghanistan's southeast. The environment suited them and their puritanical, reactionary, fearful thought. The harsh noonday light in the streets, the bleak contrast between the blinding light and the shadows in the doorways of the houses with their windowless walls. The villages that were turned in on themselves, the high ramparts around the individual houses joined to form a seamless defence against the outside world, all mirrored, and were an integral part of, the Taliban worldview. The Taliban lived in a world where differences between individuals and communities and people were profound and unbridgeable and did not just think but knew that this was a good thing. This maintenance of difference and walls was what protected them all. They were convinced that they were right and everyone else was wrong; that they had seen the one truth and it was the only truth and that no one else's truth had any validity and that they had a religious, moral and social obligation to try to impose that truth on others. Kandahar itself, once a cosmopolitan trading city, was now a harsh, arid and joyless place, a closed fortress against the 'threats' that lay outside, a desert outpost in the war against the menance of modernity and change. Kandahar, I thought, was as much a state of mind as a place.

3. Afghan Autumn

On a fine autumn morning, four months after the bombings of
the US embassies in East Africa, Ekram and I went looking for
Osama bin Laden. We were not the only ones, of course. There
were quite a lot of people, most with considerably more resources
than us, doing the same thing.

Mohammed Ekram Shinwari was in his early forties when we
met, about 5' 4" with a substantial round belly, constantly amused
eyes and a small beard. He was a Pashtun whose family were from
eastern Afghanistan though he himself grew up in Kabul. He
laughed, frequently, with his entire upper body. He spoke Pashto,
Dari (the Persian-rooted language of the Afghan Tajik minority)
and, having lived as a refugee for fifteen years in Pakistan, fluent
Urdu. His English was somewhat idiosyncratic. When I met him,
Ekram, his wife and three sons, his brother and his brother's family
were all living in a large house in the Afghan quarter of Peshawar.
Ekram had fled to Pakistan after being imprisoned for outspoken
student journalism in the run-up to the Soviet invasion. He had
then spent the next decade or so covering the war against Moscow's
forces, often travelling with the mujahideen on their raids and
expeditions. As a result, he knew everyone, knew the genealogies
of all the myriad commanders and the details of every alliance, pact
and battle. Although he had to explain such basic facts to me again
and again, he was never patronizing or impatient. He also, crucially,
knew and liked a good news story and had a deep respect for the
truth. Ekram was, if not a devout Muslim, an observant one,
rigorously keeping the fast during Ramadan and praying five times
a day wherever we were and whatever we were doing. His faith
was profoundly important to him, as was his Pashtun identity,
though never in any obtrusive way. I never heard him say anything
derogatory about any other religion and he was as critical of the

Pakistanis as he was of the Americans, his opinions based not in prejudice, but in justifiable anger at the pragmatic and ignorant policies both nations pursued towards his native country. He was also hospitable, kind and, like me, believed that no reporting should ever be done on an empty stomach. I liked him very much.

As for bin Laden, the bare facts were well known and had been widely reported in the aftermath of the August 1998 embassy bombings. Born in Saudi Arabia in 1957, the son of a devout Yemeni-born construction magnate, bin Laden had travelled to Pakistan in early 1980 to help the Afghans fight the Soviets and had used his contacts in the Gulf to raise large amounts of cash which he channelled to various factions. Towards the end of the war bin Laden decided to set up his own group to unite the small number of fractious foreign militants fighting alongside the Afghans and carry the struggle beyond Afghanistan. This, he decided, would act as 'al-Qaeda', a 'base' or 'vanguard' in Arabic, for future operations and expansion. Bin Laden then went home to Saudi Arabia, where he did very little of note until Saddam Hussein invaded Kuwait in 1990. A loyal subject, he offered to raise a legion of Arab militants to protect Saudi Arabia against the Iraqi dictator. Unsurprisingly his proposal was rejected and, soon after, bin Laden left his native land, going to the Sudan where he spent the next five years experimenting in everything from financing Islamic militants in the Balkans and the Far East to arboriculture and motorway construction.

Together, Ekram and I were able to unpick many of the myths that had sprung up around bin Laden. We interviewed scores of former and current fighters, sometimes travelling out to meet them in dismal refugee camps way off in the tribal agencies, sometimes in *qala*, the traditional fort-houses, only a few miles from Peshawar, sometimes in luxurious villas on the outskirts of the city. Often, the men would come to Ekram's house and we would sit on the cushions and rugs laid on the floor of his large front room and talk over huge piles of steaming *pulau* rice cooked with mutton, raisins and shredded carrot, local stuffed dumplings known as *manto* and *ashak*, and kebabs, all eaten with fingers and flatbread and followed by grapes or melon or pomegranate and sweet tea in very small glasses.

Such food was rare in Afghanistan at the time – indeed, it was rare anywhere – and was at least part of the reason the men came to speak to us. It was prepared by Ekram's wife, who always stayed out of sight, and served by his sons, the eldest of whom would pass among his father's guests after the meal with a beautifully engraved slender-necked silver pitcher of hot water and a bowl and a towel with which to wash their hands.

Ekram and I started with the earlier period of bin Laden's career, his time in Pakistan and Afghanistan during the war against the Soviets. We learned that, contrary to his image as a leader of a large army of foreign combatants, the contributions of bin Laden himself and the 'Arabs' to the war in Afghanistan were minimal. Most, it appeared, did not fight at all and even bin Laden himself was far from prominent, though he did take part in several battles towards the end of the fighting. It also became clear that none of the Arabs received aid from Pakistan or America, despite what was constantly said. Instead, their money had come from private and public sources in the Middle East. Ekram and I also learned about the sheer number of different militant groups left operating in the region after the war against the Soviets ended. All were focused on exporting their brand of radical militancy around the world, all ran training camps where militants from everywhere from Morocco to the Philippines learned terrorist techniques and tactics, but none were linked to bin Laden. Finally, we began to understand that the real power in bin Laden's circle, certainly in intellectual terms, was Ayman al-Zawahiri, an Egyptian paediatrician who had turned to militancy very early and had been imprisoned in his home country and tortured before coming to Pakistan to support the war against the Soviets in the early 1980s. Al-Zawahiri had experienced the rigours of militant activism at first hand, was a powerful intellectual thinker and, in many ways, was using bin Laden's money and undoubted charisma to further his own personal ambition and the fortunes of Egyptian Islamic Jihad, his own group. Though al-Zawahiri was often described merely as bin

Laden's deputy, it rapidly became apparent to us that his role was a good deal more important.

We then turned our attention to events since bin Laden's return to Afghanistan in 1996. Again we discovered that the standard version of bin Laden's career had been distorted subtly but significantly. We found that his relationship with the Taliban was far more complicated than we had thought. In 1996, for example, bin Laden had been expelled from Sudan and had been invited back to Afghanistan. But not, as was often said, by the Taliban but by three warlords. When his protectors were defeated by the Taliban, bin Laden, through cash and charisma, had partially managed to convince the new rulers of the country that he was an asset, not a liability. But, we found, the Taliban had always remained wary. They were Afghans and bin Laden was an Arab and a foreigner. They were interested in purging their homeland of corruption, he was interested in a campaign to reform the entire Islamic world. This tension had been demonstrated most obviously only a few months earlier, in September 1998, when Mullah Omar, the Taliban leader, had made it clear that the American embassy bombings in East Africa, about which he had not been consulted, had usurped his own authority. Concerned by the international opprobrium that harbouring bin Laden had brought, the Taliban had decided it would be best if the Saudi 'disappeared'. They had no idea where bin Laden had gone, they claimed, somewhat implausibly. Which is why Ekram and I went searching for him. The first place to look was Jalalabad, the eastern Afghan city that was only a day's drive from Peshawar, through the Khyber Pass.

You cannot see the Khyber Pass from Peshawar. At the western end of the rich and fertile plain around the city there is a long, blank wall of hills, the colour of rusted iron plate. The pass itself lies beyond them, protected on both sides by ranks of interlocking cliffs, dry river gullies and the trenches, bunkers and castles left by centuries of warfare. Dozens of armies, including those of Alexander the Great and the Mongols, have battled their way through its narrow defiles, and forts built by the British still exist alongside

newer ones built by the Pakistani army. The narrow road climbed
through hairpins and gorges towards the crest of the pass and then
swung in long arcs on high embankments down the other side on
to flatter ground, through a grove of slim ash trees where hobbled
camels grazed sparse grass, across a dry river bed, into the village
of Torkham and then on to the frontier with Afghanistan itself.

I had travelled through the Khyber many times and always
enjoyed it. As the pass was in tribal territory, and thus beyond the
official control of Islamabad, the authorities insisted that travellers
took a guard, usually a local Frontier Corps militiaman, who had to
be picked up early in the morning from a ramshackle whitewashed
administrative bungalow-cum-barracks in the centre of Peshawar.
You would drive out through the sprawling refugee camps in the
west of the city, across the plains and then start climbing. The
frontier itself, reached after about an hour's drive, was always total
chaos. Pakistani paramilitaries wielding lengths of cable tried to
force some order on a pullulating mass of people. Overloaded,
overdecorated coaches and trucks forced their way through the
crowds, their drivers leaning on the horn. Old men staggered under
vast bulging gunny sacks, children hauled huge and unidentifiable
lumps of scrap metal on ropes and women in burkas toted baskets
of vegetables. Next to a row of kebab stands, each with half a
dozen skinned sheep hanging behind, were the moneychangers,
all with wads of local currencies in brick-sized blocks stacked on
old ammunition boxes in front of them.

On the Afghan side, the scene was much quieter. A few Taliban
soldiers sat under a tree and an old man in a small hut with the
white Taliban flag hanging from a flagpost on its roof drank tea
and stamped visas. There was a dusty patch of land where the
trucks parked on which there always stood a jumbled collection of
old and new vehicles and drivers for hire. Ekram negotiated with
one to take us to Jalalabad, about eighty miles away.

Ekram was happy to be back in Afghanistan and joked and
laughed as we set off in a battered Toyota Corolla, singing along
to a tape of Indian film music the driver had put on as we pulled
away from the frontier. A tape of my own that I had secreted in

my bag delighted them both. Every time we approached a Taliban roadblock, the driver turned off Bootsy Collins and slipped the cassette under his seat. The checkpoints were festooned with the unspooled contents of confiscated tapes, I noticed, but Ekram assured me that the consequences of my own being discovered would probably be nothing more than a lot of shouting at him, a night in the cells for the driver and a reprimand for me. I decided to believe him. We drove down a wide valley with a floor of pebbles and rocks, through sandier terrain covered in small fields and stands of gnarled, stunted trees and then straight and fast along a good flat road across a sun-blasted gravel plain with a ruined village on one side and the refugee camp that had replaced it on the other, then on through several miles of beautifully verdant groves of orange trees with the fruit heavy on their branches. Beyond them was the city of Jalalabad itself, cupped in a bend in a broad, brown river, on a plain flanked by sandy ridges pocked with caves.

We headed for a large house on the outskirts of the city where bin Laden had stayed after his arrival at the Jalalabad airstrip in May 1996. After just a few weeks there, he had moved into the foothills of the white-capped Spin Ghar mountains that Ekram and I could see on the southern horizon and it was from there that, in August 1996, he had issued the first of a series of major statements outlining his strategy, aims and worldview. This was an incoherent, illogical, inchoate but extraordinarily potent brew made up of elements of almost every single radical Islamic strand that had developed over the previous millennium.

The basic element, the stock of bin Laden's soup, so to speak, was very clear. Muslims were at a historic low, beset on all sides by an aggressive West set on dominating and humiliating the lands of Islam and destroying the Muslim religion, either directly by force or indirectly by spurious blandishments that tempted the believer away from the true path. So far, bin Laden said, the ummah had failed to respond adequately to this threat. Muslims were weak and divided. Firm action was necessary, every woman, every man must strain every fibre to make a grand effort, a jihad.

Bin Laden focused particularly on the problems in his homeland, Saudi Arabia, where the ruling family epitomized for him everything that was wrong with the supposed leaders, religious and secular, of the Muslim community.

None of this, of course, was very new. The same thing, more or less, had been said whenever Muslims felt there was a serious threat to traditional society, culture or religious practice. In his statements, bin Laden drew on various sources, two of which were perfect examples of this kind of reaction. One was a conservative thinker called Ibn Taimiya who, following the sack of Baghdad, then the political and cultural centre of the Islamic world, by the Mongols in 1258 had called for a return to fundamentals to strengthen the ummah against the new barbarians. The second was the 250-year-old fundamentalist tradition of Wahhabism, which itself had sprung up in response to the violence and lawlessness of the Arabian peninsula in the mid-eighteenth century and had aimed to restore a golden age of peace and justice. The fact that bin Laden did not mention the various local Afghan movements that had, over the years, pursued similar projects in response to similar circumstances was evidence of how little he was interested in the history and politics of the country he was living in.

Part of the reason for this was that bin Laden was not merely drawing from radical conservative traditions, such as that informing the thought, language and strategy of the Taliban, but from a second, more contemporary strand of Muslim activism too.

Bin Laden had studied modern science at university, had worked in one of his father's companies, had grown up in a contemporary, albeit religious, environment and was thus a man of the modern world. As a student in his native land and as a campaigner in Pakistan he had met many of the most advanced radical Islamic theorists. Their key aim, though few articulated it explicitly, was not to reject the West but to borrow from the West what was needed to create the political, material and technological strength that would allow the Islamic world to compete with and defeat those who had conquered so much of it over the previous three centuries. They aimed not to turn the clock back, which they knew impossible, but to create a contemporary world, a modernity, that was more to their liking and more on their terms. So, for example, these thinkers did not want to destroy the structures of the western European modern nation state, though nations were supposedly un-Islamic, but to appropriate them to build a new, modern, Islamic society. These pragmatic thinkers had been an isolated few at the beginning of the twentieth century but had grown in intellectual strength and popularity as the decades passed. The ideology that they eventually formulated owed much to radical secular European left-wing and right-wing thought, in particular the organized mass movements of communism and fascism, and, partly as a result, they were often called 'Islamists'. On the whole, they were young or youngish men who lacked formal religious learning and had often trained in modern, pro-fessional, technical and scientific disciplines such as engineering. Their strategy was practical and proactive and they had learned from European revolutionary theory the absolute necessity of radicalizing and mobilizing the supposedly unenlightened masses through action and propaganda. Bin Laden was as much a part of this strand of thought as he was steeped in the more reactionary tradition of Ibn Taimiya and the Wahhabis.

But he and al-Zawahiri added a final element to their stew, spicing it with a range of piquant, very modern, flavours. They were ideologically omnivorous and were thus able to throw in Arab nationalism, a snarling adolescent contempt for the mundane life of those who fail to take responsibility for their own lives which owed as much to the Western romantic tradition as it did to anything else and a range of issues such as the exploitation of mineral resources and the Western domination of financial markets that were recognizable to anyone in the developing world with concerns about the negative impact of global capitalism. In addition, a range of historical references embedded in bin Laden's statements linked current events, key moments in Islamic history and mythology. So his associates became the *muhajiroun*, the com-panions who had fled with Mohammed from persecution in Mecca; his opponents were 'Crusaders'; the world of unbelief

was *jahiliya*, or barbarism, the term used in the Koran to describe
the 'pagan' chaos and violence of Arabia before the coming of
Islam, and bin Laden's own flight from persecution in his native
land became a *hijra*, the name given to the prophet Mohammed's
own precipitous departure from Mecca. More contemporary allu-
sions to objects of widespread hatred and fear were added too, so
Zionists and Jews, seen as synonymous by bin Laden and many
others in the Islamic world, became a key enemy. All these references and visual images were intended to allow bin Laden's slogans
to bypass rational thought and plug straight into the emotional and
the unconscious, something that was absolutely crucial given the
often limited literacy of the target audience in the Middle East.

In many ways, the intellectual content of the various elements
of bin Laden's manifesto was irrelevant. In a very contemporary
way it was their combination, their juxtaposition and the cultural
baggage they dragged behind them that were important. The
package of ideas, 'al-Qaedaism', was powerful and, crucially, easily
comprehensible. What it lacked in intellectual depth it made up
for in the breadth of its references, its dynamic energy and its
certainty. But though bin Laden was confident he had an effective
message and an effective strategy, he was stuck up a mountain in
Afghanistan. He may have had a message but the problem was
getting enough people to listen to it. And this, as Ekram and I
discovered as we worked our way through a number of contacts
in Jalalabad, was where bin Laden did more than merely synthesize
existing elements of radical Islamic thought and really began to
break new ground.

We spent a week in the city carefully asking what we hoped
were the right questions of the right people. This was a delicate
task but we made some progress. We heard that bin Laden had
recently been trying to buy large numbers of satellite telephones
as well as computers. One commander told us that 'some of the
Arabs', meaning the Egyptians, Algerians, Palestinians and Saudi
Arabians who made up bin Laden's close circle, had been enquiring
about restoring the old Russian communications equipment that
had been lying about the city since the 1980s. In the bazaar, we

picked up stories about televisions and short-wave radios being purchased in bulk. Someone else told us about flights to Dubai where some of the more senior Taliban, on diplomatic missions to the United Arab Emirates (which, along with Saudi Arabia and Pakistan had recognized their government), had bought both antacids and satellite dishes for 'the sheikh'. What was rapidly becoming clear was that, in addition to having poor digestion, bin Laden, who had always been interested in manipulating the media, had realized the potential of communications technology that was emerging in the mid-1990s. He appeared to have grasped how the power of modern broadcasting could help him rally large populations to his cause without long and difficult campaigns of grass-roots social and political activism. The key was effective propaganda. And television was the perfect medium to communicate his demotic, debased, lowest-common-denominator ideological package, glossing over its internal intellectual inconsistencies and making it understood, whatever the reading skills of the viewers, from Morocco to Malaysia and beyond. The new satellite television channels that were proliferating throughout the Arab world would get him heard everywhere, wherever he was. There was the rapidly proliferating, cheap and uncensorable internet too, and a whole generation who were growing up with television as their primary source of information about both their own societies and the West.

One night I sat on the open terrace at the front of the dilapidated Spinghar hotel, built by the Soviets on the outskirts of Jalalabad, and tried to connect what I had seen over the previous year or so with what I thought had been bin Laden's strategy. Superficially, it appeared that bin Laden's position had deteriorated considerably following the double bombing of the American embassies a few months before. He was now officially 'disappeared' and banned from making any public statements. But, I realized, his actual, physical location was no longer very important. Back in 1996, when bin Laden was barely known, his statements would have received little attention. Now, following the double attacks, everyone would listen to what he had to say.

Bin Laden's propaganda strategy was based in public, spectacular and violent action. This, he hoped, would weaken the enemy, boost his own profile and increase the flow of recruits and donations to his group. But bin Laden and al-Zawahiri had also recognized something else of critical importance. They recognized that spectacular violence could have a radicalizing effect on the masses who had hitherto failed to heed their call to arms. The crucial connection they had made was that the power of public violence lies as much in its effect on the audience as in its effect on the victim.

When Ekram was stopped and interrogated by the Taliban about our activities it was clear that it was time to return to Peshawar. But we had one task remaining. We had been told that bin Laden had bought a disused collective farm built by the communists called Farm Hadda about ten miles south of the city and was staying there with his family. We took a taxi through the bazaar, across an old iron girder bridge, past a group of Taliban soldiers sitting on an old Soviet tank, through a village of mud-built single-room homes and out on to a dirt road beside a canal running between regular, if overgrown, fields and up to a checkpoint at the gates of the farm. We stopped a few hundred yards away. The men guarding it were Afghan, not Arab, and told us that we could look around if we wanted to but that we would find no trace of bin Laden. They were not lying. There was nothing in the ramshackle collection of old sheds and defunct agricultural machinery that indicated the presence of the world's most wanted terrorist. This was actually something of a relief. We turned round and went home. Not until much later did we find out how close we had been.

The Western media's interest in bin Laden, though intense in the summer and autumn of 1998, waned rapidly. I spent the winter travelling extensively in Pakistan, doing a number of stories in India, reading and working on my Urdu and Arabic. Yet it was Afghanistan that continued to draw my attention and I found myself constantly looking for excuses to return.

I had always wanted to meet Ahmed Shah Massood, the legendary guerrilla commander whose tactical brilliance had made him the most effective and best known of the mujahideen leaders who had fought the Soviets. My opportunity came in the late spring of 1999, six months after Ekram and I had been in Jalalabad looking for bin Laden, when it became clear that the Taliban were massing large numbers of troops for a major offensive against Massood's base in the Panjshir valley seventy miles north of Kabul. I rang the *Observer*, persuaded them to cover the expenses of the trip and set off, flying first from Islamabad to Tashkent, the capital of Uzbekistan, and then driving via Samarkand to the Tajik border. From there I planned to drive to the Tajik capital of Dushanbe and hitch a ride on a helicopter to where Massood was based.

Before leaving Uzbekistan, I had canvassed local opinion about the security situation in Tajikistan. The vicious civil war that had racked the central Asian state in the aftermath of the collapse of the Soviet Union was more or less over but large groups of bandits, renegade troops, warlords and Islamic militants still ran significant parts of the country. I knew the political situation was fluid, with rapidly shifting alliances and truces between the various groups and the government, so had made sure that my projected route had run through pro-government territory. Sadly, everything was somewhat more fluid than I had anticipated. I had spent an extra night in Tashkent, getting extremely drunk in a nightclub with a group of arms dealers, and then loitered for an extra day in Samarkand enjoying the spectacular medieval Islamic architecture. This was a mistake as during that 48-hour delay several key militias on the road to Dushanbe decided to go freelance.

There was no sign of any problem to start with. After the avaricious and aggressive Uzbek border police, the Tajik customs and immigration guards, despite their bandanas, tight T-shirts and heavily muscled torsos, were refreshingly amiable, demanding nothing more than a $5 cash 'special visa fee' to enter their country. Once across the border, I hired a battered Lada taxi and bought some salami and four round flat loaves of sourdough bread, some cold beer and a big bag of bright red cherries. Within an hour or so we were climbing through the foothills of the Pamir mountains.

The first indication of trouble came when we rattled to a halt in a small, shady village before a makeshift roadblock comprising an old swing-gate and a small group of men wearing dirty combat kit and carrying guns. Their commander opened the passenger door and beckoned me out with the muzzle of his Kalashnikov. He took my passport and then ransomed it, demanding note after note of Tajik roubles to be laid among the tea cups and stale bread on an old school desk that sat in the shade beside the road. Every time I paused in counting out the notes his men swung their guns towards me. When we reached 800 Tajik roubles I realized that this particular game could go on for a long time and handed the commander a pen and suggested he named his price. Illiterate, but too proud to admit it, he wrote down 1000 R – about 70p. I had several thousand dollars in cash in my shoes so this seemed very reasonable. A few miles on the same thing happened. This time a little more money changed hands, the scene was a little uglier and the threats a little sharper. I was marched to the edge of the road and made to stand facing over a huge cliff that dropped down to a fast-moving mountain river.

We drove on, steadily climbing. Then came a third checkpoint, just past a tiny, pathetically poor village and immediately below the 11,000-foot pass that led over the final range of mountains and down to Dushanbe. The militia stopped me again, gave me the same bullying sneers, the same demands for cash with a rubbed forefinger and thumb, the same Kalashnikov muzzle thrust through the car window. This time I did not get out of the car, relying on a bewildered smile and the patiently repeated half-lie 'but I am just a journalist travelling to your capital to meet your president. All my documents are in order. Here's my visa, look. *Khorosho. Khub.*' The stand-off went on for some time. Then, very deliberately, the largest, ugliest militiaman reached into the car, into the bag of cherries on my lap, ate one, spat the pip into the car and waved us through.

Through our filthy back window I could see a frantic argument among the militia taking place as we chugged away up the dirt track towards the pass. Within thirty seconds half a dozen of them had piled into a large old Volga saloon and set off after us, leaving the cherry eater, responsible for letting such a prime looting opportunity go wanting, alone at the checkpoint. There followed a farcical car chase, conducted at about 15 miles an hour in twenty-year-old vehicles up a mountain road little better than a broad goat track. It was horrendous. Before we had gone half a mile it was clear that, despite its load, the soldiers' car was gaining on us, albeit only incrementally. I made universal 'go faster' signals at the driver. He made universal 'I am going as fast as I can' signals back. As we got higher we went slower, the Lada shuddering with the effort, and though the soldiers' car slowed too it was clear they were still gaining, pointing weapons at us out of the windows, waving fists and shouting. We carried on up the hairpins. The top of the pass looked impossibly distant. Soon both cars were travelling at the speed of a middle-aged jogger. We crept around another hairpin. They were still there, gaining on us, forty yards away now. We painfully hauled ourselves around another bend, the Volga now thirty yards behind. And another: twenty yards. Then came the penultimate turn before the pass. Both cars were now moving at walking pace, coughing and backfiring. I was frantically calculating distances and options. Could I make a run for it? But where to? Maybe there was someone at the top of the pass? Maybe I could call the police? But the militia were the police. And then I noticed that they had not come round the corner behind us. Thirty seconds passed, then a minute, and they still were not in sight. Then we made the final turn and could see them, two turns back down the hill, with stones wedged under their car's wheels and its bonnet up, their guns shouldered. I looked at the driver. He looked at me. We both made 'thank Christ/Allah for that' gestures. Two hours later we were in Dushanbe. A week after that I was on a helicopter into Afghanistan.

By early June, when I arrived in the valley to seek him out, Massood had been in the Panjshir valley for several weeks and knew that the time for preparation was nearly over and that the year's fighting would begin very soon. His days were a flurry of hurried meetings with all his various sub-commanders, who each had his own loyal band of soldiers and who together comprised his 10,000-strong force. It took me two days to trace the Commander, as Massood was known to everyone, to his father-in-law's house in the small village of Bazarak. Massood, then aged 48, spoke to me sitting, unsmiling and preoccupied, his thick black hair and beard flecked with grey, at a desk in his library on which were a radio, a pen and a single notepad for writing orders. Through the windows I could see a river, a patch of grass, some slender poplars with yellow leaves, a rocky hillside and a blue sky ribbed with thin, high white cloud. There were hundreds of volumes on the shelves of the library, in Arabic, Persian, Urdu, Pashto and various Western languages. Many were religious, volume after volume of Koranic exegesis, discussions of Islamic law and practice, the works of major Muslim thinkers, but there were rows of other more secular works too, works on Mao Zedong's theories of guerrilla warfare, economic analyses, a history of Marxism. Massood said he was confident that his troops would repel the Taliban assaults, adding that, though the offensive would 'cause few problems', he was ready for peace talks. 'We don't want to rule the country. We just want a representative government for all Afghans,' he told me. 'I am looking forward to the years when I do not have to fight.' Both statements were probably true.

By noon the interview was over. It had not been particularly illuminating but I was not bothered. One of the interesting things about Massood was the way he had been mythologized by Western journalists, especially in France, as some kind of Afghan secular liberal democrat and I had just wanted to meet him in the flesh. Actually, despite the image projected in the West, Massood was a man of profound faith. In many ways, he was a classic political Islamist, taking, as the books on his library shelves showed, what he needed from the West and grafting it on to local practices. Indeed, twenty-five years previously, he had tried to lead a revolt aimed at seizing power in Kabul and Islamicizing the state. Religion also played a powerful role in the lives of his soldiers, though they, without the benefit of the Commander's university education and his exposure to international political Muslim thought, preferred the traditional, folksy, moderate and tolerant Sufi-influenced style of Islam with its shrines and saints and amulets that was practised in most of Afghanistan. As with the Kurdish peshmerga, their faith was ever-present but almost invisible, part of their culture as much as anything else.

I wandered out of the house and walked into Bazarak to find some lunch. It was Friday and there was no one on the streets. A small congregation had gathered for Friday prayers at the mosque. The mullah there told me Bazarak had once been a village of 400 families or around 3,000 people. Five hundred were killed in the war against the Soviets and 500 more in the fighting of the early 1990s. Another thousand or so had fled, most to Pakistan. A few days earlier the valley had been bombarded by one of the few jets the Taliban could fly. There had been fighting down on the front lines, thirty miles away, the mullah said. I hired a battered Russian-made car and, with a young soldier who spoke Urdu as a guide, headed south.

By early evening I was on the northern side of the same front line I had visited so many times from Kabul. I wondered if the Hazaras were still in their bunkers. It seemed unlikely. In Ishka-shim, a village set halfway up one of the forested hillsides on the flanks of the hills that rimmed the plains, I found three teenage soldiers sitting on an ancient Soviet-built tank parked in the ruins of a ruined royal summer palace eating fresh mulberries, drinking yoghurt and listening to the dull rumble of the artillery on the front line a few miles to the south. Their commander had pulled them back from their bunkers and their trenches to avoid exposing them to the bombardment that was meant to soften them up for the Taliban attack and so now, along with a score of their comrades, they sat and waited, their weapons spread among the marble terraces and the broken colonnades. The sun was low, its warm rays splintering through the rows of trees and hedgerows, bathing the plain below the villa in a spray of honey-coloured light that obscured the damage done by decades of war, depopulation and disease.

The three young fighters were 15, 16 and 18 years old, had been fighting for a year and were full of bravado. 'I am ready to fight and I am as strong as any other man,' said the youngest, Mohammed Gul, puffing out his thin chest, skinny arms folded across a Kalashnikov. 'First we must win this war, then I can go to school.'

Gul insisted that I see the gym he had set up. Under the trees of what was once was an ornamental orchard, the boys had lined up different-sized mortar bombs as dumbbells and were using an old ammunition box as a bench. They told war stories with the same studied nonchalance with which I, as a teenager, had told tales of how much I had drunk. Gul's ambition was to be allowed to use one of the two RPGs, rocket-propelled grenade launchers, distributed to his thirty-man group.

'Last year the Taliban came at us when we were in the front line and they came in straight lines,' he said. 'We were in our positions so they couldn't see us and it was easy to shoot them down. I don't know how many I killed but it was a lot. When they come this time I want to have the RPG so I can kill more.'

Massood withstood the offensive of 1999 and, by the time the winter came, had retaken all the ground he had lost in the fierce fighting of the summer. The Taliban were running out of men. Many of Mullah Omar's original band had been killed, the tribes who had supported them were getting tired and the medressas in Pakistan were exhausted. The small group of leaders was becoming increasingly isolated and increasingly dependent on Osama bin Laden and the radical militants. In December, the UN passed sanctions against the Taliban regime, restricting trade and financial activity with Afghanistan. As there was little of either, the sanctions had no real effect beyond increasing the profound sense among the Afghans that they had been completely abandoned by just about everybody.

I made another trip to Kabul just before the end of 1999. It was cold and wet and there was little electricity and everyone, myself included, devoted a significant proportion of their time simply to staying warm. I have many memories of that last trip to Kabul before so many things changed. For some reason the memories are very visual, like postcards or snapshots taken hurriedly with a cheap camera. I can see malnourished infants in the children's hospital on the outskirts of the city with pinched faces in which pulsing veins, as blue as slate, were very clear under the stretched, pale skin. I can remember the small acts of everyday defiance that allowed the people of the city to keep their spirits alive: shoes, bright red and shiny patent black, white and green, with a gold bow or a plastic flower, that were visible under the uniform blue of the burkas that were compulsory for women outside their homes. In the evenings, the men got together for sly sessions where they watched Western videos on strictly illegal VCRs and wore leather jackets, frowned upon as 'modern' if not actually forbidden. In the centre of the city, down a narrow side street six inches deep in mud, a semi-clandestine bird market flourished. Every few weeks the city's pigeon fanciers illegally raced their birds. 'How do you stop a hundred birds in flight?' one professional breeder asked me and shrugged.

Down one ragged street close to the near-derelict buildings of the old polytechnic, I found a boxing gym where thirty young men were sparring, skipping and working on the light and heavy bags. On one wall was a very big poster of a sunny Newcastle upon Tyne. Wasiuddin, a skinny 19-year-old, said he lived with his family in the northern suburbs of Kabul up towards the front lines and when he was not boxing read religious books and poetry. One day, he said, he hoped to box overseas and escape Kabul. 'I am a bit of a dreamer,' he admitted. A mile away in the central Zamangar Square, an enterprising 25-year-old rode his motorbike round the inside of a thirty-foot high wooden drum watched, five times a day, by a small crowd. He made enough to pay for food and fuel for his family and was a hero to hundreds of scrofulous seven-year-olds.

And I can remember sitting in Kabul's only restaurant and hearing there was to be another execution. A woman was to be killed. At the football stadium, a mullah was addressing the crowd on the cold terraces, explaining that the sentence of death had been passed because of the gravity of the offence. The woman, after trial in three courts, had been found guilty of killing her husband with a hammer. The mullah quoted the relevant references from the Koran and the Hadith, the collection of anecdotes about the prophet Mohammed that are a key source of Islamic jurisprudence. Young Taliban fighters with black turbans and relaxed young faces swaggered by in small groups. Many were on a break from the front line and those with grenade launchers or heavier machine guns wore them like trophies.

I watched the men sitting around me. Most showed little animation, talking quietly among themselves, cracking open pistachio nuts and dropping the shells on to the concrete under their plastic shoes. They did not appear to be Taliban, or Taliban supporters on the whole, but Kabulis, largely from the poor but not poorest social groups. They were taxi drivers, vegetable salesmen, mechanics. They were ordinary men.

I can remember the execution quite clearly. I can still remember hearing the mechanical rasp of the breech being worked on the Kalashnikov and being struck by how quiet it must be for such a sound to be audible in a football stadium, even from where I was sitting thirty yards away. I can remember a light breeze lifting the pleated hem of the woman's blue burka and I can remember three sharp shots cracking out, with a longer gap between the second and third. I remember hearing the sound of the shots and then seeing dust and dirt spout from the ground in front of the woman and thinking that the gunman had missed and then realizing that actually the dust had been raised by a bullet that had passed straight through the woman's head. And I can still remember how, on the third shot, a single shard of white skull flew out through the air as the top of the woman's head came away at almost exactly the same time as she toppled over. At the execution a year before, there had been an almost triumphant shout of *Allahu akbar* when the man had been killed. This time there was only a low muttering of the same words. Nobody said very much as we filed out of the stadium. There was a general sense of having seen something shameful, something that had damaged or sullied us all in some indefinable way. More than anything, there was a sense of guilt and of somehow being complicit in the act that we had witnessed. This bred a strange and disconcerting sense of solidarity.

I have thought about that feeling many times since and, the more I have considered it, the more significant it has become. It showed me how violence works on spectators, particularly those who have even the smallest sense that what they are watching can be justified in some way. This was the effect that bin Laden and al-Zawahiri had so crucially understood. If you do not act to stop something happening, if you do not wholeheartedly condemn it, then you feel yourself aligned with the executioners. There was nothing I could have done to save the life of the condemned prisoner, yet I felt partly responsible for her death. I thought about how Saddam Hussein, as I had been told in Kurdistan, had ordered his henchmen to film their acts of torture and killing, to bind them to him and each other in the mutual knowledge of their culpability. I thought of the honour killings in Pakistan and how such ritualized and overt violence not only publicly demonstrated the power of a Pashtun tribe to chastise those who transgress its rules but also bound together those who participated in, watched or supported the killing. And I thought of Chak 100P, where I remembered Muradam Mai, the supposed witch, was burned alive in the most public place available, the village square, and how the community, or at least the dominant part of it, had closed ranks behind her murderers. If you want to build solidarity, to mobilize and radicalize, then violence was clearly an effective way of doing it. And for the strategy to work as intended, the violence needed not just to be done but, like justice, to be seen to be done too.

4. The House of Wisdom

I left Pakistan in the spring of 2000, six months after Pervaiz Musharaf, an army general, had taken power in a bloodless and relatively popular coup. I returned to London to be the *Observer*'s chief reporter. This meant an end to the freedom of freelancing but a far wider remit. I flew into Sierra Leone on a British naval helicopter gunship, reported on the fates of Khmer Rouge killers in Cambodia, spent weeks disguised as a tourist amid the chaotic violence of Zimbabwe, investigated cocaine in Colombia and religious massacres in Uganda. It was exciting, varied and constantly stimulating. But, though there were major stories elsewhere, it was stories in the Islamic world that dominated the news agenda and continued to fascinate me.

The most memorable focused on a little-known war, now virtually over, in Algeria and on the two constants of recent reporting of the Islamic world: the conflicts in 'Israel–Palestine' and Iraq.

Reporting these three stories took me into an entirely new area. I was now working in what was almost universally considered the heart of the Muslim world. There were plenty of reasons to challenge that definition – such as the fact that the combined number of Muslims living east of the Arabian Sea far exceeded those living to its west – but it remained the case that in popular imagination the Middle East was the core and the cradle of Islam. I knew that, though I had learned something about how Islam worked at a personal and national level while in Pakistan and Afghanistan, a lot was going to be different.

First of all, there was clearly a whole new question of ethnicity. Occasionally in southwest Asia I had seen how a particular strand of Islam had articulated a specific ethnic chauvinism but on the whole questions of 'race' and religion had remained distinct. In the core Middle Eastern countries and the Maghreb, however, the population was very largely of Arabic ethnicity and this, perhaps slightly paradoxically, made issues of racial and religious identity sharper. Was Islam the religion of the Arabs? Were Arabs of different faiths closer than Muslims of different ethnicities? On what basis should personal and political alliances, or differences, be defined? All these questions were perpetually in play.

There were other important issues to explore too. People in the Middle East always seemed to be far more resentful and angry towards former colonial powers than people in southwest Asia. This, I sensed, was due to two interlinked factors. The first was the fact that outside Arabic nations, despite the universalizing nature of Islam, much that had come from the Middle East, including the first Islamic rulers of places like southern Pakistan and western Afghanistan, was seen as foreign. Second, the contrast between the great Arabic-Islamic empires of the seventh to thirteenth centuries, which had been based in Damascus and Baghdad, and the ease with which a massively technologically and militarily superior West had conquered the Middle East more recently was seen less and less as a personal humiliation the further you got from the Arab heartlands. It was also the case that the colonial interventions in the Middle East had taken place far more recently than in Asia and were often very much part of living memory. They had also frequently been more brutal.

However, differences could be exaggerated. It was also clear that there were many commercial, economic, cultural, political and of course religious links. A large proportion of the major movements, spiritual or secular, that had influenced southwest Asia and to a lesser extent the Muslim communities of the Far East had their origins in the Middle East. It was in the Middle East too that many tactics of violence, including suicide bombing, had been pioneered and from where much of the language and thought of the new radical 'jihadi' Islamic discourse had come. There was a lot to learn, an imposing amount of scholarship to wade through, a very technical and highly politicized vocabulary to master and it was with some trepidation that I headed, in the spring of 2000, to Iraq.

As there were no air links, the easiest way to get to Baghdad was by driving in across the desert from Jordan. Leaving Amman, the Jordanian capital, before dawn got me to the border at noon. The first thing I saw at the frontier was a huge statue of Saddam Hussein. Astride a rearing stallion, the dictator brandished a curved sword in the air. Four rockets hovered at stirrup level. Behind the statue and the official buildings, rag-pickers moved among the rubbish blowing across a cleared area among an expanse of gravel. Otherwise the landscape was simply composed of rocks of varying size and stretched in every direction almost without relief. A vague line of darker brown above the caramel and burnt-wood tones of the desert indicated the hills by the Syrian border to the northwest. The statue stood on a pedestal ten feet tall on which someone had chalked, in English, a short and understandably ambivalent sentence: 'You are welcome to Iraq'. A six-lane expressway led east to the capital.

As, like Afghanistan, Iraq was under UN sanctions and had suffered war for decades, I was expecting conditions in Baghdad to be similar to those in Kabul. It rapidly became clear, however, as we passed dozens of roadside restaurants and rows of shops full of dates, chocolates, soft drinks, soap and other goods that Afghanistan had barely seen for years, that my water filter, spare food and spare batteries would not be needed. The raft of sanctions imposed in 1991 to punish Saddam for the invasion of Kuwait was falling apart. In Baghdad I stayed at the al-Rasheed hotel which had an open-air heated swimming pool that steamed in the chill night. Its lobby was full of Middle Eastern businessmen in impeccably cut suits negotiating multimillion-pound deals with their European and Russian counterparts. Though the majority of the Iraqi people may have been suffering, some were clearly doing well.

Reporting Iraq was much more difficult than reporting Afghanistan. The Taliban's understanding of the international media was very poor and, despite melodramatic claims to the contrary by some journalists, the worst they would do if you broke their rules was expel you. But the Iraqis ran a massive and very effective operation to manage the coverage of their country. All journalists had to report to the Ministry of Information's press centre, where they were assigned a translator-cum-minder who would accompany them everywhere and report on their activities to a variety of agencies. Any stories a journalist wrote, even if filed from outside Iraq, were monitored and could result in blacklisting and the denial of future visas. The consequence was that there were only two stories that could be reported from inside the country: the impact of ten years of sanctions and the results of the low-intensity air war waged in tandem against the Iraqi anti-aircraft defences.

Fear pervaded Iraq in the same way that insecurity had done in Pakistan. It meant that conversations, translated by the official minder, were often farcical. People spoke of their 'love' for the president, his kindness and wisdom. With tears in their eyes, they pleaded their gratitude for all he had done for them. It was impossible to tell whether they had so internalized Saddam's propaganda that they actually believed what they said or whether they were merely mouthing platitudes out of fear. The power of the security apparatus also placed great responsibility on the journalist. A misreported quote, a phrase 'tidied up' to fit the sense of a story better or a wrongly spelt name could have terrible consequences. When the owner of a newly opened and, on account of its huge plastic fake turrets and battlements, clearly identifiable restaurant spoke to me about the 'problems' he had when his establishment was too busy to find tables for people connected with the ultra-rich clique that had grown up around Saddam and his immediate cronies, his words earned him a terrifying 'visit' after my article came out. He was lucky no genuine harm resulted. Others were not so fortunate. And though the brutal methods of Saddam's security apparatus were well known, writing about the continuing human rights abuses in Iraq, at least from inside the country, was impossible. Rightly, no one was prepared to voice any criticism of the president, by then in the twenty-first year of his rule. An indication of the atmosphere in Iraq was the 'thought for the day' in the *Baghdad Observer* one morning: 'Keep your eyes on your enemy. Be ahead of him but do not let him be far behind your back.' The only thing to do was to negotiate with your minder so you did not see only what the press centre wanted you to see, to remember that no one was telling the whole truth, to keep in mind that you were being sold a particular line and to report what you saw in the knowledge that there were a lot of appalling things happening in Iraq that, if you ever wanted to travel to the country again, you could not pursue. Thankfully, there were many reporters outside Iraq who continued to run stories, most of which were true, about Saddam's revolting treatment of his people and his lavish expenditure on scores of palaces. Many also, of course, wrote stories that were completely false.

Arguing over whether Saddam or the sanctions were responsible for the suffering in Iraq always seemed to me to be completely futile. An arsonist had torched his own house and the fire brigade had turned up and poured petrol on the flames. Iraq, however you looked at it, was a deeply depressing place.

On arrival in any new city, there are various places where a reporter can go to find stories. These are not, usually, ministries or embassies but hospitals, police stations and schools. On my first morning in Baghdad, with a heavy fog stubbornly refusing to clear from the Tigris, I drove in a 1975 vintage black Cadillac that had been imported long before war and sanctions, with Sa'ad, a heavy-set but somehow gentle middle-aged minder from the Ministry of Information beside me, through near-deserted streets, surprised by the sheer size of the city. The roads were broad and well lit but almost empty. Baghdad, with its stained, brutalist-style, concrete government offices, rows of decrepit tenements and scruffy markets did not much resemble the fabled city of legend. A fine rain began to fall.

The al-Mutanabi primary school, set back off a busy potholed road, was dilapidated but functioning. After tea in her office, where a single-bar heater just about took the edge off the damp cold, Mrs Sohaila Khudeir, the 48-year-old headmistress, guided Sa'ad and me through the school's chilly corridors. There was no heating, many of the windows were broken, the books were old and torn, the desks worn out but the classrooms were full. 'Before the sanctions we had new books every year but now we only get a few. The parents have to pay for half the cost and they don't have the money. We got a batch of pencils recently but they were very poor quality,' Mrs Khudeir said. 'We get around 4,000 dinars each month — not quite enough for a pair of shoes. What makes it so much worse is that when I started as a teacher, the money was good. We lived well. Now . . . nothing.' She shrugged her shoulders.

Her classrooms looked like classrooms anywhere, though with grubbier and thinner children and peeling posters and pictures of the president in each one. Mrs Khudeir told me how about two-thirds of the population of Iraq lived on food distributed by the United Nations as part of the sanctions system. Since 1996 the Iraqis had been allowed to sell some of their oil, from the second largest reserves in the Middle East, on the international market as long as the profits were controlled by the UN. However, as the food ration included only essentials such as rice, salt and flour each month, extras like fruit and vegetables had to be bought, at exorbitant prices, in the markets. As a result, few of the children in the school, which was in a relatively poor area of the city, had eaten meat for several days. A highly controversial Unicef study that I picked up from the UN's Baghdad headquarters on my way over to the school claimed, to Sa'ad the minder's great satisfaction, that around a third of all Iraqi children were malnourished.

'The level of education has been dropping for years,' Mrs Khudeir was saying. 'When I started as a teacher twenty-five years ago, everyone went to school. The government ran big campaigns. Now all the parents have two jobs and no one takes an interest in learning or their kids' education. Families will put one kid in school while their brother goes to work. Or maybe they will all go to work. About half our kids drop out.'

In one classroom a history lesson was underway. I asked what the children were taught about the current situation.

'We teach them the truth,' Mrs Khudeir said. 'They learn that the US is our first enemy and that they are embargoing us and this is affecting every part of Iraq. In geography and history we tell them how Iraq was trying to develop its potential, how it is a rich country, an oil country, but that the Zionists and the Americans are targeting any country that is trying to develop itself. They don't want any other countries to be advanced. We are sure the American people love the Iraqi people but it is just the government who are causing the problem because they are run by the Jews.' She stopped under a poster showing a pencil and an AK47 and the slogan 'The pen and the rifle have only one purpose. Even a student can be a warrior', and turned to me and said: 'The government is not making me say this, my patriotism makes me say this.'

I had been surprised to see that Mrs Khudeir, like all her female staff, was wearing a headscarf. Though just a few days in Baghdad would convince anyone that the secularism and Westernization that had characterized the Iraqi urbanized middle classes in the seventies was long gone, I had not expected such evidence of obvious faith, particularly among women teachers.

'When I was a young teacher I never wore a headscarf,' Mrs Khudeir told me. 'But now I want to dedicate my time to prayer and to studying Islamic law. We are an Islamic country.'

In the playground children chased each other but with little energy. A group of boys had made toy guns out of twigs. Others played with some clear marbles on the top of an oil drum. I spoke to Bilawal, a moon-faced 11-year-old. His father was a taxi driver and his mother was a cleaner, he told me. One elder brother worked, another was at school 'on and off' and his sisters 'helped around the house'. Yes, he said, the family ate a lot of bread and rice and drank a lot of tea. No, he had never seen Western television or magazines or anything like that. Yes, he liked to go to the shop in the market when he had a few dinars and play pool or on the computer games they had there. Yes, he went to the mosque for Friday prayers with his father and sometimes during the week too. 'If a jihad is declared to liberate al-Quds [Jerusalem] and all Palestine then I will go. Saddam is good and if all Arabs were like him then Palestine would be liberated,' he said. I could understand enough of his Arabic to know that Sa'ad's translation was accurate. 'Anyway, we will have a war here before then. The Americans and the British want to invade us.'

As in Pakistan and Afghanistan, there appeared to be little animosity directed at me personally. The children and staff at the school had been polite and welcoming despite my coming from a state that was responsible for the sanctions against them. I wondered how Londoners might feel towards Iraqis if the situation were reversed. One conversation in a coffee shop a few days later was revealing. 'Here in the Middle East, we understand that there is a big difference between the wishes of the people and the decisions of the rulers,' the owner had told me, 'We blame your leaders, not you.' It was a perceptive comment, and as close to a criticism of their own president as anyone in Iraq could come without risking life and livelihood.

Because the president was everywhere. Totalitarianism, I realized, means exactly what it sounds like it means. Saddam's power depended on fear and that fear depended on the idea that there was no one in the country who was beyond his personal reach or the reach of his proxies. So his control was total. The web of informers across his domain meant that no one could be sure that the president was not personally listening to what they were saying. Saddam was certainly always watching. On every wall, on every roadside, there was a picture of him, sometimes smiling, sometimes grim, but always watching.

The ubiquitous pictures of Saddam fascinated me. In Kurdistan nearly a decade before, it had been these images against which the peshmerga had first turned their weapons. The portraits – there must have been tens of thousands of them in the country as a whole – had enormous iconic power despite lacking any aesthetic or technical quality. To start with I avoided them, almost deliberately sitting with my back to the pictures that hung on the wall of every office, every shop and every restaurant. Then I started seeking them out deliberately, taking photographs of them and finally attending and even enjoying, in a slightly perverse way, an exhibition of 'work by new young artists' in which every single painting was a portrait of the leader.

One of the reasons I began to like this slightly bizarre genre of contemporary art was because I began to differentiate between the various sorts of pictures that I saw. Rather like the violence in Pakistan, at first the images had all been an undifferentiated mass. However, soon themes began to emerge and I realized that you could chart the whole of the recent history of Iraq, and the recent political history of the Middle East, through the daubs that defaced half the country's walls.

The pictures could be split into six main categories, each of which had been most favoured at a different period and each of which represented a key constituency within Iraq for Saddam. They thus revealed both the image the dictator was promoting at the time they were made and the ideology that was then more broadly dominant in the region. So the earliest pictures, the black and white portraits that hung in government offices, showed a youngish Saddam in the suit and tie of a political cadre. This I dubbed the 'commissar' look. The pictures, I guessed, dated from the early seventies, when Saddam was deputy president and keen to promote himself as a competent administrator. The period had been a time of astonishing growth as oil revenue flooded into the nation's coffers and a series of extremely successful mass literacy and social uplift programmes had transformed much of the country. I guessed the commissar look might have worked with the new middle classes created by the economic boom at the time in Iraq and in surrounding countries.

Then there were the pictures of Saddam the nationalist/military leader. In these he wore an army uniform and often pilot-style sunglasses. These images appeared to have been most popular in the early 1980s when, after a bloody internal coup, Saddam had become president of Iraq and promptly led the country into a costly war with Iran. Much of his regime's legitimacy at the time was based in the nationalist, aggressively secular, quasi-fascist ideology of the Ba'ath Party and all these elements showed in the bullish portraits of Saddam as the classic developing world dictator. The tricolour Ba'athist and Iraqi flag was noticeable in many of them and the absence of any religious imagery was striking.

Yet one of the key elements of Ba'athism, an ideology that flourished throughout the region in the 1950s and 1960s particularly, was a sense of solidarity between Arabs. And there was little that was essentially Arab, apart from perhaps his moustaches, about the man in khaki and shades. So regime propagandists in Iraq had clearly developed other styles as the war against Iran went on and it became progressively harder to rally support in the face of massive casualties and economic hardship. One style depicted Saddam as an avuncular tribal leader, usually wearing traditional Arab robes and headdress. These pictures would have appealed to the conservative tribal chiefs, particularly in the restive west of Iraq. A second style looted the historical tradition of the country to find archetypes and myths of Arab warriors. Again, partly to highlight the contrast between the secular Saddam and the Ayatollah Khomeini, and the respective troops on both sides, faith-based imagery was avoided during the war with Iran. So, pre-Islamic history such as that of the Babylonian king Nebuchadnezzar was preferred to later episodes and Saddam often appeared in theatrical ancient armour or on a chariot. The victories that the early Arab-Muslim armies had won over Persian forces posed a difficult problem as they were clearly very useful sources of powerful propaganda but had religious overtones. The solution was to emphasize the Arab nature of the forces deployed and airbrush out the Islamic element. A third style, which was astonishingly cynical given the narrow base of Saddam's regime in the Sunni tribes around his home town of Tikrit just north of Baghdad, subtly used details like Kurdish dress or clothes typically favoured by southern Shias to boost the dictator's appeal to other ethnic and religious factions. This latter style was, predictably, relatively rare.

The portraits also revealed how Saddam had been a decade behind the times throughout his political career. As a young man, he had been attracted by the various nationalist and anti-colonialist movements that were then sweeping across the Middle East. Yet by the time he was politically active the withdrawal of most Western powers from the region meant that the anti-imperialist ideologies were defunct. The next dominant ideology to seize the imagination of the masses was Ba'athism and other pan-Arabist, socialist-influenced political strands. Again, however, though successive defeats by Israel in 1967 and 1973 more or less discredited such ideologies in the broader Arab world, Saddam stuck with them right through to the end of Iraq's war with Iran in 1988 and beyond.

The final style of portraits revealed Saddam's ultimate manifestation. All the newest images of the protean dictator, dating from the time of the first Gulf War and growing more numerous as the decade continued, showed Saddam praying, surrounded by religious references and symbols or, if he was in his chariot or tank or even if wearing a suit or a technician's boiler suit, pointing towards the distinctive dome of the al-Aqsa mosque. Again, Saddam had been a little slow to catch up with more general trends. Populations throughout the Middle East had started turning to religion in general and to modernized 'political Islamism' in particular from the mid-1970s, not least because the latter was widely considered the only ideology in the region that had not been tried and seen to fail. Support for the 'Islamists' had grown through the 1980s. It was only in the early 1990s that Saddam had worked this out and, spotting the growing religiosity amongst his own population, had trimmed his sails again. It had not been just an image makeover, either. Saddam had set in train a raft of measures designed to rebuild faith and a politicized Islamic discourse in Iraq, playing down pan-Arab identities in favour of religious alternatives. He had banned alcohol, added *Allahu akbar* to the national flag, increased religious tuition in schools, set up radio stations devoted to Koranic readings and recruited explicitly religious militias as auxiliaries for his army. He had even ordered the construction of a massive mosque which was to have a Koran written in his blood as its centrepiece. This time, as I had seen in the school in al-Mutanabi, he was very much in tune with his population. Unsurprisingly, given the folk religion that had existed all along and the increasingly difficult economic conditions caused by the sanctions imposed by the West through the United Nations, his religious project made rapid progress. His propaganda made sense.

One Friday lunchtime, Sa'ad and I went over to the Sheikh Abdul Qadeer al-Galani mosque, a sprawling complex of white-washed sixteenth-century outbuildings, shimmering domes, offices and marble-laid courtyards which concentrated even the weak February sun into a bleaching white glare. It was very busy and a crowd of women in headscarves and men in traditional dish-dash and chequered kaffiyehs with prayer beads clicking in their hands flowed through the narrow archways, took off their shoes and filed inside. A soldier bent to kiss the mosque's huge brass doors. In the market outside, falafel sellers shouted for business.

After the prayers Sheikh Afif al-Gilani, the young and jocular imam, explained to me that his *khutba*, the sermon that is an integral part of Friday prayers everywhere in the Islamic world, had referred to the story of Job, or 'Ayub' in the Muslim tradition. He said that the president himself, whose scholastic Islamic credentials we both knew to be non-existent, had declared the current time a period of 'construction and jihad' and thus, as the imam put it, 'of passing and overcoming obstacles'.

'Islam and the Arab world are facing a dangerous time full of dangerous questions,' the imam said. 'This is a time full of threats to Muslims and Arabs everywhere. We are a nation of believers.'

If Baghdad had been depressing, then Basra was worse. In the south of Iraq, as in neighbouring Iran, the population was almost entirely Shia. Like the Kurdish north, the Shias had suffered two sets of sanctions through the 1990s: those imposed on the entire country by the international community and those enforced by Saddam. The bulk of the resources of Iraq, of senior positions in the army, the bureaucracy, the Ba'ath Party and its various offshoots and the vast proportion of commercial contracts were all reserved for Sunnis, and whereas Baghdad had electricity most of the time the south, where summer temperatures reached 50°C, got only a few hours of power a day. There were none of the new BMWs and Mercedes favoured by the new semi-criminal, sanction-busting elite of Baghdad on the streets of Basra, just the battered orange and yellow Volkswagen Passats, known as *brasilis* because they were imported from South America in the 1980s. Raw sewage drained into the rubbish-choked canal that ran through the centre of the city. In one of the few pharmacies that were still open, an old man in a frayed beige jumper, a neat if faded tie and shirt, a toothbrush moustache and thick round spectacles that magnified his eyelashes hugely was serving a long line of women in head-scarves who were very quiet and watched the diminishing supply of medicine on his shelves very closely.

In the poorest parts of the city lines of black effluent ran in shallow troughs along the sides of the dirt roads. Broken electricity cables hung like dead snakes from charred poles and the air was thick with the smell of cheap cooking oil, burning rubber and rotting animal and human waste. Long terraces of houses, built of poor-quality concrete and baking under tin roofs, had been laid out on rigid grids. Plastic bags and rubbish littered every open space. Children were shouting raucously and playing in the con-gealing pools of rank fluids at the bottom of a dried-out canal. Crows picked and hopped through the filth.

Omran Ab'd Ali lived down one narrow alley in a small house with fourteen relatives. Despite his evident sickness, there were still traces in his face of the good-looking man he once had been. He spent his days lying on a thin mattress on an old iron bed beneath pictures of Ali and Hussein, the two great martyrs of the Shia faith. The room, the largest in the house, was about ten feet wide and twelve long. There was a thin rug covering part of the floor, some stained cushions and an old fan that just about stirred the fetid air. Omran's mother, who came in to serve us water and tea, rearranged the fake leather jacket her son had slung over his bony shoulders and touched him gently on the forehead with two fingers.

Omran had been a conscript soldier in an anti-aircraft battery during the Gulf War of 1991. His unit suffered no casualties during the fighting but had been almost totally destroyed during the retreat. 'The Allies were very wicked,' Omran said. 'They were striking both the front and back of our column and our commander told us to leave our vehicles and tanks and run for it. So for three days I walked through the desert back to Basra. It was a mess, a rout. No one was in their units. The planes just kept coming. Just one kilometre took me eight hours. Most of my colleagues were martyred.'

Omran's illness developed five years later. He lifted his shirt to show me huge, swollen tumours on his neck and in his armpits. 'I've been getting treatment for two years but nothing works. But the pain is terrible. We have sold everything, the sofas, the air conditioning, everything but this fan to pay for treatment but the medicine has to come from Jordan and costs 360,000 Iraqi dinars for a single course.'

Recently, Omran said, he had become more interested in religion. 'It's because of the disease. I've got a lot of free time. I have been reading the Holy Book and even sometimes fasting.'

No one was sure whether cancers like Omran's were linked to the extensive use of depleted uranium ammunition in the area in 1991. The local doctors, the government and various international agencies said it was. The Western governments whose ammunition was blamed said it was not. There were other things that could have caused the clustering of cancer cases, far in excess of the national average, around Basra such as toxins left over from the heavy shelling the city received during the war against Iran, traces from the chemical weapons that Saddam had deployed to fight back Teheran's human waves, decades of malnutrition, or even radiation from ships sunk in the Shatt al-Arab waterway. Like the argument over whose fault the sanctions were, I did not really feel it mattered what and who was to blame. The suffering was real enough.

I followed one young doctor on a round in the Saddam Hussein Teaching Hospital. The wards stank of stale urine and blood that had soaked and stained the foam mattresses. The beds were badly rusted and there were many flies. Groups of relatives sat on the floor. Most of the women wore full black *abbayas* and many had the blue tattoos of the rural Bedouin tribes on their faces. The doctor had studied in Britain and spoke soft, excellent English. This is what I wrote in my notebook:

Fouda Rahimi, 13, student at school. Huge swelling, size of a melon, in belly. Internal bleeding. Blood spurting. Squealing in pain. Bleeding from lips. Inconsistent supply of drugs so treatment is irregular. Usually patients respond well if have drugs. Fell ill five months ago. Can't prepare platelets because have no platelets. Next case, name is London as in city. During British mandates many took names from British. Is 8 years old. Secondary cancer in vertebrae. Primary cancer not located. Collapsed vertebrae due to cancer so paraplegic. Also secondary cancer in liver, possible in brain. Palliative care only. Relatives all in black from head to toe except for faces and lapis lazuli ring on finger. From villages around Basra. Ward has stained and peeling walls . . . next case poss bladder cancer but don't know . . .

My notes continued, without much variation, for a dozen or so pages. Outside the hospital I walked a little distance and breathed as deeply as I could, the smell of decay and sickness still in my nostrils and throat. The hospital was set in waste ground on the edge of the city and I watched a group of young men kicking a football amongst the piles of smouldering rubbish and brackish puddles. An hour's drive south was the demilitarized zone and the Kuwaiti border. There was nothing there but a few old tanks, a tomato farmer, a road across the blank desert and an irritating wind. I asked the farmer if he was worried about depleted uranium. 'This is my home, my land,' he said and shrugged. 'I can't go anywhere.'

The one thing that no one referred to in Basra was the rising of 1991. Like the Kurds in the north, the Shia in the south believed that they had been encouraged to rebel by the Americans. On 15 February 1991, two weeks before the ceasefire that marked the end of the campaign to free Kuwait, President Bush had said that there was 'another way for the bloodshed to stop, and that is for the Iraqi people to take matters into their own hands'. The remark was broadcast on *Voice of America* and elsewhere, heard widely in southern and northern Iraq and interpreted as a exhortation to revolt and a promise of aid. But no help came and the rebels never stood a chance.

At the time, a few months before my own small adventure in

the north of the country, details of what had happened in the south
were very sketchy. Only a few reports got out and they lacked
credibility. But by 1999 a series of investigations by human rights
organizations had revealed the true extent of the carnage wreaked
as Saddam's forces, led by the elite Republican Guard, had put
down the revolt. A very public, very visible brutality was a central
part of their strategy, so refugee columns were strafed by helicopters, residential areas were indiscriminately shelled and thousands of young men were shot outside their homes. Somewhere
between 50,000 and 200,000 people died. Nobody really knew
the full total.

Just out of interest I asked my minder about what happened. It
was not really fair. After all, he was not a Ba'athist ideologue but
a minor functionary who did what he did because it was the only
way he could keep his family healthy. He did not bat an eyelid.
'Oh that,' he said. 'That was some bad people who came from
outside.'

The saddest place for me in Baghdad was the book market off
al-Rasheed Street where the treasured collections of the middle
classes that had been almost destroyed by the sanctions and the
regime were displayed for sale in long rows on plastic sheets on
the ground. It was here that bibliophile professors and civil servants
and doctors sold off their favourite works, sources of comfort and
consolation and joy over years, to pay for vegetables and fuel. The
scene was made all the more poignant by the knowledge that
Baghdad, a thousand years before, had been the greatest academic
centre in the world, a place where, in the huge Beit al-Hikma, or
House of Wisdom, the only remaining copies of the most important works of Greek philosophy (the rest had been destroyed in
the wars and rapine of post-classical Europe) had been translated
into Arabic by Christian scholars serving the Abbasid emperors.
Without that work, many of the foundational texts of European
thought would have been lost. The Beit al-Hikma was long gone,
of course, and there was little room for such extraordinary scholarship in Iraq now. One man sold me his *Shorter Oxford English*

Dictionary, after carefully tearing out the flysheet on which he had written his name a decade or so before and tucking it in his pocket. At one stall stacks of translated Western classics, once the staple of Baghdad students, lay untouched. 'They don't want these any longer,' the stall holder, who had been in the trade for forty years, said, indicating a book of French Romantic poetry, a Dickens and some dog-eared Shakespeare. 'Now they are just thinking about judgement day.'

Back in my hotel I tried to watch a lengthy presidential speech on state television. Saddam, standing in military uniform next to an Iraqi flag and a large quantity of pink and white roses, was wearing a blue three-piece suit. His address was followed by songs sung by rustic-looking characters in Bedouin dress carrying swords, AK47s and old rifles. Their chants were illustrated by pictures of the al-Aqsa mosque, their leader in a homburg hat and an overcoat firing a rifle in the air at a parade, Orthodox Jews praying at the western wall, Israeli soldiers, uniformed 'martyrs' marching, their leader praying, footage of missiles striking Baghdad in 1991 and Iraqi soldiers striding forward.

5. The First Boy Was Shot at Around Three O'clock

The first boy was shot at around three o'clock. He was carried past me, trying to be brave but sobbing with the pain of his shattered elbow. The next was shot at quarter past the hour and this time said nothing but gasped for air with the sucking mouth and eyes of a fish on a slab and the blood spreading across his shirt from a chest wound. The third was shot about forty-five minutes later. By early evening I had counted six seriously injured teenagers loaded into the ambulances drawn up a few hundred yards away and driven off to the hospital in Gaza City.

I was crouched by a cinder block wall around five feet high, surrounded by Palestinian youths making petrol bombs and breaking rocks to make them better missiles. Behind the wall was a warehouse and then a half-constructed five-storey block, once intended to be apartments or offices. In front of the wall, about fifty yards away, was a crossroads guarded by an Israeli army bunker surrounded by a high wire fence and dirt ramparts. The road to the right led down to the Israeli settlement of Netzarim, just visible as a line of neat white houses with terracotta tile roofs that stood out against the blue horizontal of the Mediterranean beyond. The road behind me led between olive groves and scruffy fields and small villages to the Erez checkpoint and 'Israel proper'. The road on the other side of the crossroads led further into the Gaza Strip.

All afternoon I had watched the same thing happening. The cycle was simple. It took between fifteen and thirty minutes for the youths around me to work themselves up to charge. Then, with a shout of '*yallah shebab*', half would run out into the road hurling stones and petrol bombs at the bunker, most of which missed and exploded in oily gouts of black smoke and flame. At least one of them would then run forward and try to tie a Palestinian flag to the fence around it. A single shot would ring out, dropping one of the demonstrators, a shout of *Allahu akbar* would go up from the others and the wounded youth would be carried by his peers back to the Red Crescent first-aid teams and taken to hospital.

When it got dark and the crowds showed no sign of dispersing, the Israelis decided to clear the road by opening fire with a heavy machine gun mounted on one of the tanks protecting the settlement a mile or so away. If they had fired into us all it would have been horrific. Instead they fired high enough to miss the crowd but low enough to send fat tracer rounds, flaring yellow as they streamed across in the dusk, into the telegraph poles, sending spectacular explosions of sparks into the air and on to the tarmac. At the sound of the heavier fire, everyone behind the wall scattered, most running away from the bunker towards a small group of concrete buildings a hundred yards away. From the olive groves around us Palestinian gunmen who had been watching the *shebab* during the afternoon themselves opened fire on the bunker and the settlement with automatic weapons. It was total mayhem and must have been extraordinarily loud. Yet strangely I heard no sound at all. I hunched myself behind a road sign, then realized that half an inch of tin was not going to stop a heavy-calibre bullet travelling at a thousand yards or more per second and stretched myself flat on the tarmac behind the kerbstone until the shooting died down.

For the next two weeks and on through the whole of the autumn of 2000 I watched the same scene, almost a ritual, repeated again and again as the 'al-Aqsa' intifada, named after the main mosque on the Dome of the Rock or Temple Mount in Jerusalem, continued. The word intifada means 'shaking off', and at first every day, then every other day, then only on Friday afternoon after prayers, demonstrations would convulse the Gaza Strip and the West Bank, the territories Israel had occupied, along with the old city of Jerusalem, after defeating invasion by various Arab armies in the 1967 war. The demonstrations were interspersed with Israeli incursions and rocket strikes and Palestinian attacks on settlements, cars and soldiers. I went often to the West Bank town of Ramallah, the seat of Yasser Arafat's incompetent and corrupt Palestinian Authority. There, the demonstrations, on the same stretch of road on the outskirts of town, always followed an identical course. Sometimes I stood behind the Israeli soldiers or border police and watched them firing tear gas and 'rubber bullets', thinly vulcanized steel balls, at the demonstrators a few hundred yards away. On other occasions I stood behind the demonstrators, and a convenient block of concrete, and watched variations of the scene I had seen at Netzarim junction. The violence had a formulaic, demonstrative quality and, if you did not have a profound understanding of local cultures and politics, it was difficult to comprehend what was happening or understand the complex messages that the two sides were sending to each other and to the international community. It was also hard to understand why the Palestinian youths kept putting themselves in the way of obvious and inevitable harm and why the Israelis kept shooting them.

For a reporter, covering the intifada was a nightmare. The situation was extraordinarily complicated. One reason that a huge technical and heavily ideologically charged vocabulary had emerged in Israel-Palestine (or Israel, or the Holy Land, or the Zionist Entity, or Israel and the Occupied Territories or Israel proper and Judea and Samaria or historic Palestine or whatever) was that single, simple terms could not bridge the various dogmatically held perceptions of the 'reality'. The local law of physics was that every strongly held view had an equally strongly held opposite view, every example had a counter-example, every action had a reaction and nothing was a simple fact. So half the Israeli soldiers I spoke to just wanted to be riding a motorbike around Goa or on the beach in Tel Aviv with their girlfriends while the other half were committed nationalists. I spent a lot of time with an Israeli photographer who was left wing, tolerant and horrified by what was being done in his name and spent hours listening to radical Jewish settlers, many from America, whose myth-based, Manichean worldview, reliance on selective quotes from holy texts and taste for sweeping racial and cultural generalizations were horribly familiar. I also often worked with a Palestinian who chain-smoked, drank heavily, was one of the finest journalists I have ever met and who faithfully translated the words of a militant leader on the Gaza Strip who, in the space of a single sentence, denied the Holocaust had ever happened, said 'blacks' were 'stupid', women were 'weak in the mind' and that the problem with the Islamic world was that there were too many people who smoked and drank. In fact, I swiftly learned that the Palestinian community, even when one ignored those who were full Israeli citizens, was so diverse that generalizations were impossible. The people in the Gaza Strip disliked those in the West Bank, those in the cities were very different from those in the rural areas or the urbanized refugee camps; some loved Yasser Arafat, their veteran leader, some hated him; some were profoundly religious, others resolutely secular. In a relatively cosmopolitan town like Ramallah many would be openly contemptuous of the hardline conservatives of Hamas but would shout *Allahu akbar* on the barricades. Many Palestinians were proud of their Arab heritage, though blamed the rest of the Arab world for betraying them repeatedly. America was the country they most hated, but the one they most wanted to live in. The level of political debate and conversation was immeasurably more sophisticated than I had ever heard in Afghanistan, or even Pakistan, but everyone fell back on empty rhetorical platitudes at the first opportunity. And all this was before anybody started getting seriously biblical.

Some journalists immersed themselves in the minutiae, in the enormously detailed and important history, in dozens of UN resolutions, abrogated or defunct agreements and secret deals, and in the equally complex geography, with its language of zones, posts, settlements, areas and so forth. They often found themselves either very depressed or very partial as a result. Others, particularly those who did not live in the region, skated on the surface. This, in a sense, was inevitable.

For the whole experience of covering the intifada was somewhat surreal. You could go out day after day into fierce firefights, riots, demonstrations and the hideous aftermath of suicide bombings in Jerusalem or Tel Aviv, where the body parts of innocent civilians who had been drinking a milkshake or going out clubbing were scattered over a pavement, and then return to the hotel for a beer and dinner. There were many times when I would have been covering extraordinary violence on a Friday or a Saturday and would be back in London within twenty-four hours, enjoying an afternoon in an art gallery, taking my grandmother out to lunch or having dinner in a pub with friends. It was difficult to tell what was more surreal, the violence or the normality.

One consequence was an odd detachment. One morning, as cheery Israeli soldiers waved us through the Erez checkpoint into the Gaza Strip, the photographer I was working with turned to me and said she felt like she was going into a theme park for the day. I would not have put it in such stark terms – and she herself was shot and badly injured not long afterwards – but I understood what she meant. Even if you spent long periods in the Occupied Territories, you still had privileges, such as the ability to leave, that local people were denied. And if you stayed in Jerusalem or Tel Aviv, let alone London, you were effectively day-tripping. After fifteen hours' witnessing someone else's misery, you returned to something a lot more pleasant and secure. The sobbing parents, the screams of the wounded, the smell of the tear gas, the wailing of ambulance sirens, the smoke, the shattered glass, everything that you had seen was suddenly a very, very long way away.

One afternoon in the early spring of 2001 I went to the funeral of a 13-year-old boy called Walid. A day earlier he had got up at about eight, spent the morning playing football and watching television and then had lunch with his mother and some of his twelve brothers and sisters. At around noon he had left his breeze-block house in Rafah, the sprawling refugee settlement on the southernmost border of the Gaza Strip, and taken a bus north with his friends. At four o'clock he was shot dead by a single bullet at Netzarim junction while hurling rocks and petrol bombs at the Israeli army bunker in a carbon copy of the scene I had witnessed a few months before. His mother told me that she knew her son was dead when she turned on the television to hear that an unknown boy carrying no identification papers had been killed an hour or so earlier. 'I had called to him when he left the house and asked him where he was going and I told him to come back because I knew where he was going and he said no I am going. And when I turned on the television and heard the news I shouted, "It is my son, it is my son." I knew,' she said.

Walid's funeral took place the next day, as is the Islamic tradition. A canopy had been erected on the bare concrete roof of the house to protect against the strong spring sun and dozens of chairs lined up below it. Banners and posters on the walls proclaimed 'congratulations for the martyrdom' and anti-Israeli slogans. There were several large Palestinian flags and some graffiti that referred to a prison term an older brother had served in an Israeli jail for his activities in the very similar revolt known as the first intifada thirteen years before. A row of women dressed in full black *abbayas* squatted around the bereaved mother, who was slumped on a chair, her eyes to the floor. Walid's father, a 48-year-old taxi driver, stood surrounded by other men. 'I am happy that my son is a martyr,' he said in a dull voice without looking at me. He indicated the men around him. 'They are here to offer me felicitations on this joyful day. My son sacrificed his life for al-Aqsa.'

Walid's mother said the same. 'My son is a martyr and I rejoice,' she murmured. 'I hope the intifada goes on and on. He gave his life as a sacrifice for Jerusalem and al-Aqsa and to our Palestinian nation.'

I looked into the room where Walid had slept with three of his brothers. His bed was a thin foam mattress on the floor with a purple floral cover. There were cheap Koranic inscriptions on the walls. The view from the small window was of a cinder block wall. On the door were stickers from the youth wing of Fatah, Arafat's political vehicle. 'Fatah for martyrs' said one, over two Kalashnikovs and a picture of the al-Aqsa mosque. Two young boys, Walid's second and third youngest brothers, flashed V for victory signs at me with chubby little fingers. Neither was older than five. What, I wondered, had made Walid do what he did?

Potential answers, as was so often the case when discussing politics, violence and the Middle East, seemed to oppose those who favoured environmental, social and historical factors with those who stressed individual agency. Supporters of the Palestinians usually favoured the former arguments, stressing the context of any actions, while supporters of the Israelis typically emphasized the responsibility of the teenagers themselves or those who 'controlled' them. My own sense was that there were elements within each analysis that were helpful.

Certainly, the history and current situation of the Palestinians living in the West Bank and Gaza might have been purposefully designed to create the various elements that lead to frustration and anger. There may be no direct link between poverty and militancy but there is an indirect link: poor conditions generate the sense of injustice that makes violent activism much more likely. The Palestinians in the Occupied Territories were subjected to daily humiliations and had to live with the constant knowledge that they had been denied much that they considered was rightfully theirs. They knew they had been misgoverned by their own leaders and betrayed again and again by the international community and by other Arabs and Muslims. The far higher standard of living of the Israelis next door to them or even, thanks to the settlements, among them was a constant reminder of what might have been. Even worse, the peace process of the early 1990s had raised expectations it utterly failed to fulfil. Life, for all but a tiny elite, remained harsh. And to cap it all, there were no effective non-violent avenues for protest, either against the Israelis or against the Palestinians' own ineffectual and venal leaders.

But there were other things too that had determined Walid's act, I felt. After all, there were many ways of venting anger and demonstrating frustration that did not involve a significant risk of being killed. A clue lay in the fact that Walid was clearly under some peer pressure to take the risks he did and that pressure merely reflected the expectations more generally in Walid's community. Somehow, for children like him, a violent death as a martyr had become, with horrible irony, a part of everyday life. It had been not just normalized but, even worse, turned into an aspiration.

There was nothing inevitable in this. There were plenty of

Muslims in the world who did not see a violent martyr's death as a desirable thing. Many traditions, secular and religious, venerate the ultimate self-sacrifice. Christian iconography, for example, was crammed with representations of saints feathered with arrows or with flesh otherwise mortified. Indeed, the central figure of Christianity, in stark contrast to the Muslim faith, was a messiah who died to redeem humanity. Shia Islam, with its two central figures of Ali and Hussein, one murdered and the other dying in battle against overwhelming odds, also contained a very strong tradition of martyrdom, something that helped the Ayatollah Khomenei convince hundreds of thousands of young men to charge the guns of the 'infidel' Iraqis with plastic keys to heaven around their necks. In Israel, the site of the mass suicide of Jewish rebels against the Romans at Masada was treated as a national monument. Then, of course, there were the martyrs of the Western secular tradition; those who had laid down their lives for science, for their nations, for the war against superstition, for the ideologies of communism and fascism or for basic Enlightenment values such as the right to free speech or free association. There was too, especially in the former colonies, a veritable pantheon of martyrs of national liberation. Almost all the martyrdom stories, it struck me, featured an overwhelming, often faceless enemy set against an individual. They condensed the way any community saw their situation at a given time, dramatically symbolizing right and wrong and good and evil.

But what was clear in the West Bank and Gaza was that, though the resources to encourage martyrdom existed within the cultural and religious heritage of the local population, those resources had been deliberately and actively drawn out, emphasized, promoted and disseminated. That is what the stickers and posters on Walid's bedroom wall were about. That was what the twenty-four-hour propaganda broadcast by the various Palestinian militant groups' TV or radio stations did. That was what the banners at the funeral were for. They took an often dormant element of a rich and varied cultural tradition and turned it into its defining feature. And, not least because of the general conditions of life in the Gaza Strip and the West Bank, the effort to market martyrdom worked. Indeed it worked so well that Walid's parents were unable to express the very natural and real grief they clearly felt at the loss of their son and mouthed empty platitudes instead.

Walid was one of the last to die in the first phase of the al-Aqsa intifada, By early 2001 there was a sense of exhaustion among the Palestinians and the violent demonstrations at checkpoints and elsewhere became less common. It was unclear where the intifada and the associated political manoeuvring was going. Then, in March 2001, came the first of the suicide bombs.

It was immediately clear to me that deaths like Walid's and those of the suicide bombers were completely different. Walid had died without harming anyone else in a futile youthful expression of frustration and bravado. His death was a tragic condensation of the tragic histories of two peoples. But the suicide bombers died exploding their devices in cafés and nightclubs, in pizza parlours and on buses. Their deaths were abhorrent acts which, though they could and should be studied and discussed rationally, could not be justified whatever the conditions in the Occupied Terri-tories and no matter how 'asymmetric' the struggle in which the bombers felt themselves to be engaged appeared. The difference between their acts and those of Walid, though often ignored, was essential in understanding the reasons for each and in formulating an adequate response.

The suicide bombs generated an extraordinary level of preju-diced and unscientific debate. This was partly because the bombers' actions manifested a complete disregard for life and thus struck at a fundamental of any functioning society. Many said the bombers were 'mad', though dozens of studies conducted by the Israelis and others had revealed no signs of any mental illness among them; others maintained that they were merely sexually frustrated. Such erroneous analyses were predictable, as both madness and sexual perversity (or inadequacy) have often been used by societies to label those who reject their norms. On the other hand, some supporters of the Palestinians tried to explain away suicide bombing by citing other groups that had supposedly used similar tactics over the centuries. They pointed to the Muslim sect of 'Assassins' of the fourteenth century, the Russian anarchists of the late nineteenth century, even the Japanese kamikaze of the 1940s or the Tamil Tigers in Sri Lanka in the 1990s. But, though there are some parallels, the assassins and the anarchists had attacked government functionaries or heads of state as had, largely, the Tamil Tigers. The kamikaze, of course, had targeted another armed force. Indeed even Hizbollah, the Lebanese Shia group widely credited with pioneering suicide bombings in the Middle East during the 1980s, had actually used the tactic against military targets or against embassies. The Palestinian groups' strikes against purely civilian targets were therefore new. Their 'martyrs' died in deliberate strikes against non–combatants, something that was against basic human values. If they had not been, hardline clerics and militant leaders would not have had to deploy such tortuous and sophistic arguments or make such enormous efforts with their propaganda to justify them. They would certainly not have had to devote so much time and energy to dehumanizing the victims of the attacks, reducing them from fellow human beings who ate, drank and slept, who had families and loves and hopes and disappointments, to 'Zionists' and 'Jews', all of whom, whatever age or gender or politics, were soldiers of the 'evil military Israeli state'.

But though Walid's death and the deaths of the suicide bombers were very different in many ways there was one thing that united them. Martyrdom, however it was achieved, was a public act and, as such, a means of communicating a message. This was revealed by the etymology of the words used to describe heroic self-sacrifice in both the English-speaking Christian and the Arabic-speaking Muslim traditions. Both the originally Greek word *martyr* and the Arabic *shaheed* meant witness, someone who reveals something to an audience. But what, I wondered, where they revealing?

One of the strangest experiences when covering the intifada was to watch the evening news, flicking channels between Israeli local television, CNN, the BBC and the new Arabic-language networks such as al-Jazeera, the Qatar-based broadcasters whose iconoclastic style and agenda, promoted by the local emir who subsidized the station as an instrument of foreign policy, had won tens of millions of viewers across the Islamic world. On each you could watch the events of the day played out again, edited and described by reporters or experts. Predictably, all the various versions differed. An impartial observer (not easy to find anywhere, let alone in the Middle East) who watched CNN would conclude that the Israelis were responding, albeit in a very heavy-handed fashion, to terrible provocation by the Palestinians. If they watched al-Jazeera, they would be horrified at the appallingly brutal repression and sympathize with the paltry response that was all the Palestinians could muster.

Once, of course, the ritualized public violence I had seen in the Occupied Territories would have been witnessed by only a small number of people, sometimes merely those who physically saw it. Now the same images that were the backbone of the campaigns al-Fatah and Hamas had run among the Palestinians over the previous decades to rally community support for martyrdom and suicide bombing were being piped into living rooms across the Islamic world all day, every day. Quite what the consequences of that were likely to be was unclear but they were bound to be serious. The Arab–Israeli conflict, though actually a very localized struggle, had always been signifier and symbol for a far wider range of concerns, often those of the viewer rather than those of the viewed, round the planet. For many Arabs and many Muslims across the world, I knew, the image of tanks rolling into a refugee camp in Gaza represented every humiliation ever visited on the ummah or the Arab nation or both by the West. The course of the conflict in Israel-Palestine was a powerful symbol of their own powerlessness. That sense of powerlessness underlay their sense of humiliation which, in turn, at least in the minds of many, justified suicide bombing. If propaganda worked when it 'made sense', then hundreds of millions of people were receiving the perfect preparation for future acts of spectacular violent propaganda, perhaps on a global scale. Both Walid's action and the suicide bombings were supposed to reveal – to an already receptive audience – the fact that you could and should act.

But to have viewed the Islamic world as universally supportive

of radical Islamic militancy in the summer of 2001, even of suicide
bombing in Israel, would have been wrong. Even in Gaza, the
militants were far from universally supported. The intifada, as well
as the sanctions on Iraq, the crisis in Kosovo and various other
events in the late 1990s and first years of the new millennium, had
provoked a febrile debate in the Islamic world, not a series of
immediate collective decisions by a billion or so people. One
element foremost in the minds of many engaged in the argument
about militants and militancy in the Islamic world was the experience of one Muslim country, Algeria, over the preceding decade,
an experience about which most in the West knew absolutely
nothing.

Dr Mohammed Sekkoum, a large man in a loud shirt, had lived
in two places simultaneously for seventeen years of his life. Every
waking moment, and some of his sleeping ones, had been spent
both in a large house on a hill in Algiers with a slim cedar tree in
the garden and in a narrow two-floored apartment on a public
housing project in north London a hundred yards from a busy
road. 'When I am here I am always in Algiers too,' he told me as
we sat in his scruffy lounge with its ripped sofa and scattered
children's toys and drank 'Algerian' coffee made with dessert-
spoonfuls of discounted Nescafé from the cheap minimarket near
by. 'When I look out of my window and see the traffic and the
little park, I also see the cedar tree, even when it is raining.'
Sekkoum had left Algeria in 1986 and when he returned for the
first time in August 2001 he took me with him.

I had met Sekkoum in the course of investigating militant support networks in the UK. He was 51 years old, loud, garrulous,
chaotic and hospitable, and spent much of his time advising newly
arrived refugees in the UK on their rights, on immigration law
and on how to live in Britain. He was very well known in the
Algerian community in London and was a useful man to be able
to call when I wanted to know what lay behind one of the frequent
spates of arrests, detentions or expulsions of asylum seekers in the
capital at the time.

Through the spring of 2001, over innumerable cups of his almost undrinkable coffee, Sekkoum told me about the history of his homeland, talking about how the French had colonized Algeria in the early nineteenth century, brutally crushing the resistance movements which had, as in Afghanistan in the same period or in Iraq a little later, raised their tribal and religious flags in the scrubby hills and plateaus of the interior, and then taking all the best land and establishing a local Francophone administration. Sekkoum's father was one of the many Algerians who had fought alongside the Allies during the Second World War and who, when the conflict was over, had demanded independence. Sekkoum had grown up in the midst of the bitter struggle fought by the Algerians for a nation of their own.

'I saw it all,' he told me as we sat on the plane during the three-hour flight from London to Algiers. 'I was a child but I saw people shot dead in front of me by the nationalists, by the French.' Because Sekkoum's father, a janitor, was prominent in the independence movement, the family was targeted and one of his brothers killed. However, their sacrifice meant that, when the war ended in 1962, Sekkoum's family was allowed to move into a large house in the al-Mouradiya district of Algiers that had been vacated by one of the departing French colonists. Free Algeria was governed over the next twenty-five years by a series of nationalist, socialist regimes, all of which utterly failed to solve the country's profound problems.

Sekkoum, a qualified vet, gradually found himself drawn into politics. 'After seeing everything that I had seen, who would not have been? I started working among the very poor, helping people in trouble, campaigning for improvements in the meat in the butchers' shops, for better hygiene and better conditions for animals, that sort of thing. I was angry because I saw the lifestyles of the rich and powerful through my work but when I went home we had nothing.'

Sekkoum's story came out in short bursts, the flashes of recognition, recollection, nostalgia and melancholy of an exile. His various campaigns, and a semi-professional football career, had taken up most of his time as a young man and he had avoided all main political parties until the mid–1980s. Then, though far from a devout Muslim, he became involved with the Islamists who, as elsewhere, were emerging as a major force in Algeria. The Islamists had based their campaign on doing what the secular state, for all its populist rhetoric, was too inefficient or too corrupt to do. Their cadres ran clinics, assisted in schools, helped with loans for essential construction or medical treatment, and Sekkoum, who had spent much of his life doing exactly the same thing on an unofficial basis, was attracted to their work. It was not a good time to enter Algerian politics. When Sekkoum began to attend public demonstrations, send letters to newspapers and even write some articles criticizing the government he quickly found himself arrested and imprisoned, then committed to a psychiatric institution. He managed to escape and, understandably reluctant to remain in the country, fled to the UK.

Algiers was not as beautiful as I had expected. The shoreline was a mass of docks, cranes and choked highways and the slopes of the hills across which the city lay were stacked with poor dilapidated tenement blocks with washing hanging from every window. Yet tucked in behind the docks were broad French-built boulevards and open squares, almost perfect copies of Parisian streets, and in the famous casbah, the older district in the centre of the city, old houses painted in washes of blue were built on top of each other beside white steep-stepped passageways. Set back from the broad leafy roads that curled through the better parts of town were villas covered in ivy with a view of the Mediterranean from their wrought-iron balconies.

Sekkoum's family still lived in the house in al-Mouradiya, up on the crest of one of the hills above a mass of steep alleys. His sister, Lalyia, was waiting for him and was crying as he walked through the gate in the low wall that surrounded the house's slightly overgrown garden. Sekkoum looked at an empty space in a corner and asked: 'The tree? What happened to the tree?' Next to Lalyia stood a brother, Ahmed, who held out his arms, his thin, tired and lined face creased in a grin. As the men embraced, Sekkoum traced the imaginary line of what had once been his brother's sizeable belly in the air with his open palm and asked, 'What has happened to you? What happened?'

'Mohammed, you know,' Ahmed answered, his grin slipping to a small, slanted flicker of a half-smile. 'You know what happened.'

Sekkoum had left Algeria before the real darkness descended on the country. By the late 1980s the Islamist parties were organizing massive demonstrations every weekend and the government was frightened. When in 1991 their candidates swept the board in local municipal elections and looked set to win national elections, the army stepped in, cancelling the second round of the poll and arresting the main Islamist party's leadership. With the relative moderates gone, the field was open for the hardliners, many of whom had recently returned from the war against the Soviets in Afghanistan and were still unknown to the authorities. One such man, Sekkoum's brother-in-law, who was also called Mohammed, sat next to me in the garden that first evening in Algiers, quietly tucking into his couscous.

I had noticed him shortly after we had arrived from the airport. In contrast to the jeans and shirts worn by most of the other men, he was wearing a pristine cream-coloured traditional robe, a Gulf-style checked headscarf with double cords circling his crown and was heavily bearded. He now lived in Saudi Arabia and was a businessman and religious scholar, he told me. In 1985 he had left Algeria and travelled to Afghanistan to take part in the jihad against the Soviets. 'I went because of my faith,' he said simply, and there seemed no reason to disbelieve him.

Like many of the Arab fighters in Afghanistan at the end of the 1980s, Mohammed had returned to his homeland when the war against the Soviets began to wind down. In Pakistan I had met many such men, veterans who had continued their jihad elsewhere in the Islamic world, but before travelling to the Middle East and the Maghreb I had not realized how significant the new radicalism and violence that such men had injected into existing Islamist campaigns elsewhere had been. Like bin Laden, whom he said he had met several times, Mohammed too at the time had been full of the fusion of the modern political Islamism, radical reactionary conservatism and modern revolutionary strategies that had been fomented during a decade of war in southwest Asia. In Algeria, Mohammed and his fellow veterans had arrived back at an opportune moment and, joined by large numbers of local recruits, had swiftly hijacked the Islamist movement in the country and turned it towards a violent jihadi strategy. The results were horrific.

The Algerian civil war lasted from 1991 until the end of the decade and was one of the most savage, and under-reported, conflicts of recent times. Entire villages of civilians had their throats cut: men and women, old and young. Bombs exploded in market-places. Thousands 'disappeared'. And everyone, militants and security forces alike, was implicated in massacres, torture and intimidation. At its end no one knew how many had been killed, but conservative estimates varied from 100,000 to 150,000. Inevitably, almost all the casualties had been people who were not interested in politics, in radical Islam or in anything other than living as quiet and as comfortable a life as possible with those they loved.

Yet out of the mayhem came a tiny shard of hope. For the more I learned about the war in Algeria, the more I was convinced that it contained a vital lesson about the nature of Islamic militancy as a whole. I could see in Algeria many of the things I had seen in Pakistan, Afghanistan, Iraq and Palestine: how religion could attract people simply by being useful for them in positive or negative ways, how faith-based systems could provide an attractive alternative when other ideologies were seen to be either failing or a threat or both; how propaganda worked best when it plugged into latent suspicions and resentments that were waiting for a language and an outlet, especially when many already felt a keen sense of humiliation and injustice or disappointed aspirations. But Algeria taught me something new too. As I travelled round the country, or at least the thin strip of it along the northern coast that is inhabited, I began to sense how important was the middle ground, the mass of moderate opinion, the huge weight of the population who just wanted a decent life for themselves and their friends and family.

For it was their initial support for the Islamists that had, in some ways, led to the war. And it was their eventual disgust for the militants that had ended it.

One evening I had met two men in their thirties, both of whom had been mujahideen with one of the more moderate of the Islamic groups throughout the 1990s. They said they had started fighting because they had believed that the government was corrupt and criminal, because they wanted 'justice and security' and because their political leaders had told them that a military campaign was the only way to gain power after the cancelled election of 1991. They had also been told, as foot soldiers always are, that the war would be over within months. It wasn't, of course, but this did not bother them to start with, they said, as for the first few years they had been supported by the population around them and had wanted for nothing. It was only later that things began to change.

My two companions did not refer explicitly to the atrocities of the mid-1990s but I knew what they were talking about. As the more strategically minded central leadership of the militant groups was progressively degraded through 1993 and 1994, their attacks had become more indiscriminate and more extreme. The killings culminated in a series of massacres in 1998 in which young children were eviscerated, pregnant women impaled on spikes and villages burned. Often the butchered bodies of victims were laid out for all to see, another example of a macabre spectacle of violence. Some such attacks, it is likely, were the work of agents provocateurs from the Algerian security services. But most were the work of increasingly disorganized, brutalized mujahideen. And that brutality had an immediate impact.

'After the massacres began, food and shelter became harder to come by,' one of the men told me. 'Finally, no one would help us at all, even though they knew our group was against the state, not the population.' Not only had people been revolted by the sheer savagery of the attacks but they had been hit hard in the pocket too. The war destroyed the economy and the militants got the blame. The two mujahideen had taken advantage of a recent government amnesty and had now 'rejoined society', they said.

One was now a baker, the other a fruit seller. 'We were led in the wrong direction,' the baker told me. 'We were told that all who are not with us are against us – even if they are Muslim. Now we know that isn't true.' None of the militants they knew had ever contemplated using suicide bombing as a tactic. 'The idea never occurred to us,' the fruit seller said.

There were other things, beyond the words of the repenting mujahideen, to reinforce my impression that the days of any widespread support for radicalism in Algeria were over. I drove out east to the uplands of Kabylie where, earlier in the summer, demonstrations for better employment opportunities and living conditions had boiled over into violent riots that were, I was told, partly inspired by the pictures of the Palestinian intifada beamed in by al-Jazeera and other satellite channels. There, as in central Algiers, the walls of the tenements were sprayed with political slogans. 'Gendarmes, assassins', read one, referring to the hated police who, a human-rights worker told me, were responsible for scores of deaths in custody. 'Those who are dead, don't fear death', read another. 'A nous l'Algérie', read a third, throwing the old nationalist rallying cry of the war of independence back at 'Le Pouvoir', as the ruling establishment of politicians and generals was widely known. Yet, when you spoke to them, the anger of the young men of Kabylie was expressed in democratic, not Islamic terms. Partly this was due to ethnicity, as the locals were from the Berber ethnic minority and thus to some extent associated Islamic militancy with the majority Arab population, but it was also due to the simple fact that, in Algeria in the summer of 2001, radical religion was defunct. Mohammed, the Afghan veteran, said as much when I asked him. 'We were full of ideas and anger. We did not understand democracy.'

A day or so after my visit to Kabylie I drove in the other direction, west, through stunning dry hills covered in stunted olive trees and overgrown fields to the town of Shlef, which had been a centre of the insurgency and a no-go area for government forces until recently. It seemed calm. Local administrators told me that, even at its height, the insurgency had comprised only a few thousand men. Now, they said, the number was in the low hundreds. Their claims, though difficult to verify, appeared reasonable. I spoke to a senator, a former Islamist, who explained how the government had allowed various moderate religious parties to form and sit in parliament and how that had helped to defuse potential dissent. I went to a small village in the centre of a plain of dried-out fields where a dozen people had been murdered a night earlier by a roving group of militants for no discernible reason. 'They were cut down like wheat,' said the son of one old man, a watchman at a farm, who had died in the attack. He said he had confidence in the new president, Abdelaziz Bouteflika, elected just over two years previously in a relatively free and fair ballot. 'I am not a political man. I don't understand why they killed my father. These are not Muslims who do this.' In the doorway of one of the big tenements on the outskirts of Algiers, I spoke to Hakim and his friends. They were young and dressed, like most of their peers, in a hybrid hip-hop/mujahideen style, with oversized trousers, reversed baseball caps and combat jackets. We talked for half an hour in a mixture of French and Arabic about the many problems – lack of work, recreation, homes, jobs – facing the half-million or so Algerians who leave school each year. What did they want to do? I asked. 'Smoke more hash, listen to more rap, organize bigger raves,' they said. What did they want more than anything? 'A French visa.'

On my last morning in Algeria I went down to the café at the bottom of the road that ran by Mohammed Sekkoum's house. I was returning to London and Sekkoum, happy at what he had found so far in his homeland, was going to stay on for the summer. In the café a dozen men sat on plastic chairs around old tables, smoking and arguing over coffee and croissants and the morning's newspapers. As ever, a heated discussion was underway about the state of their nation. I sat and took notes. 'Look, it's a question of time. We started the process of becoming a democracy in 1988 and we are now in the middle of finishing it. It will take as long as it takes but we are in the final stages. We should be a bit more patient,' one man was saying. 'You're a child,' retorted another.

'We exist, we don't live. I'm unemployed. I want to buy my wife a present for our anniversary but have no money. All the rich people have homes and everything. I can't even find a job. Our government is the only mafia in the world that has its own flag. If this is democracy, I don't want it.'

The men at other tables joined the argument. 'Bouteflika might be elected but he is a puppet. The army runs the country,' said one.

'No, it started in the mosques, it should finish in the mosques. There is a role for Islam,' said another.

'Bullshit, keep the mosques out of it all. Always the mosques with you people. Even in the army there are people who want change. The process has started. It can't be stopped now, just delayed a little. Let the young deal with it. Any revolution is going to start with all these spotty teenagers anyway, not us. We just talk like old ladies.'

'Who wants a revolution anyway?'

'Well, what do you want? More of the same? Something has to change, yes. The question is how.'

When I left, they were all still arguing.

In the evening I had dinner again with Sekkoum and his family. Previously I had slipped away from my secret police escort to join them. The evenings had been full of debates and stories and conversation as different people had come and gone, filling their plates with couscous at the long table set up in the garden of the big house on the hill and then sitting on the low walls around it or on plastic chairs to eat and talk. This time, my two government minders caught up with me as I got into a taxi to travel across town. They were pleasant young men about my own age who were just doing their job but their presence totally changed the dynamic of the evening. Instead of the loud and long arguments about the future of Algeria of previous nights, conducted in French, Mohammed, the Afghan veteran and Saudi-based cleric, spent two hours illuminating us all, in classical Arabic, about some of the finer points of Islamic law. Sekkoum, his friends and family, the policemen and I were all bored senseless but the episode was revealing. It was a small, subtle demonstration of defiance and it relied on religion, something the state had little authority over, to provide a space and a language in which it could be expressed. It was a useful reminder of the role religion could always play.

On the plane home I flicked through my notebooks, transferred all the useful numbers to my contacts book and wrote the date on the cover. It was the sixth of September 2001. The weather was sunny and warm. I spent the weekend at an old friend's birthday party in a cottage in the north of England, drinking beer in country pubs and going for walks over the hills. There is a temptation to romanticize those days as some kind of pre-war idyll that is hard to resist. I look back at that weekend now and wonder what the people I had met over the previous years were doing. I think of my friends among the peshmerga drinking watery yoghurt, or *mast*, to combat the late-summer heat in northern Iraq, of Majid the Yorkshireman and the other pilgrims at the Bari Imam shrine and the villagers of Chak 100P with their fat water buffalo and their new mosque and the ashes still on the ground where Muradam Mai had been burned. I think of Javed Parachar and his schools full of young zealots and the teenage soldiers eating mulberries and dreaming of mowing down long lines of Taliban. I think of Ahmed Shah Massood, who was to die the day I got back from my weekend in the country, when a bomber blew himself up in his office in northern Afghanistan. I think of Ekram, who I know spent the weekend with his family in the big, rambling crowded house in Peshawar. I wonder if the wall-of-death man in Kabul was working and I think of Mrs Khudeir at the al-Mutanabi primary school and of Bilawal, the moon-faced 11-year-old with his playground pledges of jihad against the West. I think of Osman dying of cancer and the boys at Netzarim and of Sekkoum's sister, who pressed presents on me as I left her home and whispered, 'We did not suffer so much just for this.' And I think about the 3,000 men and women who were to die when, on the following Tuesday, nineteen Muslim men from Egypt, Lebanon, the United Arab Emirates and Saudi Arabia, trained in Afghanistan and Pakistan, hijacked four planes in America.

6. A Short War in the Hindu Kush

It was dusk and the narrow alleys of Peshawar's Bara bazaar were crowded. The stall owners were banging down their steel shutters, women in burkas were noisily hustling for end-of-day bargains and the kebab vendors, their heads swathed in scarves against the dust and the pollution, were busy. They squatted by their small braziers turning the stringy, fat-streaked meat that spat above the hot coals. When it was dark, I hoped to slip past the army checkpoints by joining the crowds of labourers and shop workers heading back from the city to their homes high in hills around the Khyber Pass for a meeting with al-Qaeda.

It was 4 October 2001 and I had been in Pakistan for three weeks. I had returned to the country a few days after the attacks of September 11 and was still trying to reconcile the familiar environment with the drastically changed circumstances. Even the clothes I was wearing – the baggy shalwar kameez – felt odd. I had never worn local dress before but in the post-9/11 Pakistan it was essential. Before, a little persistence and charm would have got me official permission to travel into the Khyber tribal territories or I could have slipped across one of the checkpoints in the company of one of the tribal elders I knew. But now the Pakistani authorities had banned reporters from the border areas 'for their own safety', imprisoning several for breaking the rules, and I needed the local clothes, along with Ekram's contacts and a tall, lean-faced Pashtun smuggler called Abdullah, to get me to the rendezvous.

Ekram, with whom I had been working closely since arriving in Pakistan, had arranged the meeting a few days earlier. It had taken a lot of negotiating through intermediaries in one of the Pakistani militant groups but finally someone, a religious teacher, had agreed to speak to me. As he was coming from Afghanistan, the encounter could take place only high on the border, deep in tribal territory.

So just as the sun dropped behind the mountains west of the city, Abdullah, Ekram's brother Daoud and I climbed into the back of a pick-up truck full of Pashtun workers which drove out of the bazaar, wove a path through the motor rickshaws, the donkey carts and the gaudy over-decorated buses and headed out on to the road towards the Khyber. There was little problem with the police. Crouched in the back of the pick-up I pulled my round prayer cap down, wound a scarf round my head, rested my forehead on my forearms and pretended to be asleep, looking up occasionally to see the familiar road: the traditional walled fortified homes, the forts, the neat regimental crests painted on to the boulders, the policemen with their old Lee Enfield rifles and black uniforms silhouetted against the oil lantern burning in their sentry post, a child with a hoop, two women in burkas, a fire, the high, blank walls of rock either side of the pass.

By the time we passed through the fifth checkpost it was fully dark. We turned right on to a dirt track and bounced on into a landscape of crags and dry valleys. After nearly an hour of driving we stopped and set off on foot along a pitch-black ridge behind several armed men. It was a very clear night with a bright moon which lit the landscape all around. Great, curling reefs of stars lay across the sky. We were right on the border, dipping in and out of Afghanistan itself. In the valley below I could make out the line of what looked like the road to Jalalabad. It was extraordinarily quiet, with no sound but for the occasionally metallic chink from the weapons and the sound of our feet padding through the fine dust of the path. We marched in silence for some time and then stopped outside a huge compound with high walls set on the top of a hill. One of the armed men banged on a plain metal door. A young man admitted us to a small courtyard.

'My cousin,' said Abdullah the smuggler. He leant his Kalashnikov against a wall and disappeared into the maze of passages to find a telephone. The young man showed us a room off the courtyard and brought us green tea as we sat on cushions along the walls. More family members drifted in and sat down and then after half an hour a slim, wiry man with sharp eyes set deep in a lined face, short hair, a beard shot through with grey and no gun came in and joined us. Abdullah introduced him as a teacher of Islamic studies who had come from Kabul a week earlier, though apparently he was based in Peshawar. He looked physically fit and when we shook hands I noticed calluses on his palms. He was the man I had come to meet. We exchanged pleasantries. 'What questions do you have?' asked Daoud, who was there to translate.

'When did you last see Osama bin Laden?'

'Not recently.'

'How do I describe you? Are you an associate, a helper, a supporter, or what?'

The man smiled thinly and did not answer for a long time. This did not surprise me. Ekram had already told me that, a week earlier, my interviewee had recently boasted to an Afghan friend that his watch had been bought for him by 'the sheikh'. From other people I knew that he had been running messages from al-Qaeda to groups in Pakistan on a regular basis for several years and had met bin Laden two months before. I had also learned that he had acted as an unofficial religious adviser to several of bin Laden's aides.

'I am a teacher,' he finally said.

I asked him if bin Laden was behind the September 11 attacks. '*Bismillah al Raham al Rahim*, in the name of the almighty the all merciful, whether the sheikh Osama is involved in these acts is not important,' he said. 'I am not the sheikh's lawyer but I will explain some things to you.'

And for the next hour he did. I disagreed with most of what he said but it was not my place to argue and, besides, I wanted to understand his thinking. His logic ran like this: first, the war against America was a defensive war and that made it justifiable as a jihad according to the strict Islamic jurisprudence on just and unjust wars. Because the Muslim nation as a whole had been attacked, this jihad was an obligation for all Muslims. Second, America was a tyranny, or *zulm*, and was promoting injustice, and thus it was a religious duty to fight it. Third, though killing innocents was un-Islamic and wrong, it was perfectly understandable that people 'angry' at 'America's continued interference in the world and oppression of Muslims everywhere' should commit attacks like those on New York or Washington and 'rejoice' in them. Indeed, the teacher said, the Koran permits the use of tactics in which innocents are killed when no alternative exists. 'I believe you call this "collateral damage",' he added, using the original English-language term.

Osama bin Laden, he said, was one of the 'angry people' who, he was careful to point out, 'welcomed' the carnage in America but had not 'organized' it.

'What about America's allies? Are they targets too?' I asked.

'There are three kinds of unbeliever,' he explained, using the Arabic word *kufr*. 'Those who have attacked us and with whom we are at war, those who live in states with which we have accords and those who live happily with us in our own country. The blood of the second and third kind is as precious to us as the blood of a Muslim. But America is in the first category that we are duty bound to resist and so, if you help them, so you too become an enemy. In your Western democracies everyone votes for your governments and pays taxes and so is responsible for what their government does. That means they are targets.'

He broke off when dinner, mutton and okra, arrived. Interestingly, his argument was very similar to that used to justify suicide bombings in Israel. It had travelled a long way and I wondered how much further it might spread. The room was now full of local elders. As each arrived, usually with his eldest son, another Kalashnikov was hung from the coat rack by the door. They sat on the floor cross-legged around the food laid out in dishes on a plastic sheet, eating with one hand, not talking until the meal was over.

'How can future conflict be avoided?' I asked the teacher.

'If you want to avoid a third world war between Muslims and non-Muslims, between the West and the East, then the world community needs to ask their own leaders why they interfere with other nations' internal affairs, why they are suppressing people, why they are supporting regimes that are publicly repressing and brutalizing people, why any freedom-loving people who want to be free in their own country are called terrorists.'

There was a murmur of support from around the room. The men all spoke in rapid, animated, incomprehensible Pashto but I heard the Arabic word *zulm*, tyranny, again and again. The teacher, who clearly felt he had made his point, said little for the rest of the evening. The other guests said a lot except when, at regular intervals, they all fell silent to listen to the Pashto-language news on the BBC. Then the discussion would start again. They were unanimous. It was very sad, they said, but every generation must fight the oppressors. It was their duty. The older men present had fought the Soviets. Now, if the Americans or the British come, the younger men said, they would have their own jihad.

I slept on a rope bed in the courtyard. Dogs occasionally barked, There was the odd volley of shots but otherwise it was very quiet. The next morning Abdullah had disappeared and Daoud and I rode back down to Peshawar in the back of the jeep of a local tribal chief in his seventies who was happy to help out a 'Britisher'. He talked about the 'good old days' when Pakistan had been properly administered by British bureaucrats. As we drove, I thought about what the teacher had said about the rationale behind bin Laden's strategy. Much of it was probably true. But there was much that the teacher had omitted. It was clear, for example, that bin Laden, like many of the Palestinian suicide bombers, simply wanted to hurt people he hated and whose complacent, comfortable, confident lives he resented profoundly. Bin Laden also hoped to use violence, and of course pain and economic damage, to force concessions on some clear political demands such as the withdrawal of American troops from Saudi Arabia or an end to US aid to Israel. Then there were personal and professional considerations too. Everything I had learned about bin Laden showed him to be an ambitious, egotistic man. A successful spectacular strike, bin Laden knew from the experience of the 1998 attacks in East Africa, would trigger a flood of donations and recruits and consolidate his status as the world's pre-eminent Islamic militant leader.

But most of all, I was convinced, bin Laden wanted to use

violence, broadcast around the world, as 'propaganda by deed'. He knew that alone, or even with a few thousand followers, he could do little and that his primary task had to be to radicalize and mobilize the hundreds of millions of people in the Islamic world who had hitherto rejected his call to arms. He had sensed the staleness of politics in the Islamic world, especially in the core Arab countries where rulers or dynasties had been in power for decades. In his view Muslims worldwide were suffering a collective failure of imagination, reinforced by supine or controlled local media, and need to be shocked into action. Bin Laden was thus prepared to gamble heavily on an attack which he hoped would force the latent support he believed existed for his radical agenda out into the open and spark the mass uprising he always dreamed of.

It was therefore logical that bin Laden had picked a hate figure that was common to many people in the Islamic world. Attempts through the early 1990s to rouse Muslims on a nation-by-nation basis had foundered on the essential parochialism of much of the audience. Yet, bin Laden had recognized, a common enemy might work where campaigns against individual governments had failed. In the West almost nobody could conceive that a commercial building packed with thousands of civilian workers could be a justifiable target for a 'military' action, but in much of the Islamic world the Twin Towers had been seen as a symbol of American economic, technological and cultural 'neo-imperialism'. Simply the size of the buildings themselves reeked, in the view of many, of American and, by extension, Western arrogance. The 'martyr-dom' of the attackers added layers of legitimacy and power to the spectacle, invoking long traditions of self-sacrifice and demon-strating the willingness of some to stand up and make the ultimate choice.

Bin Laden's logic thus appeared clear. The pictures of the Twin Towers on fire, he hoped, would force into the open the usually taboo thoughts of revenge, anger, wounded pride, humiliation – all the dark sentiments that are buried deep within the minds of many people within the Islamic world and beyond it. The attack would create the complicity and solidarity that he had always hoped for. Bin Laden was appealing to his constituency, reached via satellite TV and the internet, saying: 'I know that you know that you are pleased by this and that you admire the men who did it. It may be only at some visceral, barely articulated level, and there may be many things that make you reluctant to admit it and many emotions that conflict with it, but it's there. You felt it and you are now one of us. Now recognize it, embrace it and act on it. There are many like you.' This explained a cryptic comment he had made at a press conference back in 1998 when he had told Muslims around the world that they had to 'define themselves'. He was basically asking: 'Are you with us or against us?'

I thought of Algeria and the way progressively more violent actions had led to popular support ebbing away from militants who had once been popular. I thought of the Gaza Strip and of how the resentment and anger of the Palestinians, intensified by the brutal tactics employed against them, had made the radicals' task of marketing martyrdom that much easier. I wondered if the attack on the Twin Towers was the beginning of a new global and globalized wave of terror or the final, violent eruption of a failing attempt to impose an unpopular ideology. Much depended on what strategies the West adopted in the newly declared 'War on Terror' and, of course, the reactions of the world's Muslims. I was concerned that the war in Afghanistan would play into bin Laden's hands, deepening and spreading the anti-Western sentiments already widespread in the Islamic world. The question I should have been asking the teacher in the *qala* in the Khyber Pass, I realized, was not 'What does bin Laden want?' but 'Is bin Laden's judgement of his audience right?' Will those to whom he is reaching out see the 9/11 attacks as legitimate and heed his call to arms or will they turn on him with disgust, hate and fear?

After eight weeks waiting for the Northern Alliance, the rag-tag coalition of factions once led by Ahmed Shah Massood, to move against the Taliban I decided that the war would stop for the Afghan winter and went home. I got back to London on a Wednesday night. Mazar-e-Sharif, a strategic northern city, fell on the

Friday after a key Taliban commander opened the way in return for millions of American dollars. Kabul fell two days later after carpet bombing and yet more CIA cash tore huge holes in the front lines north of the city, allowing the incompetent and uncharismatic Northern Alliance commanders to lead their troops across the Shomali plains and into the capital. I was back in Peshawar the day after that.

The city was in a state of febrile excitement when I drove in at dawn on the Grand Trunk Road from Islamabad. The Taliban, with their flank exposed now that Kabul had been captured, had just withdrawn from Jalalabad and the secret policemen of Pakistan's Inter-Services Intelligence agency were trying desperately to organize a new force to move on the city. A whole series of interlocking gears of local, regional and global power politics were meshing. The Pakistanis, who had backed the Taliban as their proxies in Afghanistan until 9/11, were stunned to see Kabul in the hands of the Northern Alliance, traditional allies of the Central Asian Republics, Iran and, even worse, India. Unless the Pakistanis could form and arm a new group of warlords and get them into Jalalabad, a second key city would be controlled by the Northern Alliance too. And to complicate matters still further, the ISI's pet commanders all had rivals who were making their own independent bids for power. A race for Jalalabad was on. There was also a race among reporters. Hundreds of us wanted to be the first into the city. The problem was that, with the border shut and skirmishing continuing all over the country, it was not entirely clear how to get there.

Within hours of my arriving back in Peshawar, Ekram came up with a potential solution. He introduced me to a minor mujahideen commander called Haji Zargoun who, after fighting the Soviets during the eighties, had become known as one of the most rapacious of the various bandits operating in the Jalalabad region during the anarchy that preceded the coming of the Taliban in 1996. Since then he had been living in Peshawar, doing little except getting fat and waiting. He was so politically insignificant that the Pakistani intelligence agencies had not even bothered to

exile him. Apparently, he was my way into Afghanistan. 'Have a
good trip,' Ekram said merrily.

We met outside the house in Peshawar that was the headquarters
of 'the opposition'. Zargoun, chubby and bearded, looked me over
with his small eyes and leered, showing stained teeth. He was
accompanied by a small and very thin young man in a dirty shalwar
kameez who cackled frequently for no apparent reason. We set
off in a taxi for the outskirts of the city, where we waited in a
woodcutter's shed as it got dark. After an hour, though there was
still just the three of us, Zargoun seemed untroubled. And then,
in twos and threes, men began arriving, coming in from all over
Peshawar and the surrounding refugee camps. Some were old
friends and comrades, others were just there for the cash or the
chance of booty and had heard about what was going on from a
friend or relative. By about ten o'clock Zargoun had gathered
about a hundred men and loaded them into a dozen pick-up
trucks. We headed up the Khyber to Landi Kotal, a rough-edged
town on the crest of the pass, where we stopped in a large walled
compound well off the main road. Weapons were handed out,
though not to me.

Seventeen hours later we were still there. Two other contingents
had joined us and there were now 300 men with a few guns, little
food and less sanitation in an area the size of a tennis court. The
men prayed, smoked strong local hashish, slept and drank tea. I
listened to my short-wave radio, learned about lots of exciting
things that were happening elsewhere, got stressed, smoked strong
local hashish, slept and drank tea. It turned out that Zargoun had
been subcontracted by a more senior commander who had little
hordes like our own corralled in compounds all over the Khyber
and we could not go anywhere until the ancient pink plastic phone
nailed improbably to the compound wall rang. At 4 p.m. it did.
We formed a long column and somewhat groggily marched down
through Landi Kotal to the main road where we flagged down
taxis to get us to the border. There we got out of our vehicles and
started walking. The village of Torkham was almost deserted. I
wrapped a blanket round my head and, so disguised, got through

two checkpoints before a policeman noticed my blue eyes. He took a step forward and grabbed me, I took a step forward and grabbed the tailgate of a passing pick-up truck and eventually covered the remaining yards to the frontier with a Pakistani policeman literally hanging on to my shirt-tails and digging his heels into the dirt. When the Pakistani dirt turned into Afghan dirt he had to let go. As we waited for the trucks that someone was rumoured to have sent to meet us the fighters bought small, sour pomegranates and battered apples from a very quiet boy with an angelic face and a hare lip. I had seriously begun to believe that I would be the first journalist into Jalalabad. Above the shed that served as a customs office on the Afghan side of the frontier the Taliban's white flag still swung limp and ghostly in the fading light. I was tempted to haul it down and keep it as a souvenir.

Once in Jalalabad, I got Zargoun to drop me off outside the Spinghar, the hotel I had been at with Ekram almost exactly three years earlier. It was open but there was no sign of any other reporters. I walked up the long dirt and gravel drive through the overgrown gardens and into reception. No one seemed to be there other than the truculent old man who had booked me in on my previous visit. He did not appear to be in the least bit surprised to see me. I was tired, hungry, dirty, with nothing other than the clothes I was wearing, my short-wave, a notebook and a pen, but I was elated.

I had been standing congratulating myself for about a minute when I heard a noise outside the hotel that uncannily resembled a coach pulling up. In fact, it was the noise of three coaches, each of which was full of reporters. While I had been waiting in the compound high in the Khyber Pass, other opposition commanders had taken control of Jalalabad and then, to prove it was theirs, organized a series of buses to bring the press in from Pakistan. So I stood watching numbly as hundreds of journalists, with all their luggage, clothes, equipment and translators, poured into the hotel and started setting up satellite dishes and portable edit suites and phoning London and New York and Tokyo. At least I had a room.

The days that followed were a rush of fierce noise and movement and sudden still moments of utter silence. In Jalalabad itself different factions faced off in the streets, teenagers who had never driven cars before looted landcruisers from the offices of NGOs and thrashed them through the city in second gear, the nights were broken by the massive noise of the American bombing that was continuing near by. One evening a couple of freelance journalists organized a 'banquet' at the Spinghar, buying a sheep to be cooked by the bewildered staff. An American photographer loudly told a supposedly amusing story about how scores of Taliban fighters had been wiped out in an air strike a few days earlier after one of them gave away their position by lighting a cigarette. His story angered me greatly, partly because I could see no great satisfaction to be gained from the world's most technologically advanced military power killing farmboys from Oruzgan province whose life opportunities had always been somewhat limited but also because I did not like having to share Afghanistan with so many other reporters.

All over the country, the press were heading for the al-Qaeda camps. I headed first to the biggest and nearest of the militant training facilities that surrounded Jalalabad, the 'Darunta camp', where I found, in addition to the obsolete anti-aircraft guns that had been the Taliban's sole defence against the American missiles and strike planes, a small compound with several rooms packed with chemicals, respirators, dismantled mines and a stack of pages taken from the *Jihad Encyclopedia*, a compilation of guerrilla and terrorist know-how compiled in Peshawar in the early 1990s. The fact that none of the chemicals – ether, acetone, saltpetre and nitric acid, lead and sodium nitrates – indicated the lab had ever produced anything other than conventional explosives did not stop the next day's newspapers labelling it an al-Qaeda chemical weapons facility. From Darunta I headed back into the city and then turned south, following the road up to Farm Hadda, the agricultural complex where Ekram and I had hunted for traces of bin Laden almost exactly two years earlier. If we had searched a little harder we would have found what we had been looking for. Round the back of the farm was a group of small houses and compounds on a hill near the house of a major warlord. This was the al-Qaeda base we had been hunting. The complex was unguarded and empty and other journalists had already looked through its score or so of bungalows and courtyards. I found a series of charred exercise books with lecture notes in Arabic, Turkish, Uzbek, Tajik and Urdu on light-infantry tactics and assassinations. A colleague found an oversized pair of long johns that he decided were bin Laden's underpants and hung them up in his hotel room.

The Taliban had left little trace behind them. Their local recruits had jettisoned their distinctive black turbans and pretended never to have been involved with the men from Kandahar. In Jalalabad hospital, several blood-encrusted Arabs lay in filthy beds receiving desultory care beside a dozen civilians injured in the bombing. A father of an injured boy told me how happy he was that the Americans had liberated his country. A doctor told me that 'Sheikh Osama' was a 'very, very good Muslim' and that the Americans hated Islam and were 'conquering Afghanistan by force'. I asked an old woman waiting for treatment for her injured daughter what she thought of bin Laden. 'What village is he from?' she asked.

On the roads, vehicles were packed with Pakistani fighters who had either joined the Taliban or were members of allied groups. They were all desperately trying to slip back across the border. At one checkpoint, now manned by men from the Northern Alliance, I found four thin-shouldered teenage Pakistanis being roughed up by Afghan fighters. One after another they were tripped up and then slapped back down when they tried to get up off the ground. One was trying to smile, his face smeared with mucus, blood, saliva and dust. I watched from the car and when, after a few minutes, the four boys were pushed into a nearby hut, I followed. Kneeling, they faced their captors, wide eyes darting around them. 'You are Muslim and Muslims do not lie,' said the largest and oldest of the Afghans, a heavy-set man in a military shirt with thick, meaty forearms. 'Why are you here? Why do you come to my home? To my country?'

The men babbled answers in Urdu, stammering and gulping with fear. They had come to visit relatives, they said. They were not involved in any fighting. 'I came to visit my brother. I am not mujahideen. *Me mujahid nahi huu*,' sobbed one. One of the Afghans searched them, finding identity cards, passports, a handful of sweat-dampened 100-rupee notes and a dog-eared folded letter which he passed to the leader. It was a letter of introduction to the Kabul branch of a Pakistani militant group that had fought alongside the Taliban during the war. The Afghans' leader read it aloud, looked at the four men kneeling before him, kicked one to the floor, beckoned to a comrade and was handed an old, foot-long bayonet. He slid it half out of its sheath and then turned to me and told me to go. I hesitated for a second, long enough to notice that the small beads of sweat on his forehead had formed in regular lines except for where there was a patch of scar tissue above his left temple. I heard very clearly the snap of a magazine being clipped into a Kalashnikov behind me. I did not argue. I walked back to the car and drove into Jalalabad, very deliberately not thinking about what I had just seen.

The next morning Ekram arrived from Peshawar and we set off down the long road to Kabul.

7. Afghan Winter

Kabul was a circus. The Taliban had left less than a week earlier and now anyone who was clean shaven or wearing a leather jacket or otherwise obviously breaking the laws imposed by the ousted regime was interviewed twice, women in burkas were tracked through bazaars by TV crews and local portrait photographers earned more in a day in tips from their counterparts from major international agencies than they had made in the previous five years. The Intercontinental hotel was packed with reporters, pro-ducers, photographers and technicians from all over the world who all wanted a room, a shower, a cup of coffee, a satellite telephone battery. I got one of the last rooms available. It had no heating, no water, draughts blasting through cracks in the walls, CNN a floor above and the BBC on almost the entire second floor below and I spent a single freezing night there before heading out of the capital, southeast, to investigate garbled reports that American bombing was killing civilians in areas which had been vacated by the Taliban.

The road led out of Kabul, through a deep defile in the hills around the city, and out into the relatively rich farmland of Logar province. Though badly hit by drought over the previous three years, it was still beautiful. The leaves on the slender poplars which lined the irrigation channels were turning red and gold and women in bright sequinned dresses and headscarves threshed straw on rush matting laid out on the dry packed earth besides their homes. The channels emptied into a fast-flowing, splashing river into which teenage boys cast lines with makeshift hooks on the end. Men on ancient bicycles weaved along the rutted roadside, squawking chickens slung over their shoulders, chased by snotty barefoot children. Yet the mud walls of the farms were pocked and battered, there were very few goats or sheep and many homes had clearly been abandoned by the owners for months at least.

Sixty miles southeast of Kabul was the newly established front line. It was manned by Northern Alliance fighters who staved off boredom and hunger with petty robbery from passing vehicles. Beyond, the road started climbing through rounded dry hills towards a pass that was little more than a notch on the fin of bare rock that was the skyline. The surface of the road was holed at intervals by perfect round craters twenty feet across left by American bombs. From the top of the pass, where a rusting ski-mobile sat next to a dilapidated hut, a small market town was just visible in the centre of a high, windswept plateau. It was Gardez, where some of the worst recent bombing had been. The acting governor of the town, a lean old man with a long white beard called Haji Saifullah, told his men to take me to a home on its outskirts. There, at 2 a.m. the previous morning, a 'land attack guided missile M114' (according to the markings on its casing) had hit the house, exploding in a ground-floor room where four teenage girls had been asleep. All were killed instantly. Saifullah had said the Taliban had withdrawn from Gardez almost a week earlier and there was no military target anywhere near the house that I could see, merely dry fields, a large tree, several camels and a well. In the garden of the house, shawls belonging to two of the dead girls still hung on a washing line, one blue, one pink, both shredded by shrapnel.

Near by, fifteen refugee families were living in a ruined school. They had left their homes north of Kabul six weeks earlier to escape the 'Amriki' bombardment but, though they had hoped to reach Pakistan, their money had run out in Gardez. Now they were trying to survive on food scraps, mainly stale bread begged from the locals. In the semi-darkness of the school's interior I could just make out wasted women dressed in rags crouched around a blackened cooking pot half buried in dead embers. They were soaking stale bread to make it palatable and hoped traces of heat in the ash might warm it a little. From the shadows an old man with a skeletal face reached out and pulled at my arm. Someone somewhere choked out a repeated hacking, bubbling cough. Outside, children with white and pinched faces leant against a wall that caught the last rays of the sun. 'We have nothing,' one man told me and shrugged. His clothes were encrusted with filth, his eyes bloodshot and his face furrowed with impossibly deep lines. He said he was 31 but looked two decades older. 'We have no food and only a few blankets. Each night for four nights a child has died. We have no money now to go back home or to go on to Pakistan,' he said. I gave him the cash I had in my pockets and told him I would tell the Red Cross or whichever humanitarian agency I could find. The man thanked me and then, with sudden, fierce strength, gripped my upper arm, pushing rough-skinned, stained fingers into the muscle above the elbow, and then suddenly let go, abruptly releasing me.

I turned and walked away, realizing suddenly that I felt brittle and imbalanced, as if a weight had shifted somewhere. The man's gesture, his fierce grip, had made what was happening to him and his family at once very real and very close. I suddenly remembered the four Pakistani teenagers on their knees in the hut in Jalalabad and then, for no obvious reason, saw the face of a woman I had interviewed in Peshawar a month before who had lost her children in a crowd when fleeing Afghanistan and never found them again. I felt nauseous and leant against the car for several minutes. A firefight sputtered into life some distance away and then died out. I got into the vehicle, sat for a little while longer and then drove away, first to the Red Cross office, which was empty, and then back to the house on the outskirts of Gardez where I had spent the previous night.

Gardez, along with the neighbouring provinces of Paktia and Paktika, was being contested by two different warlords. There was the governor, the mild-mannered Haji Saifullah whom I had met earlier, and then there was Bacha Khan Zardan, a former mujahideen commander and tribal chief. Zardan was staying, like me, in the house owned by a wealthy local businessman with his entourage of 100 soldiers and tribal chiefs. There was plenty of room on the floors of the three huge rooms of his 'guesthouse' to accommodate us all.

I got back to the house at about 5 o'clock. It was Ramadan and no one had eaten since dawn but, before breaking the fast with the traditional dates, the men all prayed together. An old man stepped forward from the ranks and led the rest through the familiar ritual. I sat at the back by the wood stove and some oil lamps and watched their shadows flicker across the weapons stacked against the far wall as they faced Mecca and knelt and touched their foreheads to the carpet to signify their submission to God. Afterwards, we ate and Bacha Khan spoke to me during the meal, spooning great handfuls of meatballs, sauce and rice into his mouth. He sat with a cushion behind him, a pistol on his hip, a leather belt of short, snub bullets across his barrel chest and a Kalashnikov by his side. His long moustaches hung over heavy jowls. He told me that four journalists had been killed on the Jalalabad to Kabul road the day after I had travelled along it and offered his condolences. The country was 'an anarchy', he said.

Khan boasted, however, that his own fiefdom around the city of Khost, forty miles to the east, was safe. I asked him to take me there to prove it. No Westerner had been to Khost for years and I knew that the city was very much the centre of the infrastructure of the various radical groups, including al-Qaeda, that had been based in Afghanistan. Not only was there a good chance that I might find documents casting new light on bin Laden's group but, after my disappointment in Jalalabad, I could also bill Khost as my own personal, if spurious, bit of 'liberation'.

I set off at dawn the next morning with Wazir Khan, Bacha Khan's 18-year-old brother, every inch the young prince in a round silver braid and sequin hat and leather bandolier and pistol. It quickly became clear that the warlord's boasts of law and order were exaggerated. I put on the local clothes I had worn through the Khyber, and rather than take the main road we set off up into the hills east of Gardez by circuitous back routes through Bacha Khan's own tribal lands.

It took all day to reach Khost. We bounced through mountain rivers and up over rocky passes at more than 7,000 feet with Wazir Khan goading the four-wheel-drive jeep up the steep incline like a rider taking a horse over jumps, bucking over fallen logs and boulders, its engine howling in its lowest gears, the half-dozen armed men in the back of our two trucks shouting encouragement, the muzzle of the machine gun mounted on one side swinging wildly. Once on the high plateau we drove across miles of what had once been forest but had now been stripped of almost all trees save an occasional stand of dry pines and infrequent small settlements, tight knots of squat flat-roofed stone and mud houses. Several times we crossed steep desiccated terraces of empty fields beside gorges gouged by seasonal flash floods. We stopped only once, in a clearing surrouned by peaks, where Wazir Khan, rightly guessing that as an unbeliever I would be unused to a day's fasting, surreptitiously palmed me an apple and we washed our faces in a mountain stream watched by an astonishingly pretty young girl with great oval green eyes and a newborn goat kid in her arms. It was hideously poor country, far poorer than down on the plains, perpetually on the brink of famine, and I saw very few living things in the course of the ten hours we were travelling.

By dusk we were back on the main road and moving more quickly across the pebble-strewn plain around Khost itself. A pile of rubble marked the site of a mosque destroyed by an American attack a few days earlier, part of a complex including a medressa and a hostel in which more than a hundred Arab militants, Pakistani students and Taliban fighters had apparently died. Dozens of multi-coloured flags planted in the shattered concrete and cement showed the site, a mass grave, was already becoming a shrine. The city itself was full of similar buildings. When the Taliban seized it in 1996 they had merely retained a governor and the semblance of an administration so, for around five years, Khost had been effectively under the control of bin Laden, his group, Pakistani militants and their allies among the local tribes. A huge half-built mosque, funded, I was told, by donations from wealthy, devout individuals in the Gulf, dominated the city's skyline. Near by was a clinic also built with Middle Eastern money.

Wazir Khan and I slept under blankets on benches in the governor's house in the centre of the city. There was no electricity and no food and the dark corridors were lined with sleeping armed men. My own satellite phone was still in Pakistan, abandoned for

the walk over the border a week earlier, so I used Wazir Khan's
to call my office. When the sun came up for a few brief minutes,
Khost was washed in a clean golden light so sharp that the outlines
of the shacks in the city's dilapidated bazaar, the men on guard
wrapped in their blankets, the dust-coated flowers beside the dirt
roads, all seemed almost mineral in their clarity. Wazir Khan drove
me out to what he called 'the Arab camp' on the city's outskirts.
It was a complex similar to the one near Farm Hadda, a huddle of
drab grey bungalows. They were abandoned and through the bare
windows I could see stained, chipped walls and concrete floors as
stark as any cell's. The wind whipped up the dust in the courtyard.

On the floor of one room I found a small plastic bag of letters.
They were in Arabic and Urdu and were addressed to Abu Sayid
al-Kurdi, chief instructor at 'New Khaldan camp'. Near by was a
page ripped from a London-based Saudi dissident publication and
a bundle of manuals explaining how to make chemical weapons,
the bulk of which had been originally published by American
right-wing militias. The letters, written by students to their tutor,
were very personal. Some referred to bin Laden himself, others
merely thanked Abu Sayid for his tuition. Others spoke of their
hope for martyrdom or their plans to return to their own homes
to set up groups. Some referred to wounded comrades, or the
problems they had faced in getting to Afghanistan in the first place.
One complained about the lack of contact between the various
national contingents in the camp and berated the instructor for his
lack of a sense of humour. I picked up as many of the letters as
I could. There was little else in the compound. I got back in the
jeep and then headed back to Kabul.

The letters bothered me. It was clear that the men who had
written them were highly motivated. They had overcome significant obstacles and had made substantial sacrifices to reach the
camps. There was little indication that they had been 'brainwashed'. The letters were thus further evidence for something that
I had long suspected. Bin laden was certainly involved in the
commission, organization and execution of terrorist attacks but his
primary role had been to facilitate, channel and assist existing

impulses towards violent activism. There was no reason to suppose
that the attraction of violent militancy, the jihad, would suddenly
disappear now that the camps were emptied.

Bin Laden clearly did not think it would. He had released a
series of videotaped statements during the war, each of which had
been watched by hundreds of millions of people. The size of the
audience was partly due to the paucity of other images of the war
but the episode was an astonishing vindication of the strategy that
bin Laden had worked out years before when he had recognized
the potential power of combining modern communications technology with spectacular violence. In all the videos bin Laden had
gone to great lengths to achieve the right iconography, kneeling
in a cave, flanked by armed aides and usually wearing a white
turban and a combat jacket over a white shalwar kameez. The
surroundings would have been immediately resonant with any
Muslim viewer who, beyond seeing a rich man who had swapped
luxury for harsh asceticism, would pick up the references to the
prophet Mohammed, who both received his revelations and hid
from his persecutors in caves. Bin Laden's dress and accoutrements
placed him in the tradition of those who had fought the Soviets,
both Afghan and Arab, without losing touch with his contemporary audience. His careful clean turban was that of a sheikh, a
wise, just and brave leader of men.

And his message was as carefully calibrated. 'America has been
filled with horror from north to south and from east to west and,
alhumdillalah, thanks be to God, what America is tasting now is
only a copy of what we have tasted,' he said in the first and
best-known video. He went on to catalogue all the major grievances that he knew were familiar to hundreds of millions in the
Islamic world, listing the UN sanctions against Iraq, the Palestinian
situation and the failure of successive regimes in the Middle East
to provide for their people. Bin Laden made a special point of
stressing the 'humiliation and disgrace' that had been inflicted on
the Islamic world since the abolition, by a modernizing, secular
regime in Turkey, of the institution of the caliphate, the original
political unit comprising all believers led by the supposedly

unbroken line of successors to Mohammed, almost eighty years before. In the first videos bin Laden was also careful to avoid taking direct responsibility for the 9/11 attacks, maintaining that he had merely instigated them. Given what had been unleashed by way of American retaliation, this reluctance cannot have been for fear of provoking his enemy. It was as if he was still waiting to see what effect his actions would have on the masses of the Islamic world. At the end of the month he felt more confident of his judgement: 'My life or death does not matter,' he said in a final statement in late December 2001. 'The awakening has started.'

The endgame in Afghanistan took place in the mountains south of Jalalabad, at the old mujahideen base known as Tora Bora. The caves at Tora Bora, which had been used by bin Laden for a short period soon after he had arrived back in the country in 1996, became one of the most mythologized places and battles of the newly declared 'War on Terror'. The caves themselves were said to be giant, reinforced concrete constructions filled with high-tech equipment (they were just big caves), thousands of al-Qaeda operatives were said to be battling to the last man (a few hundred stragglers fought a rearguard action to cover bin Laden's rapid flight) and traitorous Afghans were said to have taken bribes to allow the most wanted terrorists in the world to slip away (no army on earth can maintain a cordon when the fugitives trying to cross it are heroes to half the local population). The narrative of the Afghan war needed a dramatic denouement and Tora Bora was perfect, not least because it was an astonishingly beautiful place and the battle that took place there was an astonishingly beautiful thing.

It might be wrong to describe a battle, in which people were killed, in terms of aesthetics, but the days, and especially the nights, I spent up on the front lines beneath the great beetling rampart of the Spinghar mountains were visually affecting in a very powerful way. I had arrived in Jalalabad after a completely uneventful journey on the histrionically dubbed 'road of death' from Kabul. With a Brazilian reporter, an interesting and engaging man called Pablo who was a one-time experimental novelist and a former fashion journalist, I drove south on the now familiar road from the city, past Hadda and on up, after three hours on dirt tracks, to a spur above the deep Milawa valley where the fighters of the Northern Alliance were camped a mile or so away from the main rampart of the mountains that marked the frontier with Pakistan and where the militants, apparently led by bin Laden himself, were holed up.

Bin Laden had been in Kandahar in September and had then moved north over the following weeks, spending some time in Kabul before taking back roads across to Tora Bora. Once his location became clear the Americans ramped up an operation to kill or capture him but with only a hundred or so soldiers actually in Afghanistan their options were limited. The Pakistani army was asked to block the frontier which ran behind the mountains while two rival local commanders, the slim-wristed Francophone Haji Zaman, and the earthy, burly Hazrat Ali, were paid very large sums to deploy their fighters in a cordon around the front of the mountains and to start the push up towards the caves. They would be backed by small teams of American and British special forces who would call in strikes by the vast fleets of warplanes circling above.

From the Afghan fighters' base we had a grandstand view of the battle. In front of us was the wall of the mountain range itself, a series of ridges, black with pine trees lower down, white with snow higher up. The caves where the militants were holed up were among the lower slopes and were marked by the huge scorch marks where the bombing had carved off swathes of timber and charred the rocky ground. To our right as we looked up at the mountains was a large, barren stony plateau, unbroken by anything other than the occasional cairn or rude shepherd's hut. Around its rim, dry eroded gullies led down to small brown fields and straggling orchards. To our left, on the other side of the fighters' base from the plateau, in a deep defile, was the river that drained the meltwater from the hills above. And directly behind us was the valley of Jalalabad, in the morning ribboned with mist that lifted progressively during the day to reveal orchards and well-watered fields and houses before returning in the evening. Beyond the city, in an almost perfect imitation of the terrain on our side of the valley, farmland gave way to plateau and then a black stratum of forest and then higher snowy mountains. This symmetry resulted in astonishingly beautiful dawns and sunsets. At dawn the sun came up over Tora Bora, touching the peaks on the other side of the valley with pink and purple alpenglow. At dusk it was Tora Bora itself that slipped from white to rose until the mountains became nothing more than a luminescent white glow beneath a dark sky with thin cirrus clouds picked out by the moonlight above the summits and a wash of stars. And then there was the bombing.

The bombing went on all day and all night. During the day, when we moved up to the front lines, the strikes landed close enough for the combination of sound and earthbound shockwaves to knock us off our feet. When back at the Afghan fighters' base on the spur, two or three miles away, the air blast still plucked at clothes and the ground shook. The most spectacular were the cluster bombs, which tended to be dropped from smaller planes. There would be an explosion in mid-air, a mere puff of white against the blue sky, and then, on impact, a rolling, boiling succession of explosions as the individual bomblets detonated as they went bouncing down the slope, each sending spouts of oily black flame and smoke and lumps of rock into the air. Then there were the huge B52 bombers whose payload sent an enormous plume of smoke into the air which broadened into a small mushroom cloud shot through at its base with orange. When the B52s came in at dawn from the north the dawn light shining over Tora Bora caught their distinctive quadruple vapour trails as they approached, turning them from white to pink.

The Afghan fighters themselves were unimpressed by the spectacle or by the military technology. Many had been bombarded in Tora Bora by the Soviets and knew that, if the al-Qaeda militants kept their nerve and kept underground, their casualties would be slight. For them the campaign was neither a righteous crusade to root out evildoers nor a jihad but a hard, dangerous job. They broke their Ramadan fast with a watery chicken stew thickened with bread, carrots and onions, slept a few hours on the floor of the huts or in the open air and then headed back up the mountain in freezing temperatures with nothing more than a blanket thrown over their thin shalwar kameez. Most cared nothing for bin Laden, for the Taliban, for the Americans or for Afghanistan. Soldiering was not a profession or a vocation, it was manual labour with guns, more hazardous and only marginally better paid than the work on their land that they would otherwise be doing.

One morning, as we sat in a trench up on a front line trying to catch the warmth of the newly risen sun, a pick-up truck with blacked-out windows and four neatly packed, expensive-looking black rucksacks in the back, drew up near by. Still wearing my local clothes, plus a hairy woollen sweater and a long sheepskin coat purchased in Kabul a week or so earlier, I walked over. A window was slowly wound down by a man with blond hair, very blue eyes, a reddish beard and a suntan, wearing a mountaineering thermal T-shirt with an M4 automatic rifle between his knees.

'Hello,' I said.

'How you doing?'

'A beautiful morning, no?'

'Sure is.'

'Where you from?'

'Sir, you know where we're from.'

8. Aftermath

It was May, midnight, and I was standing outside Tent Five in Viper City in Bagram airbase on the Shomali plains, forty miles north of Kabul. Around me, but for the soldiers out on operations or on guard, 5,000 fighting men and their support staff were sleeping. For once it was quiet. There was a live firing exercise a mile or so away but the ripple of automatic gunfire, swelling and dying away in the distance, was as soft and reassuring as far-off waves. The helicopters, which usually kept us all awake as they ferried the special forces in and out of the base during the night hours, were silent. I could see them less than 100 yards away, black against the grey concrete of the runway, the swollen, fat-bodied Chinooks with their long drooping rotor blades, the squat Black-hawks, the vicious little Apaches with their narrow fuselage and weapons pods like insect legs. A huge C130 transport plane was coming in to land. It was very low and had no lights on at all and I did not hear it until it was very close.

There are two sounds that always remind me now of Bagram in the spring of 2002: the familiar, and fantastically evocative, 'thwop, thwop, thwop' of the Chinooks' rotor blades and the American soldiers and their blithe, good-natured, hearty, asinine greeting of 'Hoo-har'. There were around 8,000 American soldiers in Afghanistan at the time, though the Pentagon was coy about the exact figure, so you heard 'Hoo-har' a lot. Of course there were many variations of 'Hoo-har'. For example, the US Rangers, the specialist light infantry, shouted 'Hoo-har, Rangers, lead the way, sir!' when they met someone of a higher rank. They made the two syllables very distinct. The US Marines, by contrast, mangled it all into 'Hoonnngaaa' with a strangled semi glottal stop halfway through. The special forces, the lean, bearded men who often carried local AK47s despite having their pick of advanced weaponry, did not say it at all, being far too cool. When I eventually asked what it meant an efficient young Airborne captain explained that, technically speaking, it derived from 'heard, understood, acknowledged', thus H-U-A, HUA and so, eventually, 'Hoo-har' (or indeed Hooaah). To me, less technically speaking, it meant the Americans in Afghanistan. It meant Cheesy Nachos on the Shomali plains and sealed packs of Beef Jerky, Teriyaki Flavor and bags of Hot Tamales Chilli Sweets ('The Patriot's Choice') in the mountains above Khost. It meant Pop-Tarts in Kabul, Bibles in tactical camouflage covers on the dashboards of Humvees, the lone star of Texas flying over rows of dusty tents on a heavily mined, deforested, ruined plain that the Soviets and then the Northern Alliance and the Taliban fought bitterly over. It meant T-Rats, C-Rats and A-Rats and a loudspeaker announcing 'This is the Large Voice' at astonishing volume both to the entire camp and to no one at all. It meant QRFs (quick reaction forces) and M16s. It meant AQT (al-Qaeda–Taliban) and AMF (Afghan military forces). It meant Sharps 0.5 per cent alcohol beers and an order from the commanding officer that no privately owned weapons be carried on base. It meant 19-year-old boys from Kentucky playing ball with M16s over their shoulders before going off searching for an elusive, highly motivated and well-armed enemy who looked like everyone else in the country. It meant five helicopters flying in formation out of a sunset, flaring with their tails down and rotors back, before dropping their noses to settle in a cloud of dust on an airstrip ringed by dusty mountains. The soldiers called it 'the 'Stan'.

And this is what they scrawled on the plastic walls of the 'heads', the fetid Portakabins, where, if you went later than nine in the morning, you were greeted by a five-foot-high pile of military faeces. In Toilet 7 someone had written, quoting both Hindu scriptures and J. Robert Oppenheimer, the builder of America's atomic bomb: 'I am become Death, Destroyer of Worlds'. Someone else had added a second line: 'I am become Bored, Destroyer of Motivation'. In Toilet 9 was a scrawl which read: 'My wife Jodie is fucking someone else doggie-style and it turns me on. Am

I weird?' In Toilet 3 another explained that 'Though I walk through the valley of death I shall fear no evil . . . because I am the meanest motherfucker in the valley'. In Toilet 6 there was an astonishing variety of extraordinarily anatomically accurate draw-ings of male and female sexual organs and two jokes. 'MARINE – Muscles Are Required Intelegance [sic] Not Essential', read one, and 'How do you get away with sexually abusing a deaf and dumb Afghan woman? Break her fingers so she can't tell anyone', read the other. In Toilet 11 you could read the following: 'Newark, NJ', 'Mansfield, Ohio', 'Brooklyn, NYC', 'Quidos, New Mexico', 'Pelham, Alabama', 'Montevideo, Alabama'. In Toilet 2, for women only, a single graffito said: 'I miss my cat'.

I liked being with the Americans. They were open and welcom-ing, well intentioned and innocent, generous and unfailingly cour-teous. The ordinary soldiers were drawn from some of the poorest communities in the USA, from Midwestern industrial cities stripped of their industry, small rural towns in the Deep South, Hispanic ghettos on the West Coast. The American army would pay for a degree if you served for a relatively short period and many were in uniform simply to get an education. 'I joined up because I watched *Full Metal Jacket* too many times,' the 10th Mountain Division's combat photographer told me, referring to Stanley Kubrick's famous film about army journalists and Marines in the Vietnam War. Later, after saying that he had thrown away a Fulbright scholarship at college through partying too hard, he talked about being mortared during a set-piece battle between American troops and al-Qaeda and former Taliban fighters a month earlier. 'Now I can tell my grandchildren that I have been in the real shit,' he said. The line was borrowed from the film. Later that day I heard a Marine sergeant address a platoon. 'Listen in, ladies,' he began, as countless Hollywood drill instructors have done.

One evening a patrol from the 101st Airborne ('The Screaming Eagles') gave me a lift in their buggy down the main road. It was nearly dark and cool after the day's heat and the road was lined with men and women out running with their weapons in their hands. We bounced past the Polish engineers in Camp Abel, past the special forces compound of Diamond City and swung left into the lines of our own tents.

The men were from Alabama. Though we were in a blackout zone the patrol leader had his lights on to help find my tent. Another soldier told him to turn them off.

'I'm on fucking patrol,' he answered. 'Why do you think I am wearing my body armour, motherfucker? For the motherfucking fun? So shut the motherfuck up.' And I thought: Do they really talk like this, or have they too been watching too many Vietnam War films?

My reading material was, I hoped, appropriate to my surroundings. I had Norman Mailer's *The Naked and the Dead* and a book by an American Second World War veteran turned English literature professor, Samuel Hynes, which examined how men seek to comprehend their own roles in war and, more specifically, in combat. In all areas of life, I read, humans, when confronted by new situations which demand new modes of behaviour, look for indications of how to behave from others, often their parents or peers, or, more collectively, from the norms embedded in a society's culture, religious practices and arts. Unsurprisingly, soldiers in every war look to the previous conflict for a frame of reference. British troops in the First World War looked to the wars of the empire, romanticized by G. A. Henty and Kipling and *Boy's Own*. The American soldiers in the Pacific theatre in the Second looked to their father's generation's experience in the First. In Vietnam, American troops there looked to the war in the Pacific and it was pretty clear where soldiers in Afghanistan, with their talk of 'going short' as the end of their tour approached, the 'born to kill' and peace signs stencilled on their helmets and their references to 'the 'Stan' were looking.

The same was, in a way, true for the reporters based there too. Few of us in Bagram had spent so much time in such a militarized environment before and I certainly was not entirely sure how I was meant to behave. We too reverted to the most obvious example from our own professional history, which was not the slightly farcical first-round knockout that was the first Gulf War but Vietnam. And whether we liked it or not, we were already being conditioned. We ate army rations, worked and sweated in an army tent, slept in rows on army cots and were surrounded by the workings of an army at war. When we played football outside the huge hangar used as a 'chow hall' we frequently had to reclaim our ball from the special forces compound. Once, when we kicked it too hard in the other direction, it went into one of the many minefields around the camp. No one volunteered to retrieve it. It was all sufficiently alien for us to require narratives beyond the usual to give us an idea of how to behave, which might explain why, having found a bootleg DVD of *Full Metal Jacket* in Kabul, we watched it from start to finish on one of CNN's laptops almost every night, a worthwhile exercise even if only for the effect of the sound of helicopters fading out on screen to be replaced by the sound of real ones above us. After a week or so we could recite entire sections of dialogue.

Some of the more familiar elements of journalism did exist in Bagram, albeit in a slightly bastardized form. Every day at 9 a.m. Major Bryan Hilferty and his British counterpart would line the press up like schoolchildren in an open-air classroom on benches outside the main canteen and brief us. Hilferty would always start by reminding us why we were all there. 'Today is the 233rd day since al-Qaeda terrorists murdered more than 3,000 innocent men, women and children when they attacked the World Trade Center in New York,' he would say. 'One of those who died was . . .' And he would read out a short obituary of a victim culled from the *New York Times* website. So we heard about 'Robert McCarthy, 33, a trader with Cantor Fitzgerald who gave his wife six dozen roses on their anniversary. Five for each year they had been married and a dozen for her colleagues,' or 'Ricardo Quinn, 40, a paramedic who loved to make life-size sand sculptures on Jones Beach where he loved to go with his family.' Hilferty always ended each briefing with the same phrase. 'The hunt goes on, and the war on terrorism in Afghanistan continues.'

One morning Hilferty was joined by Colonel Patrick Fetterman, a short, stocky man with clipped grey hair wearing combat fatigues.

He was there to explain to us the role played by his unit, the 187th Battalion of the 101st Airborne, in the one 'contact' they had had with the enemy in the last ten weeks. Four suspected al-Qaeda fighters were killed after they opened fire on an Australian special forces patrol who had called for support and 200 men from the 187th had been swiftly airlifted in. The colonel told us: 'We landed on a hard LZ in very steep terrain above a village. We moved down into it and found blood traces and three large caches of ammunition. We had an overwhelming force and though some villagers were not very happy about it we asked them to unlock their doors and we went through the village. Sometimes we had to break down doors and that was hard for my guys, who are going from strong sunlight into interiors that could be hostile. Any AQT elements would not have been able to flee because we had air.'

'What's "air"?' we all asked, somewhat surreally.

'Helicopters,' he answered

I asked the colonel where he was from. 'I'm out of Fort Campbell, Kentucky, sir,' he said. 'God's Own Country.'

I spent an afternoon on the main checkpoint on the way into the base. It comprised a tent, several machine guns, two Humvees, lots of oversized, blast-proof sandbags, five young Americans and an Afghan who they had nicknamed 'Crazy'. He had learned three phrases of English: 'Fuck you', 'Suck my dick' and 'I am a crazy mo' fo''. He was very pleased with his English and used it a lot. The soldiers were doing twelve-hour shifts and were very bored. 'There ain't nothing in life you can concentrate on for twelve hours 'cept pussy,' said one. They were, however, unfailingly polite to the Afghan drivers whose battered painted trucks formed a long, hot and dusty queue in front of them. I watched as two locals on painted bicycles, one with a small plastic device which continuously played 'My Darling Clementine' fixed to a dynamo on the wheel, the other with a spray of plastic flowers on the handlebars, approached the checkpoint.

'*Salaam*. How you doing?' said Private Parker, a frame fitter in Oregon before he joined the 101st Airborne. 'My Darling Clementine' stopped abruptly.

Parker, who had never been outside America until January, had recently been transferred up from Kandahar, where there was another major American base.

'Kandahar was where God took all the shit that was left over after making the world and dumped it,' he said as he marked the two bicycling Afghans with a red cross on their hands and waved them through. In the tent the other soldiers were passing round a travel magazine full of pictures of beaches and palm trees and talking about Cuban women.

'The second battalion were down there in Kandahar but I reckon they were scared out of there. They were telling some horror stories about going up and down those mountains. Some of those guys got shot to shit. You gotta say September 11 had some good in it,' Parker said. 'Bad for us Americans but maybe good for these Afghan guys. Made us all think about the rest of the world a bit and we ain't so good at that sometimes.'

Outside the gate of the base a small market had sprung up. Half a dozen stalls had begun selling carpets, *pakol* hats, old Soviet military belts, Uzbek vodka and sizeable blocks of local cannabis resin. They also stocked hundreds of pilfered American combat rations, crates of maple syrup, giant tubs of Tang and soft drinks.

The Americans' catering arrangements, like many things in the base, remained a mystery to me throughout my stay in Bagram. Almost everything served at dinner and breakfast was cooked in Germany, flown 3,000 miles, reheated and served on disposable cardboard trays in a hangar. Unsurprisingly, most of it was virtually inedible. Lunch was an American field ration known as an MRE (meal ready to eat). There were thirty different menus. The best was no. 21, Chicken Terazzini, in which along with the main meal you got a packet of Skittles sweets, a plastic sachet of processed cheese with jalapeño peppers, some crackers and ice-tea powder with added sugar. In every MRE there was a miniature bottle of Tabasco sauce, a moist face wipe and a chemical pad that reacted with water and partially heated things.

Because the food was so bad everyone supplemented their diet from the PX, the convenience store run on base for the soldiers.

The PX sold more than 6lb bags of pretzels and beef jerky. You could buy PlayStations (and 'Soldier of Fortune' to play), CD players and a wide and up-to-date range of hip-hop, soul and R&B CDs, magazines ranging from *Sports Illustrated* to *Shotgun News*, Stars and Stripes pendants, key rings, cards and posters and 'Operation Enduring Freedom' T-shirts showing a New York fireman standing in the ruins of the World Trade Center handing an American flag up to a soldier with the words 'Over to you, buddy'. There were moist toilet wipes, tactical towels (small patches of highly absorbent camouflage material about the size of an old-fashioned handkerchief) and special forces headscarves as well as Afghan necklaces and handmade carpets with a map of the country surrounded by carefully stitched images of guns and helicopters.

After a week in Bagram we heard that Donald Rumsfeld, the American defence secretary and the architect of the American response to September 11, was going to visit the base. At eleven the next morning we all assembled on the runway waiting for him. Major Hilferty had stuck white tape to the concrete to form a makeshift pen for the press and stood with us like a mother hen by her chicks. He pointed out a transport plane with a nose that was swollen with surveillance equipment. 'We have sensitivities towards that aircraft,' he said. 'I don't know what the fuck it is but we have sensitivities towards it. So don't film it. Please.'

At 11.05 two immense military transport planes circled in from the south. Rumsfeld strode off one, was greeted by the base commander and the US ambassador in Kabul and then driven away. He was not as tall as I had expected and I noticed that the trouser legs on his plain, black suit were slightly too short and flapped as he walked, exposing pale ankles.

There were several hundred troops waiting in front of a newly built stage in a hangar near by. American stadium rock and country & western was blasting out of several huge speakers. Many of the songs were about September 11, some defiant and triumphant, others maudlin. I scribbled the lyrics of one in my notebook. To plaintive chords on a strummed guitar, the singer confessed that he was 'not a real political man', and though 'he watched CNN, he was not sure he could tell . . . the difference between Iraq and Iran'. But, he sang on, now to deeper, more powerful backing, organs and strings and brass, he knew Jesus and he talked to God and he remembered one thing from when he was young. And that was that 'Faith, hope and love are some good things He gave us,' of which, apparently, 'the best and the greatest is love'. The song was played several times.

Rumsfeld spoke for about fifteen minutes about the war on terrorism and how Afghanistan must be rebuilt so it never provides a safe haven for 'enemies of the US and the Free World'.

'This is a momentous time,' he said, 'and you soldiers have a momentous mission.'

'Hooar.'

'You have been commissioned by history.'

'Hooar.'

'When the war is over, and it will be over, you will be able to say I fought with the coalition forces in Afghanistan.'

'Hooar.'

One morning I wandered over to the camp chapel. It was one of the biggest single facilities on the base and offered nine services a week: Gospel, Jewish, Liturgical, Korean Protestant, Latter Day Saints, Seventh Day Adventist, Protestant, Muslim and Roman Catholic. While I was there a special forces soldier walked in, placed his gun on the floor, knelt, prayed for a few minutes, stood up, picked up his weapon and left. Though I liked the Americans' frank honesty, can-do attitude and energy, I was profoundly uneasy about the obvious religious faith that so many of them displayed. I could see how much confidence it gave them and how useful that was, but I could also see the ease with which that confidence could slip into arrogance.

The Americans' confidence was also clearly rooted in the resources that they were able to deploy. These were astounding. The sight of the serried ranks of planes and helicopters on the strip at Bagram was genuinely eye-opening. If I, with my own limited experience of Afghanistan, felt the sudden arrival of the 'green machine', as the US soldiers called the army, to be a bizarre and shocking intrusion then I could only imagine what the Afghans themselves thought. As my newspaper was less wedded to the story of the troops deployed to assist 'the hunt for bin Laden' than other British publications, I was able to drive around much of the country to find out. Up in Bamiyan, the stunning central highland valley where empty hollows in a cliff face marked where the Taliban, under pressure from Kuwaiti and Saudi clerics, had demolished the two huge and ancient statues of the buddha just over a year before, I found desperate poverty but little resentment of the foreign presence. South of Kabul, in the areas dominated by Pashtun tribes around the city of Ghazni, there was also plenty of cautious goodwill towards the Americans. It quickly became apparent that most Afghans, as I had begun to learn during the fighting of the autumn and winter, were not at all unhappy that someone was coming to help them at last. The fact that the Americans, British, French, Spanish and all the others who were coming to their aid were not Muslim did not apparently matter as long as the new arrivals spent the cash necessary to rebuild their country. The general population's sympathy was, of course, finite and largely contingent on relatively rapid progress in solving the huge problems facing the nation and, though no one doubted the huge amount of work to be done to raise the standard of living in one of the poorest countries on earth to a halfway decent level, many were, at least at that stage, justifiably hopeful.

I also drove down to Gardez, not least because I was still troubled by the memory of the refugees I had found in the derelict school there five months before. The school remained as before but, people in adjacent houses told me, the survivors of the families who had been living there had left some weeks earlier. No one knew where they had gone. New refugees had taken their place among the ash and the rubble and the blackened walls but, though they too were homeless and hungry, the warmer weather meant that they were not, at least, dying of hypothermia in the night. This made me feel a little better.

Gardez had other problems, though. Bacha Khan Zardran had

not only failed in his bid to take over the city but had been forced out of all those areas he had seized in the days after the fall of the Taliban by Hamid Karzai, the new American-backed Afghan president. The warlord was now holed up in the hills I had crossed on my trip to Khost six months earlier and could do little more than sulk, firing mortars fairly randomly into the surrounding valleys and towns. Predictably, civilians died. I visited a man whose wife and five-year-old daughter had been killed by one such attack a day earlier. 'I know it is God's will but I simply ask why, after so many bad things have happened, my family was taken from me,' he said.

Kabul itself had been transformed into a bustling, hustling metropolis. I remembered Ariana Square, in the city centre, as desolate and windswept. Now there were huge traffic jams, stretching back past the packed prison, past the smart internationally trained Afghan soldiers outside the interior ministry, past the police station with its new radio system and the ranks of pristine, white, luxury landcruisers outside the United Nations offices and on past the newly refurbished embassies of a dozen foreign powers. Opposite the park in the centre of the city a row of new restaurants was doing a brisk trade. There was even a computer shop and an internet café. A mobile phone network was being set up. The downside, of course, was vastly increased crime, rents so high that even relatively prosperous refugees who had returned to the city could barely afford adequate accommodation and, in the bazaars, illicit whisky at $100 a bottle, Manchester United shirts for $50 and, if you knew who to ask, hardcore pornography featuring dwarves and obese women. However, Ekram, when I went to see him, was very happy to be back and was making plans to bring his family over from Peshawar. The last of my concerns that the war in Afghanistan might be counterproductive, provoking rage in the Islamic world generally and miring the West in a guerrilla war in which what remained of the country would be decimated, left me when Ekram and I returned to Jalalabad in October 2003. In a newly refurbished school in the south of the city, hundreds of girls, so many that they had spilled out of the classrooms and filled the gardens outside, were talking, shouting, reading, being sent to stand in corners and scribbling on slates or ragged exercise books. As a scene, it might well have been unrepresentative, even mawkish, but, to my own great surprise and Ekram's utter astonishment, I was profoundly and genuinely moved, so much so that he had to complete our interview with the headmistress alone as I stood under a large ash tree outside and took several deep breaths and blew my nose a lot.

Yet, in terms of the 'War on Terror' that President Bush had declared in the aftermath of 9/11, Afghanistan was the easy bit. It had been relatively simple to identify the individuals responsible for the attacks on New York and Washington and to destroy their protectors and their bases. The militants and the Taliban between them provided a tangible target which the massive technological and military superiority of America could, just about, engage and the campaign fought in the autumn and early winter of 2001 was, but for the escape of the al-Qaeda high command from Tora Bora, a success. It was also, despite my misgivings, necessary. Allowing such a large and effective militant infrastructure to develop in Afghanistan over the previous two decades had been a catastrophic error on the part of Western governments. The campaign to remove it actually had widespread support, even in the Muslim world, as the failure of Pakistani radical groups to mobilize larger rallies opposing the war showed. For the Afghans, as I had found out, pretty much anything was better than the status quo. The question in the spring of 2002 was: what next?

The problem was that no one was very sure who or what the enemy was. There had been little discussion at a senior level about al-Qaeda before 9/11 or during the autumn of 2001 and there was little to inform, in a sensible and unpartisan way, the discussion after the Afghan campaign's end. The result was a vacuum filled with analysis based on poor, partial sources and defined by previous ideological positions. While in Pakistan and Afghanistan I had been ignorant of much of what was being said about Islamic militancy in Britain and America. On my return I was stunned to find that what I felt strongly was a completely erroneous idea of the nature of al-Qaeda had established itself as the conventional wisdom. Al-Qaeda was seen as a monolithic organization, much like traditional terrorist groups from the 1960s and 70s, with a defined hierarchy, members, cadres, cells and operatives around the world. Worse still, a whole series of groups, from all across the Islamic world, which had nothing to do with bin Laden and whose existence had barely been known in the West before 9/11 were now designated as al-Qaeda or al-Qaeda affiliates and bin Laden was almost universally depicted as a James Bond style villain sitting in a cave with a bank of computers orchestrating a global campaign of violence. More generally, terrorism, or at least its 'Muslim' variety, was often depicted as an act of irrational rage or a visceral hate of wealth and freedom and an integral part of a plan to conquer the world. Clearly, the implication was, there was little point in looking for 'root causes' and anyone who did so was 'soft'. Suicide bombers were said to be mad or motivated by sexual inadequacy and policymakers apparently needed to remember that resolute and determined action would deter terrorists while weakness would encourage them.

This package of ideas, the 'hard' counter-terrorism discourse, dominated the debate for a variety of reasons. First, it reflected the sympathies of those formulating strategy in the White House and those who elected them, resonating broadly with a culture that stressed individual agency and industry over 'society' and 'environment' as determinants of behaviour, success, failure and history. Second, it was favoured by the overwhelmingly conservative defence establishment and security industry in America, in Europe and round the world. The nature of the men who specialize in counter-terrorism or security, many of whom are former soldiers or policemen, ensures a heavy right-wing bias in their collective contribution to policymaking and public debate. A third reason for the dominance of the right-wing paradigm was its overwhelming popularity among unsavoury governments around the world. For governments such as those of Algeria, Uzbekistan, the Philippines and Russia, attributing long-running local insurgencies to al-

Qaeda, the newly discovered international bogeymen, was extremely useful, simultaneously releasing a flood of diplomatic, military and financial aid from Washington while also obscuring the role that their own corruption, nepotism, repression and mismanagement had played in fomenting violence. A fourth factor was the broad complicity of the media in both the UK and the USA. With a few exceptions, journalists were, through ignorance, deference or laziness, happy to accept what politicians and 'security experts' said and, pleased to have found a new and snappy label for the otherwise rather opaque new threat, were content to blame pretty much any attack anywhere in the world on 'al-Qaeda'. And a final reason for the dominance of the right-wing discourse was the weakness of the left's response which varied from facile anti-Americanism to a reliance on broad liberal theories that lacked rigour and clarity. In addition, there were very few voices on the left, or even in the centre, who could talk with the authority and certainty of their opponents.

The result of the skewed debate over the nature of the threat that had, apparently, suddenly emerged in September 2001 was immediately visible in policy terms. The main thrust of the strategy of the 'War on Terror' was, naturally, determined by the White House and relied almost exclusively on traditional 'hard' counter-terrorist tactics. America set about turning itself into a fortress, while outside the USA intelligence assets and troops were deployed, with all their magnificent hardware, to hunt down and eliminate the bad guys. Some lip-service was paid to establishing greater democracy and economic growth in the Middle East but the complex roots of Islamic terrorism, the variety of the Muslim world, the importance of winning the crucial middle ground, of countering the ideology that fuelled support for the militants, were matters barely discussed. The lessons of decades of counter-insurgency warfare, as well as the lessons of recent events in Algeria, Afghanistan, Israel-Palestine and elsewhere, were forgotten or ignored. Force was, by and large, met with force.

To add, almost literally, insult to injury, public opinion in the Islamic world, in a way that must have delighted bin Laden, was repeatedly offended. A series of gaffes – President Bush's repeated references to a 'crusade' against terrorism being only one of many – outraged already oversensitive audiences. Repressive regimes were courted and supported. 'Moral clarity', an old Cold War term that meant not being bound by 'outdated liberal values', led directly to a series of appalling human rights abuses in new prisons at Guantanamo Bay and in Afghanistan that sullied the name of America and lent credibility to the old charge, so widespread in the Muslim world, of double standards. Given that the single most obvious theme in all my conversations with Islamic militants over the years was the idea that they were under attack, the cumulative impact of these various errors was predictably catastrophic. The widespread support that America had enjoyed in the aftermath of September 11, even in the Muslim world, rapidly turned, or returned, to profound hostility. And there was worse to come.

The assumptions behind the counter-terror strategy adopted by the White House, and thus largely by America's allies, in the aftermath of the 9/11 strikes were heavily influenced by the legacy of the Cold War. Then, too, conservatives in America and Europe had attributed terrorism or insurgent violence around the world to shadowy networks run by a central committee and, in the course of denying that socioeconomic grievances such as poverty or repression were relevant to the appeal of left-wing ideologies, suggested that state sponsorship of terrorism was the critical element instead. With the Bush administration including so many, such as Rumsfeld himself, who had been deeply involved in the contest with the Soviets, this continuity was to be expected. It was not just the soldiers and the reporters at Bagram who were re-fighting old wars in their heads.

In a different situation this might not have been too much of a problem but in the supercharged atmosphere of 2002 it had grave consequences. The stress on the state sponsors of terrorism, as opposed to more general 'root causes' of terrorism, led American policymakers to one conclusion. In the minds of many influential senior strategists, the greatest threat to the 'civilized world' came not from an amorphous and confusing constellation of independent radical Islamic groups articulating long-standing social, cultural, political and economic grievances in religious language but from a single state: Iraq.

9. Back to Kurdistan

I spread the photographs out and stood back. Ali Hamad Massood, the mayor of Qala Diza, looked at them silently, moving them around the glass top of his desk with the tips of his fingers with a delicacy I had not expected in such a large man. A minute passed. The office was the same as all the others in northern Iraq, indeed in all Iraq. There was a picture of a political leader on the wall, in this case Jalal Talabani, the veteran head of the Patriotic Union of Kurdistan, several vases full of garish plastic flowers set on low coffee tables made of ornately carved, heavily varnished cherry-wood and several large green sofas on which sat around half a dozen slightly overweight men, all with moustaches and stubble and thick fingers that clicked orange or red prayer beads. In front of each was a small glass of tea, so heavily sweetened that its bottom third was pure sugar. There was a strong smell of stale sweat. The mayor looked up, walked round his desk, grasped my hand, threw an arm across my shoulder and pulled me to him.

'I am very pleased to see you,' he said, or rather he told Ala, my interpreter who was sitting a few feet away, who told me. 'As you were here as a peshmerga then you are our great friend and very, very welcome to Qala Diza. And as you have come back after ten, no, eleven years we will consider you as if you have been a peshmerga for all this time.'

I had been trying to travel back to Kurdistan for several years but none of the surrounding powers on whom access to the Kurds depended were allowing transit. However, in the summer of 2002, old contacts in the Kurdish Democratic Party in London had been able to negotiate my passage with the Syrian authorities so I flew into Damascus from the UK and drove overnight across the desert to the far northeastern corner of Syria where a border crossing was open. Beyond the frontier, a semi-autonomous Kurdish state had survived for over a decade within borders that had pretty much been set by the fighting of the summer of 1991. I had been stamped out of Syria by a bored functionary and then had carried my bags down a sandy track between high walls of bulrushes to the banks of the Tigris.

This far north, the great muddy river of the Iraqi plains was cool, swift running and clear enough for me to see the pebbles, each a different shade of grey or brown, of the river bed. It was only a few feet deep. The boatman had beached his craft, a broad, flat-bottomed canoe, on the gravel of the far bank and, the only passenger, I had stepped out into what, according to a sign painted on a nearby wall, was 'Free Kurdistan'. I had been extremely happy to be there and extremely happy, in a way I had not expected, to see that Free Kurdistan still existed.

I had headed almost straight for Qala Diza, the ruined town I had been shown a decade earlier, and, whether the mayor meant what he said or not, was very touched as the men sitting in his office stood around the pictures, laughing, pointing to old comrades and talking of the past. No one in Qala Diza, nor indeed in Kurdistan more generally, had had an easy time between my two visits. The war of 1991 and the UN sanctions that followed it, their impact doubled by the discriminatory measures taken by Saddam against the Kurds, had destroyed the local economy. Even food had been scarce for several years. Though there had been a free and fair election held swiftly after the conflict of 1991, the Kurds' political leaders had been unable to overcome their age-old habit of internecine warfare and rivalry and had managed to fight a vicious civil war until 1998. Four years later, though tensions had relaxed and the economy had begun to pick up rapidly, there was still a checkpoint on the road between Arbil, the main base of the KDP, and Suleimaniyah, the headquarters of the PUK, and as I drove through Kurdistan I could see that reconstruction over the previous years had been patchy. Much of the country was still desperately poor and the sites of thousands of the villages that had been destroyed by Saddam's troops were now barely distinguishable mounds on distant mountainsides, their inhabitants working overseas or long since sucked into the rapidly growing cities.

But Qala Diza had been completely rebuilt. There was a bridge now across the Zab, the road into town was metalled and the plateau of rubble that I had seen in 1991 was buried beneath a new, slightly scruffy city with bazaars and dusty strips of wasteland and brand-new homes in haphazard rows built alongside the steep defiles that drain down to Lake Dokan, which still shimmered in the distance beyond the green plain.

'This city was 100 per cent Kurdish and so 100 per cent of it was destroyed,' the mayor was saying. 'Everyone was deported to the collective villages a hundred or so miles away. So everything you see here is new. There are 48,000 people. We have built nineteen primary schools, seven secondary schools, three clinics and three hospitals.'

I picked out the picture of the pharmacist who had run the makeshift clinic in the ruins of the city in 1991. I had never learned his name. Who was he? I asked. Was he still alive? His name was Mahmud Hamza, the mayor said, and gave me his address. I pulled out another picture, the one I had taken of a girl sweeping the patch of dirt in front of her ruined home. Who was she? Everyone crowded round the photograph. She was Zara Mohammed Hama and she lived round the corner.

The mayor told us to drive down a dirt lane between rows of low cinder block houses built on the more marginal lands on the southern rim of the city and turn left. The wealthier parts of town had been rebuilt with concrete and the roads had hard surfaces and even, in places, pavements and gutters. Here, piles of gravel and cement lay in the street, drains and sewers were still being dug and electricity cables swung loosely between tilted wooden poles. Dogs lay in the shade with their tongues out. Children played in the water from a spring that had been channelled into a concrete tank. Then I saw a plain red dress, bright even in the midday sun.

Zara was in the garden watering a square of very green grass that was surrounded by delicate peony, frangipani and jasmine. I stayed in the car as Ala spoke to her and watched as the pair were joined by a third, much older woman from within the house, who was clearly Zara's mother. Then the three women turned and together beckoned me in. Ala had explained why we had come and they were laughing. Zara's mother drew her identity card from a small purse to allow me to note down her name, Ayesha Ibrahim Hassan. I read that she was 60 years old.

We sat down on thin rugs on the floor. Ayesha, a tall, slim woman with large eyes and a straight strong nose and slightly downturned lips which had drawn down long lines in her cheeks, had six other children. Zara, Ayesha said, had been born in 1976, in the village three miles away where the family had lived for nine generations. Though her husband had died in 1986, she told me, life in the village had been 'excellent'.

'We were totally self-sufficient,' she said. 'We farmed our land and everything that we wanted was there. Then the Iraqi government came and burned the houses and we went to Qala Diza. Then the Iraqis came again and destroyed the town here. We were sent to the collective villages and life was very difficult. There was no water and the homes were just concrete and one room and very hot, and there was no school or shops or anything. Several of my children fled to Iran. Finally, after all the fighting, we were able to come back. We were very happy to come back even though we had no home. God knows we were happy.'

While we were speaking Zara listened and fanned herself with the picture from 1991, taking quick looks at it when she thought no one was watching. She had not changed much and had the same thick brown hair and eyebrows and slow, self-conscious smile and big, dark eyes of her mother. The long red dress she was wearing was almost identical to the one in the photograph. She said very little but was listening very closely. I saw her turn the picture over and trace the forms of the letters in English and Kurdish script on the back. It was clear she had difficulty reading them, though they spelt her name and her address.

'We were very shocked and surprised when we got back to Qala Diza,' her mother was saying. 'Nothing was standing. The Iraqis had destroyed everything. So we set about building it again.

We built a room every two years and then the garden and the little courtyard.'

The house the family had built comprised a single set of four cinder block walls, thirty feet long by fifteen wide, that had been divided to make one room for sleeping and another for eating and receiving guests. A raked corrugated-iron roof had been placed over the four walls. Additionally there was a small extension, also made of cinder block, which was used as a kitchen. In it I saw a small gas burner with a single old iron hob, a grate for a fire, a stack of blackened pots and pans and a few bags of rice, salt and onions. On the wall were pictures of an unidentified saint. An outhouse served as a toilet. Beyond the small, tidy garden I had noticed on the way in was the 'courtyard', a small patch of yellow gravel and a low wooden fence.

A young boy, a neighbour whom Ayesha had despatched when we had arrived, returned from the bazaar with soft drinks for Ala and me. We sat and drank. Zara remained bashful. 'Everything is fine now,' she said. 'We will be better, inshallah. I would like to see my brothers but they are working in the cities. I have never been to Suleimaniyah and I would like to see it.'

Ayesha broke in fiercely, almost impatient with her daughter's quiet words. 'If there is a new war I am not bothered if my house is destroyed again as long as it is not Saddam who does it,' she said. 'We will just build another one.' Zara was holding the picture I had taken more than a decade ago up to the light filtering through the smoke that curled from the embers in the kitchen hearth. When we left, the two women stood on the grass of their garden, surrounded by the flowers, to wave us off.

Dr Mahmud Hamza, still smart in a white shirt and neat trousers, tried to smile when I showed him the picture of him standing in his makeshift clinic in the ruins of the city eleven years before but failed. A severe stroke a year earlier, just after his forty-first birthday, had made it very difficult for him to speak. We sat on the terrace of his new house, a substantial structure with two floors and a large walled compound around an impressive garden, and his wife interpreted what he said to Ala who translated it for me.

'I know, I know,' he said as we asked him if he remembered me. 'You left very soon. But we were very happy to see you and we were very surprised as well. There was lots of cholera and no medicine. Now a lot of things have changed.'

He held up the picture again and spoke haltingly, unable to move his lips to form the words. 'Yes,' his wife said he said. 'I look at the photograph and I am happy because this is me.' She smiled to herself, closing a hand on her husband's.

We talked for a few minutes longer. Mahmud told me about his children and the vegetables he hoped to grow in his garden and asked about pharmacies in the West but he was visibly tiring. When I stood up to leave, he leaned on a cane, forced himself to his feet and with an enormous, juddering, straining effort, shook my hand.

The man I most wanted to meet was Firyad Barzani, the dashing peshmerga and KDP official who had looked after Iain and me in 1991. I had been told that he was now based in Salahadin, the hilltop town where the KDP had their military headquarters, and was still a peshmerga, though it was unclear what his job now was. I reached Salahadin late one afternoon and, unwilling to wait until the morning, wandered into the main military base to find Firyad's office. Our reunion, I felt, should not be put off any longer. Eleven years was long enough. Firyad, I was sure, would now be a major commander, in charge of hundreds of young peshmerga. We would reminisce about old times, laugh about what a poor soldier I had been, talk about the battles he had fought and the men he had killed, the long and bitter civil war and, over a bottle of whisky perhaps, forge a great new friendship. I found Firyad's office in the section of the base dealing with publishing. A peshmerga guard told me to wait, entered the office, came out and told me to go in. Firyad did not recognize me and, even after ten minutes' conversation, I was not entirely sure he remembered me at all.

But then I barely recognized Firyad. He had been in his early thirties in 1991, but had looked younger. Now he was gaunt and a close crop could not disguise grey and thinning hair. He smiled with difficulty and moved nervously. I remembered him as fit and athletic. Yet his jeans and a shirt seemed to hang off his spare hips and shoulders and when I handed him a sheaf of pictures of our time together in 1991 he barely looked at them. He now worked in publicity, running radio programmes, a magazine and literacy classes for the troops, he said. He had published a book of speeches by KDP senior commanders, he said proudly. A book of aphorisms had also been produced and a biography of Hitler translated from Persian and a collection of obituaries of *shaheed*, martyred pesh-merga, too. He was very busy.

I asked what had happened to the other men in the unit. Ibrahim Mustafa, the man we called the Commissar, had developed very bad kidney problems as a result of his bullet wounds and was in Iran seeking treatment. Abdul Rahmani, whom I remembered as a lean and fit-looking fighter, had gone on to be a 'big commander' but had been killed in the civil war between the PUK and the KDP. Others were dead too, or crippled, or overseas. We spoke for a little longer. There was not much more to say. Firyad had got married. He had two children now. They were both well. He had been to America. I took a photograph of him outside the office and then went back to my hotel.

The Kurds were free, more or less, I thought as I walked back to the hotel. Saddam now left them pretty much alone in their enclave. I had seen signs of growing prosperity, at least for some. There was a big supermarket now in the city of Dohuk where you could buy anything from a BMX bicycle to imported frozen meat and there were restaurants with menus offering French wine and 'Chateau Bryan' steak. Their clients were local merchants, many of whom were making huge amounts of money from smuggled oil, and workers for the United Nations, who earned twice as much as a local government minister. Qala Diza was a thriving city once more. The Kurds had a functioning parliament and, now that the civil war was over, some degree of law and order. The sky was still a stunning clear blue; the yellow of the plains still stretched across distant horizons as you looked south, the long grass was still washed in different directions by a fast-changing wind; the dark ridge of the mountains still hung on the skyline beyond the forests and fast-running rivers to the north. People were, within bounds, relatively content. But those I had known eleven years before were either dead, ill, broken or mired in illiteracy and a poverty so profound they barely knew how poor they were. I knew there was a lot to be pleased about and I was deeply happy that the Kurds, after suffering so much, after shooting themselves in the collective foot so many times, had just about reached some kind of stability, however relative. Nor was I disappointed that no fireworks, no national holiday, no personal epiphany, had greeted my return. I had expected none. But that evening I did not feel much like celebrating.

I had dinner with Shireen Ahmedi, a politician and women's rights activist. I had been asking some of the KDP officials about honour killings in Kurdistan and had been directed to her, the only female member of the party's ruling council.

Ahmedi was born in 1967, the daughter of a famous KDP activist, and had been completing a law degree at university in the ethnically mixed city of Mosul on the edge of the Kurdish areas of Iraq when an Iraqi attack in 1988 had forced her to flee with her family to the Turkish mountains. The family stayed in a village, where she spent hours each day fetching water, until the uprising of 1991. She did not want to talk about her life, she told me. 'Ask me about women,' she said. So I did.

'At first I was not interested in women's issues,' she said, 'but during the 1991 fighting and afterwards I became involved in interrogation.'

'Interrogation?'

'Yes. I was asked to be in charge of the interrogation of a prison. I dealt with the women prisoners.'

'What sort of interrogation?'

'I was in charge of getting people who betrayed the Kurds to talk.'

'How did you do that?'

A pause. Then a very indirect answer.

'I was very angry back then.'

We moved from the hotel garden to the dining room. Ahmedi was wearing a white headscarf, blue trousers and a matching jacket with big padded shoulders and was carrying a black bag with a gold chain. I wondered about the headscarf. Ahmedi guessed what I was thinking.

'You know the veil was a Byzantine tradition? Even before the coming of Islam?' she said. 'In Kurdistan, the full veil was imposed by the Ottomans. It is not a Kurdish tradition at all. Certainly not for tribal women. You can't wear a veil when you are working in the fields. Nor do you need to. The Iraqi government encouraged women to wear veils. Before the uprising 65 per cent of Kurdish women wore veils. Now only 25 per cent do.'

Another 'tradition' that had been imposed on the Kurds was the legislation concerning violence towards women, Ahmedi told me. 'The law was changed by the governments in Baghdad. Now Iraqi law supports a man who murders his wife or daughter if he thinks she has committed some sexual offence. I have been fighting this in our parliament. Most of the men there have helped me but some religious conservatives have obstructed me. But I know that Islam does not support honour killings. There are many verses in the Koran that say that women should be protected.' And Ahmedi started quoting line after line, exploding with religious references, political slogans, facts and statistics, her English syntax disintegrating as the sentences poured out.

'A deputation of moderate Muslim clerics went to the parliament to stress that Islam does not endorse this violence. Often the women are just killed on suspicion. We got it through parliament, the law against honour killings. We got it through. I am happy about the law but the problem is civil society. I have counted 372 women in the KDP area that have been killed since 1998. In the latest incident a girl was killed by her uncle because he wanted her to marry his son and she refused so he made a moral accusation against her and killed her. This happened in Arbil, in the city; she was 22; the family was a rural family and did not realize it was wrong.'

She paused. Another KDP official had mentioned the case to

me before and it had interested me. In Pakistan it had seemed that it was not the most conservative societies that were full of men committing violence against women but those in the midst of change. The women killed on the North-West Frontier died because they were trying to exercise rights of which they had been completely unaware a decade or so previously. Similarly, women who were subject to violence in the Afghan refugee camps or in the huge shanty towns on the outskirts of cities like Karachi were merely acting in ways that were far more appropriate to their new environments and thus confronting and transgressing customs designed for rural village life. In Afghanistan, I knew, attacks on women in the western city of Herat had actually risen since the fall of the Taliban, confirming the theory that it is change and the possibility of greater freedom for women that sparks violence towards them. Then there were, of course, the many attacks in those communities most exposed to radical and rapid change: immigrants in the West. As elsewhere, an integral part of the violence against women seemed to be that it was public or at least very publicly acknowledged.

'In villages no one imposes rules on women,' Ahmedi was saying. 'It is when they come to the city that they start imposing rules on women. Women in Sweden, France and the UK are killed for the same reasons and women who go to Europe and get educated and come back to their villages have stones thrown at them. This is a society in transition.'

She paused.

'You know the real problem? The real problem for us?'

I shook my head.

'It's the Saudi Arabians. It's the Wahhabis. But you need to talk to the religious people about them, not me.'

She gave me the names of some of the more moderate clerics who had helped her.

I asked why she was wearing a headscarf.

'I'm told it suits me,' she said.

Ala and I hired a taxi and headed east towards Suleimaniyah. Eleven years before it had taken days of driving on the back roads in the mountains to get across the north of Iraq. Now, even though the quickest route via the city of Kirkuk was still in the hands of the Baghdad regime, the journey took just a few hours. The road led first through rolling hills and plateaus, where small houses lay scattered like seeds that had rolled into the folds of the landscape, and then up through the steeper ridges of the main granite foothills of the Zagros mountains, past massive, grey crags and outcrops. One marked a lay-by where a series of roadside restaurants served traditional Kurdish food, watered down curd with lumps of ice floating in it to combat the summer heat, bowls of *fasoli*, or haricot beans in tomato sauce, *awe marish*, or chicken broth, chunks of fowl or lamb served on rice with lentils and noodles, stewed apricots and kebabs. The road then ran straight towards the southern shore of Lake Dokan before curling down through a series of broad gullies, each composed of dozens of other smaller gullies. Their grassy slopes had yellowed in the summer heat and gnarled olive trees cast small shadows which sheltered goats and their shepherds and small groups of brightly dressed women. A final left turn by a huge cement works and a checkpoint manned by peshmerga from the PUK, the eastern-based Patriotic Union of Kurdistan, and an old airstrip took you into the city of Suleimaniyah.

The front lines were forty miles south of the city and did not appear to have moved significantly since I had last been in northern Iraq. Saddam had sent his troops into the Kurds' enclave on several occasions – most notably, and most successfully, after being invited in by the KDP during the civil war among the Kurds – but along most of the front most of the time not much happened. The Iraqi troops occasionally took potshots at Kurdish shepherds who wandered too close, mines laid in no-man's land killed or maimed on a regular basis, Kurds crossing the front line to visit relatives or search for work were harassed and often beaten and robbed but Saddam knew that a full-scale invasion of the north, with the inevitable casualties, humanitarian crisis and eventual Western response it would bring, was simply not worth trying. He contented himself instead with a concerted programme of ethnic cleansing in and around Kirkuk and covert operations designed to weaken the Kurds' always fragile unity. Shortly after arriving in Suleimaniyah Ala and I drove down to the scruffy town of Chamchamal. Beyond the last slums, where refugees from Kirkuk were living, was a broad valley of cornfields and a row of low hills that reminded me of the South Downs of England, except that the South Downs do not have a row of bunkers and trenches along the top. Through binoculars I could see Iraqi soldiers sitting on the top of the trenches filling sandbags. They were almost certainly conscripts. Many were likely to be Shias from the south and as unhappy to be where they were as the Kurds were to see them there. Ala, a staunch PUK activist and a native of Kirkuk, borrowed my binoculars and watched the troops. 'Soon the Americans will come and sweep them off the hills,' she said, waving an arm dramatically. 'Then I can go home.'

One of the clerics that Shireen Ahmedi had mentioned helping her in her campaign to reform the laws on violence against women and marriage was the imam of Suleimaniyah's largest mosque, Majid Ismael Mohammed. We met in his simple offices behind the mosque where the bustle of Suleimaniyah was nothing more than a distant hum and young students walked along quiet corridors carrying books. Occasionally there was an outburst of laughter or the sounds of an argument, reasonable and forthright rather than heated or strident. Ismael Mohammed, a tall, thin man with warm eyes, wore the white, tightly wound turban and long grey robe of a Kurdish cleric. He was preparing for the afternoon's service but had some time to share tea. He was, like most Kurds, a Sunni from the Shafai school. He explained to me how, nearly a thousand years ago, Sunni Islam had been split into four main schools, all of which differed in their practice and theory, by religious authorities of the Arabo-Islamic empires. The schools, named after their most pre-eminent jurists, still determined practice in much of the Islamic world. The most rigorous and conservative, the Hambali school, predominated in Saudi Arabia and the Gulf and was best represented by movements like Wahhabism. The less conservative Hanafi school covered Iraq, Turkey and most of south and southwest Asia. Malikis were found in the Maghreb and sub-Saharan Africa. Shafais, Ismael Mohammed said, were known for their moderation but, though strong in the Far East, were a minority in the Middle East.

Though his family were from Suleimaniyah, Ismael Mohammed had grown up among the substantial Kurdish community in Baghdad until discrimination forced him to flee to Iran in 1985. His life over the following decade or so was an astonishing example of the interconnectedness of events in the Middle East, linking internal upheavals in Saudi Arabia, the war against the Soviets in Afghanistan, the conflict between Iran and Iraq, domestic politics in at least four countries and religious debates across half the region. History, for him, meant more than a subject at school or a section in a bookshop.

Ismael Mohammed's life also showed how national boundaries – very recent developments in much of the region that he had lived in – could be transcended, or at least ignored. He had spent his years moving around a religious, social and political network that, almost like an entirely alternative system that could be mapped over its secular counterpart, spanned dozens of countries. Where one system comprised states, governments, customs officials and borders, the other consisted of linked seminaries, senior clerics, schools of thought and places with particular religious significance. Of course the two systems met frequently, particularly where local clerics had been co-opted by a given regime or where, as in Saudi Arabia, religious and secular establishments were difficult to separate, but it struck me that Ismael Mohammed navigated his way through life with a map that was often very different from the one I used. His personal landscape certainly included a range of different features that were entirely absent from my own.

On arrival in Iran he had been interned in a refugee camp where he had come into contact with radical preachers. His own background was tolerant and ecumenical, like that of most of the Kurds, but the certainty and force of the radical message projected by the teachers in the refugee camps' schools attracted him. The men were Wahhabis, ultra-conservatives from Saudi Arabia, who had fled to Iran after being involved in an abortive rebellion against the regime.

'I come from a big religious family and my great-grandfather actually married his son to Christians. But in the refugee camps in Iran we knew nothing,' Ismael Mohammed said. 'We were refugees, scared and confused. We saw the medressas, the religious schools, and the teachers there were our first real teachers. We believed what they told us.'

The refugee camp lessons lasted for almost a year. When the Iranian authorities found out what was happening, Ismael Mohammed said, they closed all the schools and told the radical teachers to leave. Taking the most committed of their students with them, most of the Wahhabi preachers headed to Pakistan to fight the Soviets.

Ismael Mohammed too travelled to Pakistan but swiftly decided that the harsh brand of radicalism current in Peshawar and else-where at the time was not for him. He studied with moderate clerics in the eastern city of Lahore and then returned home in 1993, about the same time as many of the hardline Kurdish militants who had fought in Afghanistan. Since his return, he had sought to guide the local community towards a 'centre path of Islam'. I asked if he believed he had a political role.

'Of course,' he said. 'How could I not have when I stand before my congregation on a Friday and deliver the sermon? I have to talk about things that are relevant to them and that means talking about real life.'

I mentioned that on the drive over from Arbil I had seen dozens of new mosques by the side of the road, each with IIRO painted on the side, the initials of a major quasi-governmental Saudi Arabian charity. Ismael Mohammed leaned forward and rested a single finger on my notebook.

'Those mosques were built by the Saudis and they pay for their preachers to run them. They have a very intolerant, very fierce type of belief. This kind of preaching is the biggest threat,' he said.

I could understand Ismael Mohammed's animosity towards the Saudi Arabians. Events in the kingdom had exerted a malign influence over much of his life. It had been Wahhabi preachers that had first led him, as he saw it, astray. Then he watched how those hardline ideologies had been reinforced by the war in Afghanistan, where the Arab radicals were heavily funded by private and public donors in Saudi Arabia. Then finally he had watched Muslims in his own country come under the influence of Wahhabism, exported as part of a deliberate policy by the house of Saud to boost their religious credentials in the Islamic world. The same, I knew, had occurred in Pakistan, Afghanistan, East Africa, the Far East and the Maghreb. Tolerant, pluralist styles of worship, often incorporating pre-Islamic traditions or the ideas of the Sufi mystical strains of Islam, such as those I had seen at the Bari Imam shrine outside Islamabad many years previously, were being shouldered aside by the angry, harsh, rigorous strand of the faith that had originated with a dissident cleric in the Arabian peninsula a mere 200 years before.

'Two years ago I set up a union of more than a thousand moderate religious scholars and preachers in Kurdistan to fight the extremists who are filling the heads of the villagers and the young with these bad ideas, but we are very poor and we don't have the funds to combat these big Saudi Arabian organizations that are coming in here,' Ismael Mohammed was saying. 'They are giving aid to orphans and widows and set up their preachers in villages and build big new mosques for them and we cannot compete with all of that. You have to fight the Wahhabis on their own ground, on ideology, with true religious ideas about the true nature of Islam, an easy true Islam with friendship for all other religions. Now the Wahhabis are very strong and aggressive and some of our own scholars are afraid of them and afraid to preach what they want to preach.'

Every evening when I was in Suleimaniyah I left the new hotel and went for a walk. I could hardly remember the city from when I was there as a student so meandered at random through the parks and open, tree-lined streets. Somehow I always headed north or east or south. Late one afternoon I realized why. At the end of a street less than a mile to the west of the hotel, I saw, as we drove swiftly past, a bullet-pocked, semi-shattered shell of an office block, all square concrete windows and jutting moulded concrete cubes, painted pink. It was the 'Amna Securita', the Red Security.

The Red Security was where Saddam's Mukhabarat intelligence services had been based. It had been the site of four days of fierce fighting in 1991 when the people of Suleimaniyah and the local peshmerga had risen against Saddam. It was one of the first buildings attacked in the city and many of the Iraqi intelligence officials, possibly hundreds, who were based there had been massacred. The bodies had been cleared away when I had seen it in 1991 but I could still remember the stench and the filth that had coated the courtyard. In the rooms inside there had been worse. The largest cells measured twenty feet by thirty and had each held around 100 prisoners. Space was so restricted that each man had his own floor tile. Near by were smaller cells for solitary confinement or torture with small windows through which the jailers pushed faeces or the underwear of raped relatives and hooks in the ceiling from which prisoners were suspended. I had been walking in circles to avoid it. When, one morning towards the end of my stay in Suleimaniyah, I finally worked up the courage to walk round the complex, I found the cells had been cleaned and were to be preserved as a museum. After eleven years, naturally, the smell was gone. The hooks on the ceilings were still there.

10. Secrets and Lies

The Kurds had their own security services, of course. The PUK's was based in a nondescript compound in the north of Suleimaniyah full of battered jeeps and men in jeans and shirts with handguns shoved through their belts. They had two jobs: the first was to counter attempts by Saddam's agents to destabilize Kurdistan and the second was to combat the radical Islamic movement that, between 1991 and 2002, had sprouted like a weed in their homeland.

The chief at the local security service headquarters was Wasta Hassan. Wasta is Kurdish slang for 'foreman' or 'boss' and Boss Hassan was in his early forties, short, with thick black hair brushed back from his forehead, a long moustache and broad shoulders. He wore jeans with a 9mm pistol tucked in the waistband, a light checked shirt and a leather jacket. He was a veteran of scores of armed encounters and talked and walked quickly, slapping his men on the back, shouting orders or jokes or insults as he moved among them. He treated the prisoners, who were held in cells a few steps from his office, with a weary nonchalance, and, like most of his men, wore shades more often than was strictly necessary. Wasta Hassan had clearly watched rather too many American detective films, but then so had I and I liked him.

Wasta and I got on well. For several hours one morning I talked to him about Pakistan, Afghanistan and al-Qaeda, explaining the set-up of the training camps there and of what I knew about the linkages between the militants in southwest Asia and those in Iraq. An American reporter and friend expressed surprise when I told him about these conversations, saying that they raised serious ethical questions about contacts between journalists and intelligence services. I shrugged and said I had seen the discussions as a genuine exchange of views between two people interested in a specialized field, not as assisting the authorities. I also pointed out, probably somewhat defensively, that, unlike some reporters, I was profoundly distrustful of all intelligence services.

I had learned early on in my career that there was a big difference between knowledge and intelligence and that 'secrets' were as likely to be wrong as right. In the early nineties I had seen intelligence dossiers on Islamic militants in London compiled by the British domestic security service which had contained basic errors. In Pakistan I had watched as Western and local intelligence services pushed particular agendas in the media, feeding journalists completely unsubstantiated information in the knowledge that its source would invest it with a degree of utterly undeserved authority. After September 11 there were dozens of such operations, ranging from the placement by Middle Eastern intelligence of false stories depicting bin Laden as a teenage playboy who had suddenly got religion to a British operation which aimed to blame al-Qaeda for much of the heroin being imported into the UK, a charge which was completely baseless and, given what bin Laden had in fact done, completely superfluous too. Then, of course, there were the myriad governments claiming, via selected leaks by 'intelligence sources', to have suddenly discovered 'al-Qaeda' cells on their soil. The most egregious of these claims came from the Macedonians, who simply shot dead a group of Pakistani asylum seekers and, having dressed the corpses in combat uniforms, announced they had struck a major blow in the 'War on Terror'.

This background gave my meetings with Wasta Hassan an added significance. Over the previous months I had been increasingly frustrated by my inability to rebut misleading statements by commentators or analysts or politicians which invoked the magical 'security sources', particularly those who insisted on linking Saddam Hussein to al-Qaeda. Just speaking to Wasta Hassan meant that I was at least one stage closer to the original source of the information. Even better, Wasta Hassan allowed me to interview pretty much anyone I wanted in his prison.

Over tea in his office, Wasta explained the roots of Ansar ul-Islam, the local militant group. Many were familiar, similar to those underlying the development of radical groups in Pakistan, Afghanistan, Algeria and elsewhere. So there was the local tradition of the use of Islam to aid resistance to outside interference, the widespread disappointed aspirations following the 1991 Gulf conflict, significant social and economic stresses in the mid-1990s, the activity of Saudi-funded preachers and meddling from the Iranians looking to use Kurdish Islamists as proxies and a generalized, incoherent sense of 'injustice'. There were also two influxes of 'Afghan veterans', the first arriving in the early 1990s, the second arriving after the recent American-led campaign against the Taliban. In addition, there was the simple fact that the two main local Kurdish political parties, seen as responsible for many of the problems, were nationalist, secular and socialist in inspiration. Religion had become a natural rallying point for opposition as a result.

One of the first militants I spoke to was a 25-year-old called Rebuar Khadir, the son of a Suleimaniyah shopkeeper. He had given himself up to the Kurdish security services a few months earlier and described his induction into radical militancy lucidly and intelligently as Ala and I sat with him in a disused office adjacent to the prison. Khadir told me that he had not been particularly religious but a more devout older brother had introduced him to representatives from one of the more moderate Islamic groups when he was at Friday prayers at a local mosque. Lectures on the Koran had been followed, after several months, by more political speeches. Eventually, not least because he would be paid a small salary, Khadir had joined one of the politically active Islamic groups and, in February 2002, had made his way to an enclave in the hills north of the city of Halabjah where Ansar ul-Islam was based. He was shocked at what he found. 'They were in charge of a few villages and were trying to run everything like the Taliban and the locals didn't like it much. And then they were all talking about liberating Palestine,' he told me. 'I was interested in liberating Kurdistan from the unbelievers. I couldn't understand why they were so angry and so excited about something that was happening so far away.'

Khadir told me that there had been a steady radicalization of the group over the previous years as they had developed ties with the hard core of al-Qaeda in Afghanistan. In the summer of 2001, he told me, the leaders of the main Islamic groups in Kurdistan had visited bin Laden in Afghanistan and requested assistance. They had received money and training and, in the aftermath of the war in Afghanistan that autumn, had given shelter to around a hundred militants fleeing the American-led assault on their bases. This was an important point as it proved that Ansar ul-Islam was neither part of a single global jihad led entirely by bin Laden nor dedicated merely to a local project but, like so many groups, a hybrid of the two. It was this ambivalence that led to Khadir, after several months in the mountains, becoming disillusioned and, scared and homesick, giving himself up to the PUK.

The second prisoner I saw was Didar, who was only 19, and bounced into the room with a loud *salaam aleikum* and a smile. He had a thin, youthful beard, medium-length brown hair, acne, an old green shirt and striped baggy trousers, and long, rangy limbs. He spoke fluently and rapidly and without contrition but with an odd bashful self-consciousness, like a child confessing to smashing a window with a ball. He told me he had been born into a large and relatively wealthy family in Arbil and had left school at 16. He had kicked around home for a bit and then, though his family had not been religious, had begun spending more time at the mosque. Like Khadir, he was invited to join a Koranic study group where, after a few early lessons in pure theology, the tone hardened and he found himself being taught that jihad was the duty of every Muslim. Within a month or so he was at the mosque every night. The teacher told him all about bin Laden and the new party the students would form in Kurdistan that would be part of al-Qaeda. He was, he told me, very excited.

In November 2001 Didar was told by his teacher that a group of militants had announced a jihad in Kurdistan. The two men travelled by bus to Halabjah, from where a taxi took them up to Ansar's headquarters in the hills. 'It was a dream come true for me,' Didar said. 'I wanted to take part in the jihad so much. I had learned how God will reward me in paradise for my jihad. It was a big adventure.'

After two weeks his parents tracked Didar down to the camp and came to see him. 'When they came to me I held them and kissed them and my mother asked me to come home with her,' Didar said. 'But I refused. We sat outside the camp to talk. I was crying. So was my mum and so was my dad. They prayed for me to come home. But I thought, this is a jihad, and I had been taught that the jihad was more important than going back with my parents.'

For the next three months Didar was instructed in the same syllabus as had been taught in the Afghan camps: basic infantry tactics, explosives, urban warfare and assassinations. The instructors, unsurprisingly, were all veterans from Afghanistan, as were the leaders of the group. The idea of 'martyrdom operations' was first raised by the Arab instructors but it was Didar's friend, Hisham, a 22-year-old whom he had met in the mosque at Arbil, who started talking seriously about participating in suicide attacks. Removed from the wider community, it appeared that it was the views of his immediate new companions that most influenced him. I thought immediately about Walid, the boy who had died on the Gaza Strip, and of an academic in Israel who had spoken to me at length about the importance of small-group dynamics in the decision to become a suicide bomber, speaking of 'fictive kin' or groups as substitutes for families as being a key element, not just in recruitment, but in the progressive formation of a bomber's mentality. I remembered too a former Irish Republican Army trainer and double murderer who, over a pint in a London pub, had told me that he could do nothing with teenagers who 'went home' every night. 'Give me three months with them in a farmhouse in the hills and I'll give you a killer,' he had said.

'Hisham said we should do it together,' Didar was saying. 'He quoted all the verses of the Koran and repeated the prophet's teaching and every day we talked about it. I told our leaders that I was ready and they called me on the radio and they showed me the jacket and demonstrated how it worked. Then we had lunch.'

As we talked Wasta Hassan, who had been working on papers

at his desk, went to a cupboard and pulled out the jacket that had been taken off when Didar had been arrested. It was a sleeveless jerkin made of blue nylon and had a slab of explosives over the chest and another in the small of the back. A separate belt, also stitched from the same cheap fabric, contained more explosives. At the end of twisted wires were two small metal switches, one for the jacket and one for the belt, which clicked back and forth with a satisfying, firm metallic tick.

'What date was this?' I asked.

'It was the twelfth of June,' he said. 'I know because it was the World Cup.'

'You were watching the World Cup?'

'There were no televisions because they are forbidden. But I was following it in the newspapers.'

'What was your favourite team?'

'England.'

'England is your favourite team and you are about to blow yourself up in the jihad against unbelievers?'

'Politics is one thing. Football is something else. I used to play right-back for Dadowan team in Arbil.'

'You don't think it's odd for someone who is about to die to be following the World Cup?'

'It seemed normal.'

On the day before he was supposed to die, Didar was driven to a house on the outskirts of Halabjah. He had spent most of the previous week closeted with the leaders of Ansar, praying, listening to lectures about his duty, the oppression of Muslims and the paradise that awaited the martyr. The plan was to launch a diversionary attack and then the suicide strike. Didar was told that when he heard shooting the next morning he was to make his way to the local PUK office and blow himself up. He ate dinner and then watched a Jackie Chan DVD with his host. 'I knew that it was my last dinner but I didn't think about it,' he told me, smiling his odd, slightly bashful, slightly cocky smile. Earlier he had laughed when I had trouble pronouncing some Arabic words. His apparent phlegm had begun to irritate me.

'So after the Jackie Chan film you just went to bed and dreamed of seventy-two virgins?' I asked.

'I didn't dream. I slept fine. I knew I was going to paradise so was very calm.'

'Did you have an alarm clock? Weren't you worried about oversleeping? It wouldn't look very good if you didn't get up in time to blow yourself up, would it?'

'Like I said, I was thinking about paradise.'

'Did you think about your mother?'

'No. All my mind was on paradise.'

The first attempt was aborted when the diversionary attack failed. Didar was taken back to the home of the group's leader, a Jordanian Kurd, and spent another three days there. On the third day, after dawn prayers, he was taken back to Halabjah again and dropped at the same house on the town's outskirts. It was a small house made of mud and stone with three rooms, and though Didar heard his host's wife and young children he never saw anyone. Finally it was time to get ready again.

'I slept until lunchtime and then prayed and ate and then waited until the end of afternoon prayers and then put on my jacket and went to the bus stop. I was calm and not at all nervous. I got on the bus that went through the bazaar to the PUK office.'

'Aren't the PUK Muslims?' I asked. Didar looked at his feet, his odd smile disappearing for a moment.

'They are unbelievers.'

'But so are the English football team.'

'That's different.'

Wasta Hassan, still at his desk in the corner of the room, snorted in irritation. 'I'm a Muslim, believe me,' he said, stubbing out a cigarette in a saucer. 'Just not one like you, thankfully. All this crap about paradise. There is nothing in the Koran that promises anyone like you paradise.'

Ala smiled faintly as she translated what he had said. Didar continued his story.

'I left the house with the man I had stayed with. He came to the bus stop with me. It was about 5 p.m. and I was warm because

I was wearing the jacket under traditional Kurdish clothes. I was not nervous. I got on the bus and the man paid the driver a dinar and I sat down. There were three other passengers.'

'How did it feel?' I asked, thinking of the character in *The Secret Agent*, Joseph Conrad's extraordinarily perceptive novel about terrorists in London at the end of the nineteenth century, who enjoys the sensation of power he has while sitting on the upper deck of a bus with a bomb and a detonator in his hand.

'Did you feel strong? Did you feel like a hero?'

'I just thought of paradise. It was ten minutes on the bus and when I got off it I saw the office, the target, and I walked up to the peshmerga at the door and gave him the name of a man who I thought would be inside and said I had come to see him and when the man came out I was going to press the switch but the peshmerga asked, "What is that underneath your shirt?" and I said, "Nothing" and he asked again and I did not think of anything and I said, "It's TNT" and then they arrested me. I was glad. I knew the men there were from Arbil and I did not want to kill people from my own town. I didn't want to die.'

'So you didn't want to do it?'

'A human being is always changing his mind. When I think about it now I know it was a mistake.'

I spent dozens of hours with different prisoners during that week in Suleimaniyah but it was the last interview that I conducted, tired and slightly bored, that proved one of the most fruitful. It focused on the alleged links between al-Qaeda and Saddam Hussein, a topic that had been much discussed since the attacks of September 11, 2001 and would take on a huge significance over the coming months.

It was about 10 o'clock in the morning and already stifling, the heat reflecting from the whitewashed courtyard outside and glaring in through the window. Wasta Hassan had gone to a meeting, leaving me with Ala and a prisoner called Mohammed Mansour Shahab. An hour earlier I had seen some pictures of him holding a bloodied knife over the corpse of a man who had been strangled with a length of blue cord. Dressed in a pale shirt and grey trousers, he was smiling at the camera and appeared remarkably relaxed, given that he was holding the man's right ear, which he appeared to have just severed, in his fingers. Now he was sitting in front of me, smiling again and wearing plastic sandals, a checked shirt and baggy traditional Kurdish trousers.

He had been arrested early in 2001 trying to cross from Kurdistan into Baghdad's territory. The gruesome pictures had been printed from an undeveloped film found in his pocket and had resulted in a seven-year prison sentence. For the first six months of his imprisonment he had kept his story to himself. Then, in October 2001, he told a fellow prisoner who told the guards who told Wasta Hassan. When, in the early spring, a reporter from the *New Yorker* magazine was in Suleimaniyah, Shahab had told him too. The resulting story was published with the headline 'The Threat of Saddam' and announced that 'the Kurds may have evidence of [Saddam's] ties to Osama bin Laden's terrorist network'. Though there were a number of possible links between the Iraqi dictator and al-Qaeda included in the article, Shahab's story was prominently featured.

Shahab said he was an illiterate Iranian smuggler who started out running TVs and videos across the marshy Iran–Iraq border before graduating to a two-way trade running Iranian weapons into Afghanistan and Afghan drugs back into Iran. After delivering a major consignment of ammunition to Kandahar he had been introduced by a contact there to Osama bin Laden in late 1999. For the next year, Shahab said, he bought guns from Iran and handed them over to his smuggler associate at the border on the understanding that they were for al-Qaeda. He met bin Laden again, in a cave in the mountains, and was thanked for his help and asked for more weapons 'if he could get them'. Then things got more complicated.

First, Shahab said, an Iraqi smuggler called Uthman asked him to travel into Iraq for a secret meeting. There, he met Saddam Hussein's brother-in-law who asked him to take ten air-conditioning units across the border into Iran. Six months later he was given 300 82mm mortars and 400 rocket-propelled grenades and was told to take them across to Iran too. With five others Shahab drove the munitions to the border in three trucks, transferred them on to boats, crossed the marshes to the Iranian side, put the consignment back on trucks which, he said, were then driven away to Kandahar. Finally, in early 2000, there had been a last meeting in Iraq at which Ali Hassan Majid, known to the Kurds as 'Ali Chemical' for his enthusiastic execution of Saddam's orders to use poison gas on them in 1988 and 1989, asked him to smuggle a consignment of thirty refrigerator motors into Iran, the housings of which appeared to have been reinforced and filled with some kind of fluid that, he was told, was extremely dangerous. They were, Shahab said, chemical weapons. Once he had got them into Iran his contact took them on across the border and on to Kandahar to bin Laden. And there his story ended.

Shahab's tale was widely reported in America and in some British publications and found its way into various speeches, with various sources quoted, by various figures in the Bush administration. It was promoted as evidence of the link between Saddam and al-Qaeda. Shahab's story apparently confirmed that one of the most notorious men in Saddam's regime, with a proven track record in chemical warfare, was secretly sending fluid-filled containers to Osama bin Laden. Or at least it would have done, if Shahab had not been a liar.

First, there were significant inconsistencies between what Shahab told other reporters and what he told me. He told the *New Yorker*, for instance, that he had met bin Laden in a tent, not a cave, and claimed he himself delivered the liquid-filled fridge motors to the Taliban personally. Then there were the practical problems with his story. The consignment of weapons that he had described smuggling for the Iraqis would, I calculated, have weighed more than 20 tonnes. It would have been simply impossible for six men to load and unload that weight (twice) in five hours.

It was also perfectly clear that Shahab had never been to Kandahar. When I asked him to describe the city he said it was 'dirty', which was true, and was entirely composed of mud houses, which was not true at all unless a lot of very quick demolition and reconstruction work had taken place since I had last been there. So why was he lying? Probably, as Wasta Hassan admitted, because his sudden conversion from two-bit brutal smuggler to useful source might well get him a few years off his sentence. And from where did he get the idea or material for the lies? Televisions were introduced into the cells in the prison in Suleimaniyah a month before the September 11 attacks.

By the time I returned home at the end of August 2002, the decision to invade Iraq had already been taken in Washington. It seemed to me to have been based on fairly straightforward reasoning. It was not, I felt, a war for oil, which could have been obtained by concluding the sort of preferential agreement that Saddam had been indicating he wanted for years, nor for global supremacy, which it would not achieve. It was, quite simply, a war for security based on the perception of a significant present or potential threat. In the minds of senior figures in the American administration, Iraq posed a danger to the United States and therefore had to be dealt with. Their view, which was entirely comprehensible, was that nothing that might lead to another September 11 could be ignored. They also felt, less reasonably, that the decade-old policy of containment of Iraq had failed and that the United Nations, and the international community the body supposedly represented, had proved itself incapable of confronting the threat Saddam posed. America had to act to protect itself. It was as simple as that. And if it had to act alone, so be it.

Of course there were other currents of thought too. Several major figures in the White House, influenced by an odd and irrational stream of pseudo-scholarship, had seen Iraq as a source of terror and Islamic radicalism for many years. Others believed that the nineties had seen American liberals fritter away through fecklessness, a lack of determination and insufficient 'moral clarity' a historic opportunity to remake the world in the image, and the interests, of 'the greatest democracy ever known'. Still others had a grand vision of remaking 'the Islamic world' through enforced change in Iraq. They argued that unleashing the power of liberal democracy, even if freedom arrived riding on a tank, would slice through the Gordian knot of Middle Eastern politics, forcing regimes from Riyadh to Algiers to reform and provoking a surge of social and economic progress that would simultaneously 'drain the terrorist swamp', preserve the strategic position of Israel and secure the world's access to the region's natural resources. But, despite all these various currents of thought, the principal idea underpinning the invasion of Iraq remained relatively simple: to do whatever needed to be done to make America safe. The British prime minister and most of his government were manifestly sympathetic to the Americans' decision and followed in their wake. The problem, of course, was that the threat, both from Saddam and from Islamic militancy, was wrongly analysed. All the thinking about how to deal with that threat, however reasonable, was predicated on the mutually reinforcing falsehoods that Islamic militancy was the result of the actions of a single group, or even a single individual, and that Saddam was on the point of developing nuclear, chemical and biological weaponry, if he did not have them already. It was easy to make the mental jump to linking bin Laden with Baghdad and thus increase the threat exponentially. Once you did, given the prevalence of the 'hard' counter-terrorism discourse, only one line of action was feasible. The result of these cumulative and self-reinforcing failures of judgement was a very significant strategic error.

The six months from August 2002, when I got back from Iraq, to February 2003, when I returned to Kurdistan to cover the war, saw a concerted effort by the American and British governments to rally public support behind the invasion of Iraq. Though perhaps not intended to be, it was one of the biggest ever deceptions of democratic populations in recent history. It bewildered me, shocked me and profoundly shook my faith in the political institutions of Britain and other nations. I did not think that politicians in the UK or America were deliberately lying to the public, but I did think they were deliberately presenting a very one-sided case.

And given that the evidence they presented was based on almost entirely false information, it did not really matter whether the deception had been intentional or otherwise. The outcome was the same.

The process of building support for a war in Iraq did not rely entirely on the actions of the British or American governments, however. As ever, the propaganda had to make sense. The governments' failure to comprehend the true nature of the threat merely reflected a broader confusion among their electorates over the reality of modern Islamic militancy and the dangers of the post-Cold War world. They also reflected a general sense of profound unease, exacerbated by sensationalist reporting and often clumsy and alarmist government statements. In addition, government statements also played into a broad and growing prejudice against Muslims and Arabs which made populations in the West far more susceptible to the suggestion that, in Saddam or al-Qaeda, they faced the latest manifestation of historic Islamic or Arab hostility. Long-standing cultural traditions dating from the Crusades and beyond made derogatory or inflammatory comments about Muslims far easier to assimilate. So, for example, the idea that Oriental despots are duplicitous and cruel, a strong element of Western literary and visual tradition, meant that Western audiences were predisposed to believe that Saddam, who often had displayed both characteristics, was lying when he claimed that he had no weapons of mass destruction. Historic ideas of the threat from 'the Turk' or 'the Mussulman', a given in Western public discourse for many centuries, meant that the latest propaganda about the threat in the East plugged into profound, pre-existing prejudices. Yet, important though this may have been, the key to the successful process of marketing the invasion of Iraq was, especially in Britain, the myth I was busy trying to unpick in Suleimaniyah: the supposed infallibility and impartiality of our security agencies.

In Britain intelligence material was fed into the debate in a variety of ways. Senior parliamentarians and editors received briefings from ministers of the 'if you had seen what I had seen' variety. Politicians' speeches referred elliptically to 'the threat'.

Senior policemen spoke of 'dozens' of averted al-Qaeda attacks but released no details. Two government 'dossiers', both supposedly based on secret intelligence material, were released. One, based not on the amazing ability of the British government to gather secret information but on a PhD student's research that had been downloaded from the internet, was a farce. The second dossier, issued by the government with the approval of MI6, was at least based on genuine intelligence material. Sadly, most of that material proved to be a mixture of half-truth and outright falsehood. Predictably, both dossiers ramped up the threat posed by Saddam's weapons of mass destruction and, though they did not actually say that al-Qaeda was linked to the Iraqi dictator, implied that it was only a matter of time before such a connection did develop. These dossiers were backed up by repeated public and parliamentary statements which received saturation media coverage and had a major impact on what was a febrile public debate.

In America, a similar process was unfolding, though with judicious leaks replacing dossiers and far less public argument. Claims that al-Qaeda and Saddam were jointly responsible for 9/11 persisted despite American intelligence agencies rapidly distancing themselves from the idea. As ever, however, early impressions counted and the idea of a nexus between bin Laden and Baghdad remained largely unchallenged in the minds of many Americans. The situation was exacerbated by Iraqi opposition groups with clear agendas funnelling defectors of varying reliability to intelligence agencies and media organizations on both sides of the Atlantic.

The marketing campaign for the war in Iraq climaxed with the address of Colin Powell, the American secretary of state, to the United Nations general assembly in New York in February 2003. Most of his speech was devoted to Saddam's supposed WMD programmes but Powell also spoke about the Iraqi dictator's links to bin Laden. Of course his entire case was based on secret 'intelligence' and his statements, though carefully worded, seemed to sum up all the worst elements of the analysis of al-Qaeda and Saddam. The idea that Islamic militancy was a nebulous movement based on personal associations, not hierarchic structures, simply had not sunk in. Instead, it was the old story of international organizations, state sponsorship and psychopathic leaders. The possibility that al-Qaeda was more of an ideology than an organization, and that Muslim radical activism might be exacerbated rather than countered by the invasion of Iraq, simply did not seem to have registered.

My own quandary in the run-up to the conflict was straightforward: I did not believe the intelligence, was deeply concerned that a war would fuel violence by strengthening the perception that the West was committed to a Crusade against Islam and was very angry at the way the government was manipulating public opinion. I was also concerned at the possible violations of international law, though accepted that such legal restrictions were often deeply flawed. I was concerned too that any war, however swift, would consume resources that could be far better employed elsewhere, in rebuilding Afghanistan, for example. But I also knew that all my Kurdish friends, all the Kurds I spoke to in Iraq and all the Iraqis I spoke to outside Iraq wanted the invasion to happen. So, I felt sure, did the vast bulk of the silent population within the country, especially the 55 to 65 per cent who were Shia. My reaction might have been an emotional one, but it was powerful. Who was I, I asked myself, to tell people whose families had been wiped out or who lived in fear that they were wrong to want to be freed from that terror? Who was I to tell them that they did not understand complex international issues and should accept that their own liberation was not worth the price that the international community more generally might have to pay? In addition, I was deeply saddened by arguments of many of the 'peace' campaigners which seemed to be based more in a fear, even a hatred, of Bush and the USA than in any genuine sense of sympathy with the Iraqi people. The repeatedly stated observations that Saddam should not be dealt with because 'there are lots of other dictators and repressive states' and that the West had supported the one in Iraq seemed utterly banal. Surely if there are so many dictators, any attempt to remove one should be welcomed? And inconsistency does not necessarily imply hypocrisy. The idea, expressed to me by one campaigner, that Saddam was genuinely moving towards a multi-party democracy, was simply ludicrous. And there was always the argument, which seemed to me to have some validity, that, as the Americans were clearly committed to the war come what may, the UK would do best to support them in the hope of having some influence on the execution of the campaign and its eventual consequences.

But I was not sure. Like most people, I came to no clear conclusion on many of these questions. I felt it was the right war for the wrong reasons, and at totally the wrong time. I even went, for an hour anyway, on the anti-war march in London. Much, I felt, depended on the successful reconstruction of the country after any conflict. If Iraq, as a result of the deposition of Saddam, became a prosperous and secure country, able to choose whatever type of political system its people felt happiest with, in charge of its own foreign policy and economy, then the disruption of the war would be worthwhile and a strong signal would be sent to Muslims around the globe that the West was not actually set on dominating and dividing the Islamic world. If the reconstruction of Iraq was botched, then the long-term consequences could be disastrous.

In the end, like many others, I never made my mind up. My emotional and moral support for the Iraqis who wanted to be freed by the Americans and my more reasoned concerns about the repercussions of a war were not reconcilable. Unlike many others, however, I did have a personal and intellectual way out. As a journalist I had the luxury of being allowed, indeed encouraged, to be distanced. So I retreated behind my professional disengagement, as I had, in part, in Pakistan and Afghanistan. The war would not make a major difference to my life, I felt. I did not risk losing my home or relatives, I would be able to return to my nice flat in north London at its end. There was a slim chance of being killed or injured, certainly, but I was not planning on taking any major risks. I cared about friends in Iraq, I cared about the strategy in the War on Terror, I cared about the consequences of the war for all those I knew in Afghanistan, Israel, Palestine, Algeria and elsewhere but, when I began to make final preparations for it, my interest in the impending conflict had been reduced to the bare professional essentials. I was going to the war to do my job, to watch, to take notes and because, in February 2003, there was nowhere else I wanted to be.

11. The Magical Misery Tour

It was a beautiful afternoon. After weeks of drizzle and cloud, the skies, except for the strands of brown smoke that hung over the bridge in the valley, were clear and blue and very big. The American jets were tiny, sharp, metallic shards of light very high and very far away and barely got any bigger when they descended to release their missiles and bombs.

I was about twenty miles south of the Kurdish-held city of Arbil. It was about 1 p.m. and I was watching a battle, lying just behind the crest of a small ridge midway between a row of bunkers where there were some American special forces soldiers and a river over which there was a strategically important bridge. The peshmerga who had been massed around the American positions had attacked the bridge during the morning and the Iraqis had withdrawn before launching a counterattack that had just been broken up by air strikes. Through the cheap binoculars I had bought at the airport on leaving Britain nearly two months earlier I could see a small convoy of Iraqi tanks and trucks on the road that led away from the bridge on the southern bank. Several of the vehicles appeared to be on fire and there were figures lying immobile on the road beside them. There was still fighting in the village on the approaches to the bridge nearer to me and smoke came from somewhere among the flat concrete roofs of the houses and shuttered shops along the riverside. The fighting had set light to some of the long grass that covered the open, rolling hillsides and fields either side of the bridge and the smell of the burning was not unpleasant.

I was just thinking about walking a little bit further down towards the action when the first shell flew high over with a long screech, cutting out a few seconds before it impacted with a loud crack around 200 yards away. With a dozen or so other reporters I scrambled off the ridge, down a small bank and dropped into a

ditch beside the road that led down to the village. Almost immediately, a second projectile impacted with an astonishingly loud,
tearing, cracking sound into the rocky ground where we had been.
Then a third shell came in and then there was a pause. I had cut
my forehead, elbows and the bridge of my nose when I jumped
into the ditch and I ran a fingertip over the cuts and tasted the
blood and the burned smell of dust in the air and wondered what
to do. I had been shelled several times before in Afghanistan and
elsewhere and it had never lasted for very long so I was not unduly
concerned.

I considered my situation. I had walked to where we were,
worried about presenting too big a target in a car. As most of the
other reporters in the ditch, mainly TV crews with heavy cameras
and equipment, had driven, this, it now appeared, was a mistake.
It was true that the jeeps, lined up and gleaming in the sun along
the road just to my right, had attracted the fire in the first place
but they also provided a means to get back to safety. Even as I
thought about this, there was the sudden noise of engines and
those reporters with vehicles had gone and then came another
screeching howl and the shelling had started again.

The next shell landed about 100 yards below where I lay. A
fourth landed 150 yards above me. A fifth, closer now, landed
below, sending a spout of flame and black smoke and stones and
soil into the air. There was the strong smell of cordite which
suddenly reminded me of bonfire night and fireworks at home.
Another pause, and then several more shells in quick succession,
each closer still, below and above where I lay, each ploughing up
a fountain of stones and metal that pattered down around me.
Whoever was firing was 'bracketing' the position, firing either side
with a steadily decreasing margin of error. My ears were ringing.
Four more rounds came in at intervals of about a minute. Each
seemed to get closer. I very much wanted to dig myself into the
ground, urinate or both. Then I heard another shell coming.

The ditch was shallow but the high bank on one side and the
raised road on the other provided relatively good cover. The road
that led back up to the American bunkers and safety was a strip of

exposed tarmac across open fields and a very stupid place to be. Yet, by the time the next round arrived, I was already halfway along it, slowed by 35lb flak jacket and helmet, feverishly muttering, 'This is fucking bad. This is really fucking bad,' between rasping breaths as I tried to sprint. I cannot remember the exact thought process that led me to leave the ditch and start running, though I can remember the sudden and absolute conviction that it was the only thing that I could conceivably do. This, I thought later, was panic. There was no instant of blind terror, no loss of reason, merely an overwhelming sense of astonishingly acute discomfort, a sense that my immediate environment was as insupportable as a hair shirt crawling with vermin and that only this particular course of action, though it was in fact the one that would expose me to the greatest danger, was absolutely, immediately and incontrovertibly right and necessary. I can also remember, as I tried to run up the road, the sense that the huge open blue sky arcing overhead was impossibly big, impossibly bright and filled with lumps of fast-moving metal and explosive swooping towards me like giant bats. I can remember feeling my tongue very large and very dry in my mouth and the weight of the flak jacket on my shoulders and my knees jarring as my boots hit the hard surface and being suddenly very angry rather than scared.

The shelling continued. As each round came in, I threw myself flat, waited until the debris had stopped falling, got up, wiped sweat and blood from my eyes, started to run again, panting hard and swearing, before, as I heard the screech of a new round, throwing myself flat once more. When, after what seemed to be a long time but was probably only a couple of minutes, I saw a small group of reporters in a shallow ditch just set back from my road on my left. I dropped into it, breathing hard, coughing with the effort and suddenly violently indignant. 'This is fucking ridiculous,' I said to no one in particular. A shell came in but landed several hundred yards away. 'I mean, the whole thing is a fucking outrage,' I said. The others in the ditch were pointing to a path that led through grassy fields and abandoned trenches back to the American bunkers and relative safety. I knew from Afghanistan that the most likely places to find landmines were in old military positions, along roadsides or on paths in long grass. And so, judging by their conversation, did the others. As they started out in single file, I developed a sudden interest in tying and retying my bootlaces and then, having let them get some distance ahead, followed, treading carefully in their footsteps.

Back in the rear positions, I felt first relief, amusement, a detached interest in my own behaviour, some anger at the TV crews who had disappeared quite so quickly, and then, very rapidly, a powerful sense of elation and of vindication. But for a few cuts and bruises I was fine. It was only a minor incident that had lasted for no more than twenty minutes. It was hardly worth mentioning to anyone. Personally, however, I knew it was important. Finally, at long last, my Iraq war had started.

It was 4 April 2005, three weeks after my thirty-third birthday, and I had been in Iraq for six weeks. I sat beside one of the bunkers dug by the American special forces units enjoying the sun on my face, with Diyari, the young Kurdish mechanic whom I had hired as a driver, and shared some cold grilled chicken and flatbread and drank some warm Coke and then, this time in our battered old Toyota Landcruiser jeep, headed back down towards the bridge. Diyari was laughing as he drove between the craters left by the morning's shelling. I pointed to where I had lain and where I had run and we looked at the brown scorch marks and the incisions the shrapnel had made on the tarmac. The metallic specks of the jets were still there high above, the smoke still rose from the village and the burning vehicles and the smouldering grass. The peshmerga had stormed a set of Iraqi trenches on the far side of the bridge and wounded men were limping back with soot-blackened faces and blank, wide eyes. We stopped the car and I got out but they did not want to be interviewed. I saw a couple of photographers I knew a short way away in a mortar position and waved and they waved back. There were two dead Iraqis, their bodies turned to charcoal, their teeth grinning in blackened, burnt flesh, pinned beneath a smouldering truck. A pick-up truck driven by two civilians bounced past us out of the village with a looted fridge in the rear. There was a lot of firing on the Iraqi side of the river and I could see figures moving over the ridge opposite. The sky was still blue. There was a slight breeze. It was still a beautiful afternoon.

For a long time it had been unclear whether I would get into Iraq at all in time for the war. The Iraqi authorities refused to give me a visa and, after my experience in Bagram a year earlier, I did not like the idea of 'embedding' with a fighting unit as an official correspondent. For a while it looked like I would be stuck in Jordan or Kuwait, waiting, as I had done in Afghanistan, for the borders to open when the war was half over. Then I heard that the Turkish government was to open its southeastern border, closed for more than a decade, to journalists who wanted to attend an Iraqi opposition conference to be held in Iraqi Kurdistan in the first week of February. The border would be open for one day only. I picked up my flak jacket, some warm-weather clothes, my nuclear, biological and chemical warfare suit and $10,000 in cash and flew to Istanbul, where I boarded an overbooked flight to eastern Turkey, then a packed bus, then a taxi.

Silopi, the border town that I had passed through on my way to join the peshmerga in 1991, had not changed much. The news that the Turks might open the border had spread quickly and the town's grimy hotels were packed with reporters, cameramen and photographers, all there to get into Iraq, none sure whether the Turks would deliver on their promises, all greeting one another, swapping rumours, reminiscing about Kabul, the intifada, the Balkans, catching up on who had been hired by or was sleeping with whom or had won what award or had landed what book contract. Fixers, drivers and translators hung around the hotel lobbies hoping for work. Some reporters were gung-ho, such as the Frenchman known universally as 'the Frog of War', others were more phlegmatic, such as the Russians who seemed to sleep all the time. A Chinese journalist wore a suit and spoke no English. His only baggage appeared to be a black attaché case.

We were loaded on to coaches and then unloaded an hour later. We checked out of our hotels and then checked back in. We signed our names on lists and then found that other lists had been drawn up. We drove to the border and then were turned round by the Kurdish border guards. Two American journalists had themselves smuggled across the frontier under a cargo of potatoes in a metal coffin in the back of a truck usually used for transporting illegal immigrants in the other direction. Others started arranging to march over the snowbound mountains. The Silopi town governor, a mild-mannered civil servant in a blue suit with small glasses, very straight black hair and a small moustache, almost provoked a riot when he said that journalists would not be allowed to take their satellite telephones across the border. There were fistfights as some journalists sought to 'calm' others. I ended up hitting a hysterical pipe-smoking French journalist in a black polo neck. I was not sure what had annoyed me most, the hysteria, the polo neck or the pipe. Intermittent rain and sleet turned the streets of Silopi to mud. The only thing that lent any dignity at all to the proceedings was the presence of Don McCullin, the war photographer whose autobiography had inspired me to set off for Iraq myself twelve years before. McCullin, who was 68 and far more famous than any other journalist covering the war, was calm, quietly spoken and modest. Finally, in a steady freezing downpour, five coaches full of 100 or more journalists crossed the border and started crawling along snowbound roads through the hills of northern Iraq. It took thirty-six hours to reach our destination, the city of Arbil. Standing in the muddy forecourt of a dingy trucker's restaurant during a lunch stop on the second day, Charlie Sennott, a veteran reporter from the *Boston Globe* whom I knew from London, indicated the row of buses with his cigarette. 'Welcome,' he said, 'to the Magical Misery Tour.' It was, I thought, a nice description of our profession.

However, though we were all very pleased with ourselves for actually getting into Iraq, it rapidly became clear we were in completely the wrong place. Within a few days of our arrival the Turkish parliament refused American forces permission to cross their territory, effectively ending the Pentagon's plans for a northern front. Their decision meant that the war would be fought, at least to start with, in the south of Iraq, around 1,000 miles away from where we were. Those of us in Kurdistan, without any way out of Iraq other than via, as one reporter put it, 'the Laura Bush memorial terminal at Baghdad airport', were stuck. 'Jesus, I told my wife I'd be back in three weeks,' said Charlie.

Personally, perhaps because I was without wife or children, I was just glad that I was not stuck in press conferences at the main coalition headquarters in Qatar, on a ship in the Arabian Gulf, confined to a military camp in Kuwait with an army minder, in Washington or in London. Also, after following their story for nearly fifteen years, I wanted to see what was going to happen to the Kurds. And I needed time to sort out all my logistics. I drove over to Suleimaniyah and, once I had found a hotel room, drew up a list of what I needed: a driver with a good vehicle, a translator, a reliable source of good petrol, containers for storing the extra fuel, spare food, spare water, tanks for the water, a generator, extension leads, tarpaulins, blankets, a heater, at least two local mobile phones, radios if I could find them and an expanded first-aid kit. I hired Diyari as a driver. He was in his early twenties, had a roguish smile and an earring in one ear and was relaxed enough to be good company and eager enough to be a good colleague. I also hired Jazza, a young student who spoke both Arabic and Kurdish, as a translator. Jazza was neither relaxed nor good company. After several days' search, I found them both flak jackets and helmets and two brand-new Iranian military gas masks. The masks were a complete joke, of course. Even my own expensive suit, mask and vaccine set did not come with anything that could actually detect chemical or biological agents. If we did get gassed, we would know it only when one of us keeled over. Most journalists faced the same problem. When I visited one TV crew's rented house in Arbil I was introduced to their two canaries, Diehard Two and Diehard Three. Diehard One had expired the previous week from overeating.

Then, with our logistics arrangements made, we waited. It has been said that war is nine-tenths boredom and one-tenth fear, which for a combatant is almost certainly true. For a journalist war probably involves less fear, less boredom and more worrying.

Charlie and I combined resources, not just for companionship and security but to bring down costs and give us both a reserve vehicle and a spare satellite phone.

The wait was punctuated by odd episodes. There was the football match between an Iraqi side from Baghdad and Arbil's local side. Arbil won 2–1 and when the match was over the visiting team got back in their coaches and drove across the front lines back to the capital. The Kurdish spectators had chanted 'fuck the Turks' throughout. When the American bombers started to strike Kirkuk and the Iraqi positions around the city we rented an empty house in the town of Chamchamal. Evacuated by its owners because of the persistent shelling of the town, it had been stripped of everything except power sockets so we slept on the concrete floors in our sleeping bags, our useless NBC suits to hand, listening to the American raids on Kirkuk, the desultory mortar fire with which the Iraqis replied and, on my short-wave radio, the real war in the south. One evening two sodden Iraqi deserters, both senior officers, appeared in the street outside, cold and scared and shaken by the accuracy of the missiles which were picking off their command bunkers one by one. 'If they came and fought us on the ground, we would fight,' they said. 'But we cannot fight them like this.' I thought of Ala, my translator the previous summer, and her fervent wish for the arrival of the Americans and wondered if she and all the other Kurds who had expressed the same desire to me over the previous weeks would come to regret their enthusiasm for the war. Then I went to see Wasta Hassan, my security service contact, and interviewed Mohammed Kassm and decided that, come what may, they probably would not.

Mohammed Kassm was a former Iraqi Mukhabarat intelligence service torturer who had been captured by the Kurds two years earlier. He was 39, 6' 4" and weighed sixteen stone, with small eyes, slightly pudgy cheeks and grey-flecked hair. He was wearing a washed-out red sports shirt, grey tracksuit trousers and broken plastic sandals. His hands, I noticed when he was brought out of the cells and sat down at a desk in an empty office in the security services headquarters, were very large.

Kassm had joined the Ba'ath Party at the age of 15 in the year that Saddam Hussein seized power. 'From the beginning I believed in it, like a Marxist believes in Marxism or like a Buddhist in Buddhism,' he said. 'In those days the Ba'ath Party was not like it is now. It was not compulsory.'

By the time Kassm was 16 he was working for the Mukhabarat main office in Baghdad. By the time he was 20 he was, full time, five days a week, an interrogator. 'At first it was difficult for me and then it became more easy. Torture is like anything. You get used to it.'

Kassm, sitting across the desk in an upstairs room in the security service offices, gave no indication that he felt any shame whatsoever. I could imagine him as the school bully, stealing the lunch money of small kids, enjoying the power his sheer physical size gave him. If you have been a torturer, I thought, you either stay a torturer or you fall apart. He seemed almost proud of what he had done. He did not look like he was falling apart.

'All the opposition know me. I am very intensive in my questioning,' he said and smiled. 'Anyway, they can't recognize me.'

'How did you torture people?' I asked him. He chuckled and sat back with his fingers laced over his belly.

'There are multiple ways. We hoist them over a bar with their arms behind them, We use hot things like an iron on their skin. We use an electric cable – here, here and here,' he said and indicated ears, tongue and groin.

'How about fingernails?' I said, thinking of a waiter who had served me a day or so earlier whose fingers ended in smooth nubs of skin.

Kassm looked insulted. 'That's an old technique. We don't do that any more. Though we did occasionally cut off or amputate toes or fingers.'

'Did you interrogate children?' I asked.

'Sometimes,' he said and shrugged. 'We tortured everyone, men, women and children.'

'Who was the youngest?'

'Newborn babies, I suppose.'

'You tortured newborn babies?'

'Well, not exactly, but sometimes we brought in newborns and threatened to starve them to death to get their parents to talk. We might starve them a bit for effect but we wouldn't kill the child. That was a pretty effective technique actually.'

'And the older kids?'

'We would hit five- or six-year-olds with a cable.'

'What about rape?'

'My team did not do that but we had a specially designated rape unit.'

'You have a wife?'

'I have been married twice and I have seven children.'

'And you went home to your wife and kids after a day of torturing people?'

'You are a journalist, I am an interrogator. I got paid, got overtime, bonuses, holidays. It was a job.' And then he added, as if aware of the inadequacy of what he was saying, 'I was following orders. Saddam is responsible for these things. Saddam made us into killers. During the time of Hitler was there any German soldier who could reject his orders?'

'Would you fight for Saddam if you were free now?'

'The men of the Mukhabarat are frightened now,' he said. 'They have blood on their hands. They have to stick with Saddam or they will be killed by the population that hate them.'

I asked Kassm about his background. He was a Shia Muslim, he told me, and grew up in a poor village in the south of Iraq with six brothers and three sisters. His father, a farmer, had borne his own scars, a mesh of cicatrices across his shoulder-blades which were, Kassm claimed, the result of being tortured by the British in the 1920s. 'They hit my father with cables,' he said.

The overture to our war came when thousands of peshmerga backed by American special forces moved against the strongholds of Ansar ul-Islam, the radical Islamic group to which Didar the failed suicide bomber and the other militants I had interviewed in Suleimaniyah the previous summer had belonged, north of

Halabjah. The group had spent the winter and early spring fortifying their positions in and around the scattered hill villages close to the Iranian frontier that were their base. Though Ansar ul-Islam detested Saddam, it was also violently opposed to the Americans and their local allies and, given the group's position deep within Kurdish territory, would have to be eliminated before any real movement against Baghdad from the north began. With Ansar ul-Islam's numbers boosted by local recruits and a steady stream of fugitives from Afghanistan who had managed to slip through the ring of fortifications and guard posts that the peshmerga had set up on the plains below the militants' strongholds, no one expected the battle to be easy. It finally came at the end of March.

Over the previous weeks Charlie and I had made regular visits to the front lines beneath the Ansar ul-Islam positions and, using contacts built up on those trips, we were able to evade the Kurdish officials trying to keep reporters away from the battle and watch the last hours of the fighting from the house of a militia commander on the plain just below the headquarters of the militants. The battle resembled a miniature Tora Bora with the militants up in the mountains, the special forces and their Kurdish allies pushing up from the plain, the purple evening sky lit up by orange flashes from the bombs and tracer fire from where resistance was continuing. When we finally slept there was one position high on a rocky crag that was still holding out and was the target of many bombs and missiles. In the morning all resistance had ceased and Charlie and I drove up through the aftermath of the fighting. Peshmerga wrapped in blankets slept slumped against dry-stone walls, their rifles piled in pyramids muzzle against muzzle, blackened kettles sitting in the embers of small fires. A corpse of a young man, an alleged spy executed by the militants, lay by the side of the road, one rigor-mortised arm pointing skyward, his mother keening beside him in the dust. In the rubble of Ansar ul-Islam's headquarters I found exercise books like those I had found in the al-Qaeda camps in Afghanistan, a very rudimentary chemistry lab, miniature calendars printed with pictures of Ansar ul-Islam's leaders

and a letter written by a Kurdish suicide bomber called Abdul
Ghani extolling martyrdom and telling his parents that he had left
money with Uncle Ferraj to pay the 100 dinars he owed to a local
shop owner called Bilal. The locals were not bothered by the
huge hole ripped in their mosque by an American missile. 'The
extremists are gone and that's what matters,' an old man told me.
Though the Kurds claimed to have killed most of the 600-odd
militants who had been based in the enclave, many of whom had
been foreign fighters who had fled the American campaign in
Afghanistan, there were very few bodies. We were told there were
hundreds buried in caves further up the hills but it seemed more
likely that the vast majority of the militants had escaped, either
into Iran, where the authorities were no friends of either the Kurds
or the Americans, or through the peshmerga lines.

The destruction, or dispersal, of Ansar signalled the end of our
phoney war. This was good as almost everyone was getting irritable
and claustrophobic. 'We all have a bad war now and again,' said
McCullin, which was scant consolation as we watched tank battles
in the south on television and read other reporters' award-winning
despatches. For a week, sharp skirmishes flared rapidly and then
died away along the length of the northern front like a fire trying
to catch in damp wood. To the south the American troops were
closing on Baghdad and, with Ansar cleared from their rear, the
Kurds intensified their pressure on the Iraqi lines. It was during
this chaotic, messy period that several journalists in northern Iraq
were killed or injured and I got caught under shellfire at the bridge
at Khazer and it was clear that the real conflict was getting closer
to us every day. In the evenings reporters sat in the garden of
the hotel swapping stories from the day, pausing as bombing
rattled the glasses on the tables. Then Baghdad fell and everything
happened very quickly.

The news that the capital was in American hands reached the
north on the evening of 9 April. I spent the night in a peshmerga
position close to the front lines south of Arbil. Early the next
morning it became clear that the Iraqis had either pulled back or
collapsed entirely along the entire northern front line. Diyari and

I drove to a town called Machmur, thirty miles beyond what had been the front line twelve hours earlier, and found the local Ba'ath Party headquarters on fire and a dozen Iraqi soldiers sitting disconsolately among triumphant peshmerga. A teacher who had led a local clandestine resistance network hugged and embraced me, crying as he stammered out his gratitude and thanks and pleasure at his 'liberation'. A bureaucrat who had worked with the Ba'ath Party drew me to one side and said that not everyone who had been a part of the organization was 'bad' and asked if I thought the Americans would put Ba'ath Party members in prison. It was unclear whether the townspeople were rioting or celebrating or both. I filled a notebook in less than an hour, as much through my own excitement as that of those I was interviewing, and then, hearing that 'something was happening in Kirkuk', Diyari and I set off east down narrow, straight roads through open grassland. The roads were empty of any traffic and, detouring to the north to avoid the fighting we could hear to the south, we drove at speed through scattered villages and oil fields, all eerily deserted. At first we saw no one but then small groups of men, all bizarrely wearing nothing but their underwear, began to appear, walking by the side of the road away from the city twenty miles ahead of us. Soon we passed larger groups, still all in nothing but baggy, off-white underpants, long johns and vests or T-shirts, trudging down the verges of the road, some waving at us and smiling, others scowling, and we realized that they were Iraqi soldiers who had thrown off their uniforms and dumped their weapons and started walking away from the fighting. Somehow we appeared to have got to the Iraqi side of the front lines. A few miles further on a thick stream of men were walking down the side of the road and though most were still half dressed, many were wearing the dusty brown trousers or shirts of their army uniforms. Another few miles on, the crowd became even more dense and soon the men we saw were still wearing their uniforms and suddenly we were driving through a horde of men in khaki, all unarmed. Diyari looked at me, eyes round with astonishment. We kept driving, past lines of tanks, armoured personnel carriers and trucks, all left standing, intact and empty, some by the road, others lined up in the deep grass of the rolling hills around us, their desert-brown paintwork incongruous in the green landscape, and then, as we approached the outskirts of Kirkuk, we saw that the soldiers either side of us were not only in their uniforms but were armed and as we drove past, Diyari thumping the horn to clear a passage, they laid their guns on the ground and raised their hands in the air forming a corridor of upheld arms. And then finally there was Kirkuk, with a cavalcade of pick-up trucks crammed full of peshmerga pouring down the main road from Suleimaniyah and Arbil, crowds hauling down statues of Saddam or torching his picture, crushed corpses of Iraqi officers in the streets with their brains spread around them and the air full of celebratory volleys of automatic fire and the acrid smoke of the burning administrative offices and the roads littered with official-looking sheets of paper and a traffic jam of looters forming on the road in from the north and car thieves with guns and teenagers filling wheelbarrows with bottles at the huge Pepsi factory on the outskirts and a cheap hotel just off the main square where Charlie and a few other journalists had taken a room and were brewing coffee on a camping stove on the floor.

Mosul fell the next day, in much the same fashion and with much the same scenes. On the Saturday we tried to get from Kirkuk to Tikrit, Saddam's home town and only eighty miles from Baghdad, but fighting and armed bands of robbers had blocked the road. A French TV crew tried it and got shot. So did CNN. I drove down one back road until I saw several corpses on the verge and then turned back. I filed my piece for the *Observer* over my satellite phone with my computer propped on the bonnet of the car. The dateline was 'Jason Burke, outside Tikrit'. A colleague, stuck in the Coalition press centre at Doha in Qatar, rang me. 'We're all outside Tikrit, mate,' he pointed out, not unfairly.

We set off again the next morning, driving along a narrow pitted road which lay on a slight embankment running through the oil fields around the edge of Kirkuk and then across the rust-coloured flat desert that spanned northern central Iraq. We passed large stretches of long grass and some trees where there was water and sometimes square fields laid out beside low flat-roofed farms with decrepit tractors standing next to them in puddles of oil. Occasionally we came across a small village of rundown houses and shuttered shops. We had no trouble on the road and drove through the eastern part of Tikrit where a grain warehouse was on fire and then across a badly damaged bridge across the Tigris and into the centre of the town. On either side of the main road lay the huge walled complexes of Saddam's palaces and, parked beneath the crenellations and portraits of the dictator, there were rows of American armoured vehicles. The city had fallen to a force of US Marines after a short firefight about twenty-four hours earlier. The soldiers had been in motion all the way from Kuwait and had now come to a halt and seemed slightly unclear about what to do next. Saddam's home town, where many had expected to see a desperate last stand, had fallen with little resistance, and there was nowhere else for them to go. The tanks and armoured personnel carriers stood with their engines idling, the soldiers sitting or standing beside them, washing clothes, borrowing reporters' satellite phones to make a first call home for weeks, smoking. There was a sense of anticlimax. The war, it seemed clear to pretty much everyone, was over.

Walking through the empty streets I found a platoon of Marines fanning out across the acres of rubble that was all that remained of the Mukhabarat headquarters to the north of the town. They were led by Specialist Hemming from Milwaukee who told me they were 'looking for contact'. This, he translated, meant they were 'looking for someone to shoot'. There had apparently been reports of a sniper close by.

The platoon moved off through the twisted girders and shattered concrete, taking up positions behind 60-tonne chunks of wall thrown like dice by the massive air strikes, covering each other carefully, quiet and methodical. I followed, tripping over lengths of barbed wire and making too much noise and then loudly apologizing. Hemming and his men had been fighting for a month without pause; they were dirty and dusty and their uniforms hung from them, softened and moulded by weeks of wear, like folds of old, leathery skin.

For me, after nearly two months with the Kurdish fighters in northern Iraq, this was something new. As in Afghanistan the year before, the sight of American troops triggered a series of powerful memories, almost all of which were cinematographic. The men were moving through a grey urban landscape under a dull, flat, cloudy sky laced with thick coils of oily smoke. American helicopters rotored slowly above the shattered buildings. I could hear the distant grinding and clattering of tanks. Broken glass, wire and smashed concrete cracked underfoot. It all seemed astonishingly familiar and, after a moment's puzzlement, I suddenly realized why: I had walked into *Full Metal Jacket* again, the Vietnam War film I had watched so often in Bagram airbase a year before. In the opening sequence of the second half of film, American Marines fan out to hunt a sniper in the rubble of Hue City. They move through broken, bombed-out, grey rubble under a sky the colour of cigarette ash. I knew that my double vision was ridiculous, completely unprofessional and possibly dangerous too but could not help myself. Overhead, both in the film and in real life, Huey helicopters wheeled through plumes of soot. When I reminded myself that any moment a sniper might open fire, I immediately thought of what had happened in the film. Telling myself that the Ba'ath Party did not have female snipers, as the Viet Cong did in the film, did little good. The whole thing, I felt, was becoming ridiculous. If the Marines knew what I was thinking they would laugh at me. We stopped and took up positions behind a long low wall. Hemming's radio crackled. Some of the Marines sat with their backs to the wall, their rifles between their legs and their helmets tipped back, and lit cigarettes. Others surveyed the rubble ahead of them through their rifle sights. Hemming called over to Vroman, a 19-year-old from New York, and Norr, 21, from Michigan, and told them to 'get on point'. Then he looked around him and turned to me and asked: 'You seen that film *Full Metal Jacket?*'

I walked back to the car and sat in a queue of journalists' vehicles as we waited for the Americans to clear some mines from the road. I accepted a photographer's unexpected and welcome offer of a cannabis-laced cigarette. Everything felt so final that I almost expected to see The End in huge letters across the sky.

Tikrit was indeed the end, at least for me. I stayed on for a week, reporting on the violence in and around Kirkuk as Kurds sought to oust Arabs from lands and houses that, in some instances, they had once owned. I also wrote about the role religious networks were playing in maintaining basic services and law and order in cities. In Mosul, a call from the mosques stopped the looting. A second call brought the restitution of a large proportion of the goods stolen over previous days. In Kirkuk graffiti appeared on walls, not far from where the biggest statue of Saddam lay like a felled tree, proclaiming the old slogan: 'Islam is the solution'.

12. The Debacle

I was back in Iraq within two months, driving in from Jordan on the fast straight highway through the western desert. Baghdad was a febrile, exhausted city with a population running on nervous energy, hope and fear in equal proportions. It was June and the city was baking in the full heat of an Iraqi summer. There was little electricity and, though the wealthy suburbs and the main hotels had generators, most people just sweated. The looting of the first few days after the regime had fallen, during which almost all the main government buildings except the Ministry of Oil had been gutted, was well over and now American troops patrolled the streets and enforced a haphazard law and order.

But nothing anywhere was certain. The power could go off at any time, for any duration; mobile checkpoints could turn a usually clear road into a two-mile-long traffic jam; telephones or the television would work and then cut out abruptly in a hiss of static, government offices would change their function overnight, police stations would open and then close a day later, hospitals and clinics would stock random drugs in apparently random quantities; one day there would be plenty of petrol, the next day there would be a riot when the pumps ran dry; the markets would suddenly be full of melons but no cooking gas; the next day, they would be full of gas but no melons. Most uncertain of all was the political situation. One American appointee to the position of de facto governor-general, a retired senior military officer, had just given way to another, a former businessman named L. Paul Bremer III, but no one knew quite who was in charge, of what and with what legal authority. Attempts to rationalize things invariably just added to the confusion. The city, and the country as a whole, was oddly suspended. There was a strange sense of hiatus, of a pause, as if everyone were drawing breath, looking about them, trying to make sense of the new landscape. If Tikrit had seemed like a full stop, then Baghdad in the summer of 2003 was a hyphen.

For the journalists, insulated as we were against the worst of the uncertainty and physical discomfort by our dollars and hotel facilities, Baghdad was not an unpleasant place to be. There were hordes of us, packed into the Palestine off Sadoun Street by the banks of the Tigris or in the al-Hamra in the wealthy, relatively leafy suburb of Qarada. The latter had the great advantage of a swimming pool, the existence of which was kept, by common consent, from all our offices, and steady supplies of cold Amstel beer. There was also little sense of immediate threat. We could drive anywhere in the country, talking to anyone we wanted. We could even listen to the newly revived Baghdad FM playing hits from 1985, the last time the station had been able to buy Western records, as we sat and sweltered in the traffic, and in the evenings we could join the hordes of Baghdadis who promenaded beside the newly reopened grilled-fish restaurants beside the river on Abu Nawas Street, named after a famous eighth-century poet, playwright and bon viveur, or go to one of the various parties thrown by one of the TV networks, get drunk and watch the tracer fire unleashed by nervous American guards. Some, such as the one involving the naked table tennis tournament, were memorably debauched.

With hindsight, of course, the trigger-happy sentries were far from the only signs of the trouble to come. When I went over to the Green Zone, the fortified secure area in the centre of the city from where the brand new Coalition Provisional Authority was trying to run Iraq, I was struck by its isolation from the rest of the country. I had lunch with a press officer in the huge canteen and, as she spoke to me about all the progress that was being made across the country, tried in vain to spot a single Iraqi eating at the tables around us. When, the next day, I finally located the men who were responsible for Baghdad's streetlighting in a dusty compound on the western edge of town out towards the airport, they had no vehicles, no bulbs for the lights and no way of getting power even if they had got the lights to function. The situation at the city's various waterworks was worse. Casualties of a growing criminality – 'teething pains', according to one official I spoke to – filled the city morgue. And there were signs too of a nascent political mobilization. In the huge and desperately poor Shia suburbs in the northeast of Baghdad, the authority was not the Americans or the Coalition but a militant Shia religious faction loyal to Muqtada al-Sadr, the young and unpredictable son of a well-known cleric who had been killed by Saddam. In the chaos of the fall of the Ba'athist regime it had been the clerics who had run the lives of the million or so poor inhabitants of the sewage-filled, rubbish-strewn streets of the suburbs and the clerics had stayed in power ever since, changing the name of the quarter from Saddam City to Sadr City. In Fallujah, the Sunni-dominated city thirty miles to the west of Baghdad, people told me frankly how they wanted to kill 'the Americans and the Jews' who had invaded their country and how they were happy that their own electricity substation had recently been blown up by unidentified attackers.

And, after a long run of luck which had ensured that, despite the considerable numbers of journalists killed or injured in Iraq, no one with whom I had more than a passing acquaintance had been hurt, there came the death of Richard Wild, a young, talented and personable British reporter who was shot in the head in the centre of Baghdad in an apparently random attack. Richard had contacted me in London a month or so before his death asking for advice about whether he should go to Iraq 'to make his name as a foreign correspondent'. I had tried to dissuade him, pointing out, possibly somewhat hypocritically given my own experience with the peshmerga, that there were better and safer ways to break into journalism. But when he had turned up at the al-Hamra hotel, full of charm and enthusiasm, I had done my best to help him. He had given me a letter to take back to his parents the day before he was killed.

But, despite Richard's murder and the rumblings in the Sunni province west of Baghdad and the growing strength of Muqtada al-Sadr, the situation was very difficult to gauge. For every negative, there was a positive. So, when I arrived in a small town in the centre of the country to report on the deaths of six British soldiers in a mini-uprising a day earlier I was made welcome by the locals, even writing my story in a tea shop a hundred yards from where the fighting had taken place. For every dozen Iraqis who muttered darkly about resistance and insurrection when interviewed, there were two or three dozen more who did not. When you asked if people wanted the Americans to leave, almost everyone said 'yes'. When you asked if they wanted them to leave immediately, almost everyone said 'no'. It was evident that only a small fraction of the population favoured any resistance at all, let alone violent resistance. Just after leaving Baghdad at the end of July, I wrote that there were still plenty of reasons to be optimistic about the situation in Iraq but that if a respectable level of social, political and economic progress had not been achieved by mid-autumn then there would be serious consequences. Quite what the consequences might be, I did not know.

I found out seven months later. Following the lynching of four private security contractors in Fallujah, the American army had tried to fight their way into the city; as a result, much of 'the Sunni triangle', the Sunni-dominated, heavily tribal areas west of Baghdad, had risen in revolt. Simultaneously the Coalition Authority tried to move against Muqtada al-Sadr, blaming him, probably fairly, for the murder of a key moderate cleric the previous year. Al-Sadr called upon the militia he had spent the last six months creating and forced coalition troops and the moderate clerical factions who opposed him to effectively cede to him control of Sadr City and the two great Shia shrine cities of Najaf and Karbala.

One immediate consequence of the uprising was that the American-led coalition forces, 150,000 strong, lost control of the roads. Baghdad itself was cut off except from the air. When I headed back to the city from London to cover the upsurge in violence, the road from Jordan was unusable. Instead I found myself sitting in row 18 of a brightly painted, relatively new seventy-seater Fokker being served coffee by an incongruously uniformed and polite South African hostess and listening to the captain informing us that the temperature in Baghdad was a 'pleasant 34 degrees'.

The plane was supplied by Air Quarius, a private contractor that ran the only civilian flights into Iraq. Flying in on their planes was a surreal way to arrive in the city, with only the steep corkscrew descent to avoid missile attacks and the predominance of bull-necked, shaven-headed men among the passengers giving any clue that the flight's destination was at all out of the ordinary. In April 2003 the atmosphere on board was funereal. Not just because everyone was heading into the middle of an uprising but because the violence had brought the new threat of kidnapping with scores of aid workers, journalists and private contractors abducted over the previous week. Most had been released after a harrowing, if relatively short, detention but others, particularly the security guards, were still being held. I hoped that a ridiculous floppy white cricket hat, colourful shirt and jeans would prevent any confusion and was not pleased when, on walking out of the airport, I was greeted by a bear-like man in a flak jacket with an automatic rifle over his shoulder and a handgun on his hip who was clearly working for one of the big security companies and was there to welcome newly arriving colleagues. 'Hi,' he said to me in a broad Midwestern American accent, 'you must be Daryl. Welcome aboard and welcome to Baghdad.'

But, despite the burned-out vehicles on the airport road, new graffiti on a bridge reading 'Mercy from God please. Islam is peace. We want hope. We want peace' and a noticeable increase in blast walls and barbed-wire barriers, Baghdad did not appear to have changed greatly. There was the strong sense, which always impressed me on my arrival in the city, that the vast bulk of people, a massive silent majority, were just attempting to get on with their lives. They were just trying to get by, to put dinner on the table, locate some fuel for a generator, find a supply of electricity or simply gather the confidence to walk the streets without fear. The roads were full of the decrepit orange and white *brasili* taxis, there were hawkers on the streets and, though a few shops were shuttered, many were open and busy. Small things indicated bigger problems, however. Many of the staff at the hotels lived across the city and were unwilling to risk the journey to work. 'The first casualty of war is room service,' sniffed one colleague over dinner that evening.

The questions that everyone was asking were: How had it come to this? What were the factors that had led, so quickly, to apparently widespread, armed insurrection in Iraq? There were no easy answers.

Some reasons for the violence were obvious. Critical mistakes had been made by the Coalition Provisional Authority and by senior political figures in Washington that had made what was always going to be a hard job much, much harder. Immediately after the fall of Baghdad, the failure of American troops to stop the looting in Baghdad had shocked many. Then there had been a series of radical decisions – such as the total demobilization of the Iraqi army and an aggressive effort to clean out all senior and many middle-ranking Ba'ath Party members from the civilian administration – that had created a vast pool of unemployed, humiliated and angry men, a high proportion of whom were from the country's Sunni Muslim minority. In addition, owing to intelligence failures at least as grave as those which had led to the conclusion that Saddam had weapons of mass destruction, there had been almost no realistic assessment of the massive infrastructural needs of post-Saddam Iraq and the pace of reconstruction had been appallingly slow as a result. As the security situation had deteriorated it had slowed further, causing more resentment and thus more recruits to the insurgents. Nor was the task of the Coalition Authority made easier by the local Arabic-language media which, though often usefully challenging the official version of events, frequently allowed its own profound opposition to the war to colour its often sensational but widely credited reporting.

I went to see Hoshyar Zubari, the foreign minister of the Iraqi administration appointed to govern in tandem with the Coalition Authority through a bizarre and Byzantine quasi-democratic pro-cess the previous autumn. I had met him when he had been the spokesman for the Kurdish Democratic Party in London and knew him to be a warm, intelligent man and a plain speaker. Sitting in his office in the recently refurbished, though still fairly

basic, ministry in central Baghdad, Hoshyar listed a variety of
reasons for the crisis. First, and somewhat predictably, he stressed
the interference of foreign powers inside Iraq. Though he was
careful to mention no one by name, I knew he meant the Iranians,
who were allegedly assisting and advising al-Sadr, and the Syrians,
who were said to be facilitating the passage of weapons, men and
money to the Sunnis in the west.

'The bigger regional picture is that there are people who are
working, if not to defeat the coalition, then at least to make life
hell for us all,' Hoshyar said. Another factor, he told me, was 'the
slow pace of the political process, the constant change and reversals
of policy' which had sapped motivation and momentum and led
to a loss of faith at a grass-roots level in Iraq's new leaders. Finally,
he mentioned something that interested me very much. A lot of
the problems, he said, were rooted in the 'ideological reasoning'
of the Americans and their allies. The application of 'your standards' and 'your ideas' to a complicated and violent reality was
apparently a big mistake.

I had already noticed that many of those who had arrived in
Iraq to run the place had little understanding of the country or
Islam and little interest in the ideas, customs and sentiments of those
they were supposed to be governing. I had had an extraordinary
conversation with one official on a short-term posting from Washington who genuinely appeared to believe that radical and instant
privatization of all Iraqi national industries would be of enormous
benefit. Others simply presumed that what had worked elsewhere,
in Japan or Germany after the Second World War or in Kosovo
or Afghanistan more recently, was simply transferable. One official
document I saw actually contained a presumably undeleted reference to Reichmarks. More pre-war intelligence failures meant
the social problems of the south, a result of successive conflicts
and Saddam's discriminatory policies, had been underestimated.
Worse, there were very few people working for the coalition who
had spent much time in the Middle East or the Islamic world more
generally and even fewer who spoke Arabic. This meant that only
a tiny number appeared aware that the Americans and their allies

had arrived in a place which had an almost legendary grandeur in the minds of many Arabs and Muslims, an almost mythic status that, given the splendour of the Abbasid court that had once been centred on Baghdad and the extent of the empire then ruled from the city, was, in many ways, entirely justified. Though extreme sensitivity and respect were called for, the attitude of most of the new rulers of Iraq, though undoubtedly well intentioned, was profoundly paternalistic and thus played directly into the hands of those inside and outside the country who wanted to ensure that any attempts at reconstruction failed.

In a sense this was predictable. The occupation of Iraq was one of a series of similar Western enterprises in the Islamic world stretching back more than two centuries and was inevitably shaped by the language and ideas of those earlier projects. The very phrases used in speeches by Bush, Bremer and others in the summer of 2003 were a direct, if unconscious, echo of those that had been employed by Western soldiers and politicians for centuries. 'I come not to abolish your religion . . . but . . . to restore your rights from the hands of oppressors,' Napoleon Bonaparte declared after seizing Alexandria in 1798, the event seen by many historians as marking the beginning of the colonization of the Middle East by Western powers. 'Our armies do not come into your cities and lands as conquerors or enemies but as liberators,' said the British general F. S. Maude on entering Baghdad in 1919. 'Unlike many armies in the world, [we] came not to conquer, not to occupy, but to liberate,' said Donald Rumsfeld in April 2003. The contrast between the historical consciousness of Iraqis and others in the Middle East, for whom these invasions were all very much part of a single ongoing pattern, and that of the West, where even the war of 1991 was seen as ancient history, was striking. Though such events were enormously important in forming the views and sentiments of millions of people in the Arab world and beyond, few in the Green Zone knew much about the Iraqi Revolt of 1920, let alone pivotal and hugely symbolic events such as the 1258 sacking of Baghdad by the non-Muslim 'barbarian' Mongols. By failing to understand how decades of clumsy and cynical

Western interventions in the Middle East, as well as centuries of European colonialism, were viewed locally, the new rulers of Iraq put themselves at a massive disadvantage. In addition, their almost deliberate ignorance of local history meant that they were unable to compete with those who sought to exploit earlier episodes for propaganda purposes. As the vast statues and portraits of Saddam in medieval costumes showed, this was not a mistake Bremer's predecessor would have made.

Some of the new occupiers, of course, were far from paternalistic. They had neither good intentions nor the slightest interest in showing respect or deference to local people. One afternoon I saw two semi-armoured 4×4s with blacked-out windows pull up outside the Palestine hotel. A dozen men in black T-shirts and combat trousers got out, each carrying an automatic rifle or pump-action shotgun and handgun. One of the vehicles had clearly been shot at and the men posed happily in front of the bullet marks for photographs. I went down and spoke to them. They were mainly South African former soldiers and policemen and were working, for several hundred dollars a day, for one of the major American companies overseeing the faltering reconstruction effort. 'I tell you,' said one merrily, 'it's a fucking jungle out there.'

One problem was a complete dearth of genuine information. It was hard even for journalists living in rented houses in the city to find out what was happening on the other side of Baghdad. It was almost impossible for anyone in the Green Zone to get reliable facts on events just 100 miles up-country. Poor communications meant that administrators in Baghdad simply did not know what was going on elsewhere in Iraq. The results were most evident at the so-called 'Five Thirty Follies', the Orwellian daily press conferences given in the Green Zone by senior coalition spokesmen. On one occasion, with a helicopter downed near Fallujah, clashes in Najaf, Karbala and Sadr City, a mortar attack in Baghdad that morning that had literally shaken me out of bed and all roads in the country apparently too dangerous to drive, the chief military press officer referred to a 'slight uptick in hostilities'. When pushed on the fact that the recently recruited Iraqi government forces had deserted en masse, some joining the rebels, he grudgingly admitted that 'the progress we had hoped to make with the security was not as expected' and then fell back on clichés. 'American troops are fighting and dying to bring democracy to young Iraqi women and children,' he told us. The noise of low-flying helicopters was apparently 'the sound of freedom'. We were regularly given a 'body count' of ACFs (anti-coalition fighters) killed in 'proactive combat operations', though figures for civilian dead were impossible to obtain. On leaving the press conferences, the assembled reporters passed under banners advertising the 'Destination Baghdad EXPO 2004' and the 'Iraqi Business Development Center', the motto of which was 'helping business do business in Iraq'.

As during the months before the Iraq war, when the populations of Britain and America had been fed terrifying and largely false information about weapons of mass destruction and links to al-Qaeda, I did not think the official spokesmen were lying or deliberately trying to deceive. Instead I thought they just did not know the truth or did not want to know the truth. The result, however, was the same. The senior officials of the CPA, let alone their political masters in Washington, lived in a world of virtual reality.

Much of the criticism of coalition policy focused on the American army. Glib comparisons of American soldiers with Nazi stormtroopers or the satisfaction manifested by some in the West as American casualty figures mounted angered me greatly, but I knew that some of the charges against the American army were fair. In Tikrit I had heard American soldiers refer to Iraqis as 'Hajis', an ironic use of the term of respect used in Muslim societies for those who have made the pilgrimage to Mecca. They used it to indicate individuals, as in 'there were two Hajis in the house' or collectively, as in 'Haji was fighting back', or as an adjective, complaining about 'Haji cigarettes'. Haji was the exact equivalent of 'Gooks' or 'Krauts' or, for that matter 'Niggers', 'Yids', 'Slope-eyes', 'Honkies', 'Kaffirs' or 'unbelievers' and just as dehumanizing. Guarding the Palestine hotel was a squad of tanks, all presumably from B platoon, with names such as Blitzkrieg, Bladerunner, Beautiful Destruction and Bloodlust painted on their main guns.

I asked the American military if I could spend some time with one of their civil-affairs team, the people who they hoped would win local hearts and minds. They were overjoyed at the request and put me on a Blackhawk helicopter which, flying very low and dipping and weaving to avoid possible rocket fire, headed north over the suburbs of Baghdad, out over the fertile farmland beyond and up the line of the Tigris river towards Tikrit where the 1st Infantry Division, 23,000 strong, was based.

The '1st ID' had a discretionary development fund of hundreds of millions of dollars and it was the job of the 120 men and women of the 115th Civil Affairs Battalion to spend it. As ever with the Americans, the unit members were courteous and welcoming. They were pleased that someone was showing an interest in their work, which, despite the words of their commanding officer, appeared to be very much a doctrinal poor cousin. They took me to dinner, tried to teach me to play volleyball and made sure I knew where the showers were. And they appeared genuinely committed to helping improve the lives of the 'Eye-raqis'. When Major Donna Kentley, a physician's assistant from Santa Barbara, California, told me she enjoyed her time in Iraq only when her health education programmes, aimed at women and children, went well, I believed her.

But Kentley and her colleagues were hamstrung by the mutual suspicion of local people and the troops. The 1st Infantry Division's first casualty in Iraq had not been a grizzled infantryman but Nicole Frye, a 19-year-old from Oconto Falls, Michigan, from the Civil Affairs Battalion, and the daily attacks on 1st ID troops resulted in a steady flow of casualties. The result of the continuing attacks was that Iraq was considered 'bandit country'. 'A successful mission is one with no losses,' one officer told me. 'The rest is gravy.' Moments after talking about her health projects, Major Kentley, watching local youths play football as our convoy of half a dozen heavily armed vehicles crawled through their village, commented on the difficulty of identifying 'the enemy'. 'Weird, isn't it?' she said. 'They smile at us now but could be planting a bomb in two hours' time. We just can't tell.'

The consequences could be almost comical. When I accompanied one civil affairs officer, Major Forrest, on a short trip across Tikrit to tell a local municipal administrator that $9,700 had been made available for a new electricity transformer, we travelled with a squad of thirty heavily armed soldiers and his own close protection team. Forrest himself wore body armour and carried a 9mm handgun and an M16 rifle. When he set about telling the administrator 'the good news' about the transformer, his bulky flak jacket meant that he could not sit down in the narrow chair provided for him. Owing to problems of translation, the council worker thought Forrest was accusing him of corruption. When we left the building and a local in traditional dress stopped his vehicle close to our convoy, the infantry guarding us were only with difficulty prevented from opening fire. The car actually contained a local sheikh who had stopped by to say hello to 'his American friends'. On our way back to base, one female soldier told me she wore a scarf around her face to make her look mean. 'Otherwise they'd see me smiling at the children,' she said. 'And I've got to look mean to stay safe.'

Contributing to the mutual suspicion was the sheer insularity of most American troops. Though many of the 1st Infantry Division were usually based in Germany and others had deployed to the Balkans, few had been anywhere like Iraq before. Many soldiers expressed their surprise that the country was not just sand dunes and camels. 'I thought it would be something from the Arabian Nights,' said one sergeant, 'not with cities and stuff.' While on one patrol we slewed to a halt when a camel was spotted. The animal was actually serving as a mobile advertising hoarding publicizing the 'authentically local' cuisine of a restaurant but this did not bother the soldiers, who excitedly pulled out their cameras, taking turns to cover each other with their weapons as they took pictures. 'Now I know I'm in Iraq,' said one. 'I've seen a camel.'

As I had flown up from Baghdad I had seen the immense truck parks of Camp Victory, the American base at Baghdad airport. There were scores of such similar facilities, where the vehicles that ferried supplies and men around the American army positions in

Iraq were maintained and guarded. The system was almost entirely
sealed off from the country itself, the trucks like corpuscles carrying
oxygen around the arteries of a body, and once a soldier had
entered within he had no need for the outside world. The helicopters with their network of airstrips and pads that the senior
command used to move around the country provided another
parallel system, also almost entirely sealed off from Iraq itself. Some
troops never left the huge bases at all. At Tikrit around 3,000
headquarters and 'combat support' staff were based in a vast palace
complex built by Saddam Hussein on the banks of the Tigris. The
troops slept beneath chandeliers and wood-panelled ceilings carved
with the former dictator's initials. Much of the food was freighted
in from Saudi Arabia or Kuwait – leading to shortages of fruit,
vegetables and eggs when violence cut supply routes. The facilities
were far in excess of anything I had seen at Bagram. There was a
vast, fully equipped gym offering Taebo lessons and aerobics classes,
a chess club, a cinema and an internet café with thirty computers.
Some bases were even bigger. The huge complex at Balad, halfway
between Tikrit and Baghdad, had traffic police and a giant mess
that served corn dogs and onion rings twenty-four hours a day. It
was there that, at three in the morning, I had a short, intense and
thoroughly bizarre discussion about T. E. Lawrence's *Seven Pillars
of Wisdom* and Edmund Said's classic work *Orientalism* with a
disconcertingly well-informed 19-year-old infantryman. The conversation reminded me that it was as easy to slip into lazy stereotypes about the Americans as it was about anyone else.

    After nearly a week I left the 115th Civil Affairs Battalion and
joined an infantry unit whose job it was to patrol Tikrit. They
were much younger, much more male and much more heavily
tattooed than the civil affairs specialists. Their life consisted of
long periods of tedious 'security' duty and vehicle or weapons
maintenance interspersed with short bursts of extreme excitement.
Their conversations revolved around weapons, films, music and
video games and what they were going to do (and whom they
were going to do it with) when they got home. Politics was never
mentioned. And, though every platoon had suffered a casualty, all

the soldiers looked forward to actually being involved in combat. The 30-year-old captain in charge said he 'couldn't have been happier' to be where he was. 'I'm a professional soldier,' he said. 'Until recently I could have gone my entire career without hearing a shot fired in anger.'

The general attitude to the 'Hajis' varied. Locals who were co-operative and friendly were 'good guys' and when, on patrol one evening, we were stopped by an old man who wanted to give us information, he was treated with great courtesy. But others were treated with indifference bordering on contempt. The number of people the locals crammed into their decrepit cars was a constant source of amusement. And the sense of being a target was ever-present. When we walked through the streets of Tikrit, the soldiers happily taught slang American words to curious and unafraid children and then pointed their weapons at their parents when they came too close, shouting 'back the fuck up'.

It was the infantry who had to do 'raids' to pick up 'bad guys'. One night the target was a suspected 'ACF' financier. The captain laconically detailed the mission, sitting at an inlaid wood table in a high-ceilinged room of the palace where the unit was billeted, his men's weapons strewn over the marble floor. 'Here's the deal,' he said, spitting chewing tobacco into a plastic cup. 'The guy is . . . Mohammed al-Whateverthefuckhisnameis al-Fucking Some-thingorother.'

A sergeant took over. 'This is the motherfuckin' route to the fuckin' house,' he told the men, handing out satellite pictures. 'Remember we don't use sandbags on the heads of prisoners we use fuckin' blindfolds. And the word from the CO is we don't just smash the motherfuckin' door in, we knock first. And then the motherfuckin' door goes in.' There was a brief, and profane, discussion about what to do with prisoners. 'Jus' bring 'em to me,' the sergeant joked, rolling his eyes. 'The women, anyways.'

At 12.40 a.m. six armoured Humvees moved out of the base and drove through a silent city. At the first house the door did indeed 'go in'. Unfortunately it was the wrong address. Leaving shattered glass and cash as compensation, the squad moved on to the next house. This time the soldiers climbed into a walled garden and cut through the chain on the gate. A tall thin man, the suspected financier, opened the door, coolly picked a flower and offered it to the captain. The captain questioned him with almost elaborate politeness. The man denied everything, saying he was a taxi driver.

Outside the men talked softly. Sergeant Arthur described the silence in the mountains near his home in West Virginia. Second Lieutenant Craig talked about taking a degree in education to be a football coach when he returned to the US. Another soldier, the squad medic, talked about using his army college funding to do paediatric medicine at college. A New Yorker said he joined up after September 11 because he had 'lost friends' and 'wanted to do something'. I walked back to the Humvee and fell asleep.

When I woke up we were moving again. The captain had decided that the man was no taxi driver and had detained him. 'A taxi driver? With an orchard? And a two-storey villa in the nice bit of Tikrit? And two cars?' he asked, shaking his head. 'I find that surprising. And what's with the flower? Just too nonchalant. It's like he was French or something.' We drove back towards the base. But for the odd gunshot and an occasional round from a tank fired at suspected 'ACF' mortar positions, Tikrit was silent.

On my last morning with the 1st ID I went to see their senior intelligence officer. He had close-cropped sandy hair, very blue eyes and spoke very quickly in a strong New York accent. What was going wrong? I asked him. 'We need to get ahead in water and secure key infrastructure so we can get prosperity rolled out, not prosperity as we know it, but out in the little fucking villages. Out there he wants his water for his sheep, his cattle and a bit of electricity. They have to have that basic service. That's why he's pissed. Because a year after the war what's changed? Nothing.'

How widespread was the support for the insurgents?

'Well there are less than twenty attacks a day in our area of operations on thousands of patrols among three and a half million inhabitants in all. So you do the math. Even if each of those twenty attacks takes fifty guys, which they don't, then you are still talking about only 1,000 actives out of a population half the size of London,' he answered.

What did the insurgents want?

'What do they want? They want us out of their fucking country. They want their own government but do they know what it would look like? No. And they want electricity.'

What will defeat them?

A big sigh. 'Muqtada al-Sadr is a fake, a 30-year-old punk, an opportunistic little bastard and the Sunnis . . . well . . . as long as there are people out there who are out of work there is going to be a problem. You don't need to drink a lot of coffee to work out that the insurgency's centre of gravity is the economy.'

As I left I walked through the main operations room, the nerve centre of the 1st Infantry Division. It was set up in what had clearly been some kind of ballroom or banqueting hall under Saddam, though army carpenters had rigged a set of benches which made it look like some kind of lecture theatre in a bizarrely decorated university. Staff officers sat at the plyboard desks with telephones at their elbows linking them to all the various field units. They faced a low rostrum above which hung a huge white board which was divided into three sections, labelled 'What has happened', 'What is happening' and 'What needs to be done'. The 'What is happening' section was further divided between an enormous projected map of the division's area of operations, effectively a third of northern and central Iraq, and a series of TV screens. Two showed direct feeds from the cameras of two Predator unmanned drones, picturing a street and the back of a house, with a figure clearly moving in the garden. Next to them, two screens showed CNN and Fox News. It was an extraordinary insight into the virtual, mediatised, nature of modern conflict – fought, planned and watched in realtime, image and reality interacting in an astonishing and unprecedented way. There were the public mass TV channels, the private military pictures, different audiences, different actors and different, and partial, representations of the truth. I wondered who was watching whom watching whom. A bulletin had just started. The lead story on both CNN and Fox was the

recently revealed abuse of Iraqi prisoners by American soldiers at
Abu Ghraib prison.

The Abu Ghraib scandal had broken while I was with the
infantry. Their reactions to the horrendous stories of abuse at
the prison had varied from 'they must have deserved it' from the
infantrymen to 'now we are really screwed' from the civil affairs
officers. I too was surprised, perhaps naively. Back in Baghdad to
cover the fall-out from the revelations, I drove up to the gates of
the prison and listened to the stories relatives of inmates told me
about what was happening in the jail and felt sick.

Yet, despite the widespread anger the scandal at the prison
caused, I felt more relaxed in Iraq than I had done for weeks. The
situation around Fallujah appeared to have stabilized and there had
been no abductions for several days. When there were clashes
between the Americans and al-Sadr's militia in Najaf and Karbala,
only a few hours' drive away, I decided to drive down to cover
them, sharing a car with Rory McCarthy of the *Guardian*, a colleague and friend from days in Afghanistan and Pakistan. We were
fifteen minutes late leaving Baghdad because I had overslept. This
proved to be extremely lucky.

We had just driven through the scruffy town of Mahmudiyah,
around fifty miles south of the capital, when we came round a
bend and saw a car pulled up on the central reservation a hundred
yards away. As we got closer, our own driver slowing our vehicle,
we could see its rear window was full of bullet holes. Whatever
had happened had only just occurred as a crowd was still gathering
and other vehicles were just pulling up. As we got closer we could
see two bodies, one on the rear seat with what appeared to be a
serious head wound, the other stretched out in the dust, either
dead or unconscious. From closer still we saw that he was a
Westerner, on his face in the dirt with one thick pale arm thrown
out. I could see little blood beside him, in sharp contrast to the
mess around the body on the back seat. Sliding down in our seats
and telling our driver to keep going, Rory and I were past the
scene and accelerating out on to the open road within seconds.

An hour later we found out from our offices that the dead men were a senior Polish TV reporter and his Polish–Algerian colleague. They had driven through Mahmudiyah a few minutes ahead of us and been spotted by a group of local Sunni militants who had followed them and then, once on the open road, opened fire on their car. Their mistake was to put a sign saying 'Press' in their window. That, and being Western and in the wrong place at the wrong time had been enough to get them killed.

13. Miss Sixty

The problems that had thrown Iraq into chaos in the spring had never been resolved and it was the Shias who first renewed the conflict. At the end of July 2004 Muqtada al-Sadr's militia seized Najaf, the small city ninety miles south of Baghdad and the shrine of Imam Ali, one of the holiest sites in Shia Islam, that lay surrounded by pilgrim hotels and religious schools at its centre. The American army, backed by troops from the newly sovereign Iraqi government, launched an assault intended to force al-Sadr's men out, fighting their way though the outlying districts and the massive dusty cemeteries in which devout Shia from all over the Islamic world were brought to be buried and then moving street by street towards the shrine itself, squeezing al-Sadr's men back into the labyrinth of narrow alleys around the golden-domed enclosure of the shrine. The militia readied themselves for a bloody last stand.

The battle lasted three weeks and was one of extraordinary intensity. It was unlike anything else I had ever seen. On its penultimate day I found myself crouched behind a wall, bullets cracking and whipping above me. All the buildings around me were in ruins and the streets were filled with dead dogs and ragged, rusting coils of wire; paper and pools of oil; chunks of masonry, split pipes, scattered bricks and spent cartridges that shone like brass coins in the bright, white noonday sun. There were tanks backing and grinding to my left, rocking back on their tracks as they fired high-explosive rounds into walls less than a hundred yards away which then disintegrated as if they had been hit by a demolition ball. To my right, nosing out from a narrow lane, was an armoured personnel carrier armed with a huge machine gun that thumped like a piston-powered industrial machine tool when fired. Behind the armoured vehicles there was the American infantry, kneeling or lying in the dust, firing grenades ahead of them before edging a few yards forward, shouting and gesturing to each other. From a few hundred feet above, Apache helicopters descended every twenty minutes or so to fire rockets that brought down entire houses and shops, sometimes exposing bizarrely undamaged furniture or stock inside. At regular intervals a jet would fly in, the sound of its engines building into an astonishing, howling scream before it peeled away leaving a dramatic pause before the shattering percussion of the explosion. Somewhere in the welter of noise and air blast was the sound of the Kalashnikovs and rocket-propelled grenades of al-Sadr's militiamen and it was their bullets that were chipping concrete and plaster out of the wall above me when a metal gate on the other side of the street opened and an old man beckoned me and I ran across and in through the narrow black slot of the doorway.

Once inside, the noise of the fighting was strangely distant. We sat in a small courtyard in the centre of the house and the old man offered brackish water from an oil drum in a corner. A dim light filtered down from an opening to the sky two storeys above. The old man farmed a few small fields to the south of the city, he told me, beyond the old gate where Najaf's houses and mosques and scruffy streets ended and before the open sands of the desert itself. He had not left his home since the fighting had started three weeks earlier. Within a minute or so of my crashing through his door, all of the half-dozen reporters I was with were also squatting on his floor. The old man said his name was Saleh Alawi Jassm and he was 69 years old and still in his house, where he had lived all his life, because he was scared of it being looted in the fighting. 'I'm here just looking after my home,' he said. 'I don't blame anyone for the thefts but it happens a lot. They took two TVs, CDs, all sorts of things. I am just a farmer and I just want to get back to my fields.'

A helicopter overhead momentarily drowned out his voice. I had taken my flak jacket off and was sitting on it and holding my sodden shirt off my skin trying to dry the sweat out of it.

'This is better than 1991,' Jassm was saying, referring to the repression of the Shia revolt against Saddam in the aftermath of the first Gulf War. 'Then there was just bombing and bombing of everywhere. It was completely indiscriminate. Now at least they are targeting each other and no one is trying to kill us. The problem is that when the tank fires in the street outside, our houses fall.'

'Who is the enemy?' someone asked.

'We have two enemies,' Jassm answered. 'The Americans and the al-Sadr people . . .'

'And the Jews,' interrupted a Syrian cameraman.

'What have the Jews got do with it?' said Jassm. 'There aren't any Jews here and anyway a good, honest Jew is better than a bad Muslim.' He paused and sipped the brown water he held in a smudged glass with fingers as brown and bent as sticks. 'Like I was saying, we have two enemies, the Americans and the al-Sadr people; they are not from here, they come here and fight in the middle of our homes and we are just trying to live.'

'Do you get any sleep?' I asked.

'How can I sleep? Am I a child? Am I a child who can forget about everything and shut his eyes and sleep? Of course I don't sleep. I just sit up all night smoking cigarettes.'

Outside, the fighting had eased. There were no air strikes and the tanks appeared to have pulled back a short way. A photographer suggested taking advantage of the lull to take a shortcut into the centre of the city by crossing the front lines ahead of us. This seemed to me to be an insane risk and after a brief and farcical argument, in which I was told first that 'it would be fun' and second that if 'I didn't have the balls I should have stayed in the hotel', our small group split up and I set off, following a colleague and old friend, Stephen Farrell from *The Times*, who said he knew a safer way of reaching the shrine and the headquarters of al-Sadr's forces.

We circled around the knot of congested alleyways and old tall houses in the centre of the city, looking for a route in. Out of sight, the fighting continued, coughing into loud life and then going silent like a badly maintained engine. The streets we were walking through were eerily quiet. Though it was extremely hot we walked down the centre of each road in the sun, stepping around the debris, our hands raised in the air, aware all the time that somewhere, someone, possibly one of al-Sadr's men, possibly an American sniper, was probably watching us. Stephen and I were both wearing floppy white sun hats in a bid to make our appearance as unmilitary as possible but they seemed scant protection. When we came to an open stretch of road just before the old city, we stepped out, our white hats on sticks above us, and walked across the soft tarmac very slowly to allow any gunman to see exactly who we were, our shadows like dark stains immediately underneath our feet.

A woman came out of her house to offer us water in a tin mug. An old man leading a donkey with two baskets on its back crossed a passageway in front of us and then quickly passed out of sight round a corner. There was a sharp crack. Looking round the corner, we saw the donkey dead in the road. One of the American snipers, presumably tasked with stopping supplies reaching the fighters in the city, had clearly just shot it. There was no sign of the old man.

It took us an hour or more to reach the shrine. The passageways around the compound itself were full of small groups of young men with weapons and scrubby new beards, green ribbons tied round their foreheads and dirty bandages. The heat was still intense and the noise often extraordinary. But, despite the stunning explosions and the shock they produced, the narrow alleys of the old city provided cover against blasts even close by and, almost incredibly given the environment, many of the fighters were lying asleep on the ground, barely waking when a tank round impacted round a corner thirty yards away, covering us in dust and debris. Other fighters carried huge deep metal dishes full of rice and yellow beans, ducking and running behind the barricades of furniture and scrap metal that had been erected to give cover against the snipers. An injured man was pushed past us lying on a wooden handcart, his hands clasping his belly, blood coursing between his fingers and on to the ground, a look of dull surprise on his face.

Few of the fighters were from Najaf. I had noted when we had reached the shrine that most wore tracksuit trousers and T-shirts or faded shirts, the uniform of working-class urban Iraqi youth, rather than the more traditional robes favoured by the rural Shia population. Most said they were from the major Shia cities in the south of Iraq or from Baghdad and had travelled to Najaf at the beginning of the fighting. Though still defiant, they were clearly stunned by the firepower directed against them. They mouthed formulaic defiance about fighting 'to the last drop of our blood' against 'the occupiers' and some spoke of their wish for martyrdom. I had noticed a poster showing a portrait of their leader, Muqtada al-Sadr, alongside pictures of the leaders of Hizbollah, the Lebanese Shia militant organization, and I briefly thought of the stickers on the bedroom wall of the dead teenager in the Gaza Strip and the whole method of marketing martyrdom that Hizbollah had pioneered elsewhere in the Middle East. But it was impossible to speak properly in the noise and the dust and, without our interpreters, conversation was anyway limited to banalities. We had established that the militia were still in control of much of the old city and that any claims to the contrary were wrong and there was no reason to linger. It took us several hours to get back to the hotel that we were using as a base on the outskirts of the city. On the way we passed the corpse of the donkey shot by the sniper earlier in the day and, twenty yards further on, that of its owner, now stretched out on the street in a pool of blood.

The siege of Najaf finished thirty-six hours later when the Grand Ayatollah Ali al-Sistani, the most senior Shia cleric in Iraq, returned to the country after heart surgery in London and told Muqtada al-Sadr to leave the shrine city. The younger cleric, whose religious qualifications were negligible compared with the older man's renowned scholarship, grudgingly agreed, aware that he was not popular enough to risk a confrontation. Caught between the guns of the Americans and the religious authority of a grand ayatollah, al-Sadr had no option but to relinquish Najaf and give up his plan of using the shrine city, and the huge sums donated by its pilgrims, as a springboard to power in Iraq.

To give al–Sadr a fig-leaf for the retreat and to demonstrate his own power, al–Sistani had called worshippers from all over Iraq to travel to Najaf to pray at the shrine on the Saturday morning. During the night the Americans pulled back and, in the pale blue half-light of dawn, the pilgrims began walking through the debris-strewn streets towards the golden dome that rose above the shattered buildings. Many were barefoot with their palms turned upwards in a gesture of supplication. As the sun rose, the great dome of the shrine flared into gold and orange as the rays struck it and soon the narrow streets were packed with men walking slowly. A brief firefight between a group of al–Sadr militiamen and Iraqi police broke like a sudden squall of violence over the crowd and was gone as quickly as it had come. Not one of the militiamen emerging from their positions in the rubble was over 25. Several were former soldiers who had been demobilized a year before. They were hollow-eyed with fatigue. 'Six of my friends are dead and fifteen injured,' one told me, a green rag around his neck, his clothes torn. 'We tried to attack the tanks but it was very hard. I was never scared because I knew I would die as a martyr and that made me happy.' The shrine itself, even as medics worked to scrub the congealed blood from the marble floor outside the room that had served as a first-aid post, rapidly filled with worshippers calling out praise to Ali, the martyred cousin and son–in–law of the prophet Mohammed. At 8 a.m. the loudspeakers of the mosque crackled into life. 'To all mujahideen, you have to leave the shrine and the city by 10 a.m. These are the orders of the college of scholars.' I watched a row of fighters who had been sleeping in the corner of the shrine rouse themselves, stretch, gather their few belongings and start to move.

I thought of Jassm, the old man who had welcomed us into his home on the front line two days earlier, and hoped he was pleased. Most local people were staying away from the ruins of the centre of the city, though later in the day they would start arriving to check the damage to their homes and businesses. Few among them had anything positive to say about al–Sadr. Indeed, it rapidly became clear that the young cleric was very unpopular in Najaf

even before bringing such destruction to the city. Najaf was loyal
to al-Sistani, who had consistently called on the Iraqi Shia community to shun violence. Al-Sadr, impatient and ambitious, represented a new radical, politicized strand of thought among some
of the more urbanized Shias and his bid to seize Najaf had been as
much an attempted coup against the established clerical authorities
as a blow against the coalition and the new Iraqi government. The
college of senior Shia clerics in Iraq was called the *hawsa* and
locals explained to me the difference between the 'silent' *hawsa* of
al-Sistani and the 'loud' or 'angry' *hawsa* of al-Sadr. Though it was
al-Sistani who had Iranian roots, it was al-Sadr who was actually
the inheritor of the radical ideology that had underpinned the 1979
Iranian revolution. I spoke to one cleric loyal to al-Sistani who
had just emerged from hiding in Najaf. Shaking with trauma and
anger, he stood among the rubble of the main street next to a
wrecked pickle shop and told me tales of violence and intimidation
standing in a congealing ammoniac pool of chillies, vinegar and
cabbage. The sight of two dozen swollen and putrid corpses laid
out in a makeshift morgue in al-Sadr's office near the shrine
convinced me that his description of a revolutionary reign of terror
had not been exaggerated. Most of the bodies were of local people
who appeared to have been executed by al-Sadr's henchmen over
the previous three weeks for having 'suspect loyalties'. At least one
had a noose round his neck. The entrance to the office was
spattered with vomit.

   The successful resolution at Najaf proved a number of things.
The most obvious lesson was that it had needed a military strategy
married to a political strategy to end the stand-off. Second, the
siege had shown how, as I had learned elsewhere, insurgents cannot
win without the support of a critical mass of the local community.
However, the battle at Najaf had also shown that a very small
number of sufficiently motivated men can cause enormous problems and great harm. Despite being unable to deploy more than
1,500 fighters, all lightly armed and virtually untrained, al-Sadr
had been able to hold off a division of heavily equipped American
soldiers and several thousand Iraqi auxiliaries for the best part of a

month and had, almost as importantly, dominated all the headlines from Iraq. Finally, the siege indicated that the attempt to sideline al-Sistani by the US-led coalition throughout the previous year, largely because he was a conservative cleric with a big beard and friends in Iran, had been a serious mistake. Ideological differences within the Shia community in Iraq that appeared, at least to outsiders, nothing more than nuances had proved to be of critical importance in securing a positive outcome to a dangerous situation.

With the siege of Najaf lifted there was little to detain any of the reporters who had been covering the story. Having filed my copy via satellite phone, I left the hotel and set off back towards Baghdad. Since my last visit to Iraq three months previously there had been a steady deterioration in the security situation and in previous weeks several journalists had been abducted on the road to the capital and a number were still being held. There had also been scores of ambushes on American convoys or Iraqi government forces. I had driven down to Najaf at 4.30 a.m. when the roads had been deserted. Now it was early evening but, with all the other reporters pulling out of the city, I did not want to spend another night there.

As the local police were suspected of collaborating with the kidnap gangs further north, I was under a blanket on the back seat from the moment we left from the hotel. For a few minutes I listened to Samer, a young student who was my translator, talking in short, terse sentences with Tareq, my driver, and then lay back. I had worked with both many times before and trusted them implicitly. They too would be in grave danger if we were stopped. I watched the tops of palm trees flicker across the patch of sky framed by the car window and tried unsuccessfully to sleep. Soon, from the sound of our tyres on a newly resurfaced section of road, I knew we were close to Mahmudiyah. We had covered the ground quickly and were clearly not far from where I had seen the bodies of the two Poles. Usually garrulous, both Tareq and Samer were now silent, both smoking cigarettes, lighting one from another. Through the window I counted the wrecked pylons, counted the tops of the palm trees, idly pondered the fact that Iraq once produced 90 per cent of the world's dates, dozed, woke to visions of the body of the Polish reporter splayed out in the dust and dozed again.

Then the brakes locked and we slid to a hard halt. I could hear horns and men running and Tareq swearing viciously and fluently. Then Samer was swearing too. I could see nothing except the blanket, a slice of sky and the sunlight refracting through the windscreen.

'Samer, Tareq, what the fuck is happening?' I said.

'Jason. Is OK. Is a traffic jam. Is Baghdad. Is OK.'

Spending time in Iraq always had the paradoxical effect of making me more optimistic that the troubles of the country would eventually resolve themselves happily. For a while this puzzled me, given that while in the country I saw the fearful reality of life there up close. Then I realized that my optimism was rooted in the daily contact that I had with ordinary people, the 24 million individuals who made up the nation of Iraq, and who were neither fanatics nor victims but people whose aspirations, hopes, fears, pleasures and anguish were almost identical to my own. Every day that passed in Iraq reminded me that though men like al-Sadr or the politicians or those behind the suicide bombings that frequently killed dozens might dominate the headlines they were far from representative of the vast bulk of Iraqis and the television coverage of the country, which naturally focused on the most sanguinary episodes of any one day, obscured the reality of life for most people. So, inevitably, did my own reporting. But the often under-reported truth was that it was this massive majority who would bring Iraq out of the nightmare. And they were not composed of militants or thugs or religious fanatics. They were not repressive and devout or brutalized or violent. They just wanted to know that they could put dinner on the table for their children, to go to work or to school or get their ageing parents to a hospital, wanted merely to be able to sleep through a whole night without waking in a sweat through fear or heat or both, and they aspired only to just a little of what we in the West largely take for granted. These were the people on whom the future of Iraq depended and these were the people who, somehow, given an opportunity and despite the harshness of everyday life and all the forces ranged against them, would eventually defeat the violence.

And, whatever the coalition, the government or Washington claimed, the daily reality was undoubtedly harsh. Of course, the picture was patchy and it would be wrong to have portrayed the whole of Iraq as entirely sunk in deep poverty. The pavements of one street in Baghdad were lined with new plastic-wrapped air-conditioning units, satellite televisions and fridges and there were restaurants that cost $10 or $20 a head that were always full. But the truth was that for most of the population, life, both before the invasion and after it, was a huge struggle. Though the south of the country had been starved of electricity under Saddam, the people in Baghdad had received an almost uninterrupted supply and thus felt the constant and unpredictable power shortages badly. In the south, it was the authorities' apparent inability to ensure clean drinking water that soon began to anger many. When I visited a power station near Basra I saw why rebuilding Iraq's infrastructure was so hard, even before the saboteurs had got to work. It was not merely that the complex had clearly been on the point of total collapse before the invasion but that every link in the production and distribution chain – the generators, the transformers, the power lines, the fuel supplies, the refineries, the trucks, the bicycles that the workers used to move around the site – needed replacing. That almost every power station in the country was in the same state showed that Iraq had been a poor country for a long time, despite its oil wealth. The population likewise had been so run down over decades of war and sanctions that they had nothing left to help them through lean times. They were already running on empty.

Then there was the security situation. For many, the total break-down of law and order in many areas posed far more problems than any actions by militants. The chances of actually being caught by a bomb were statistically quite low, though obviously the prospect was frightening. But the chances of being shot by bandits, robbed, abducted and ransomed were high. People were trapped in a terrible dilemma. If they went to work or went out to try and find work, they risked death or serious injury. If they stayed at home, they would have no money and, eventually, no food. For anyone who was ill, the situation was worse still. Healthcare systems, at least for those without funds, were almost non-existent. I frequently visited one woman who had two badly disabled children, Fara and Mariam, each of whom needed constant care. I usually brought her large boxes of biscuits and fresh fruit, pretending that it was the custom in my country when visiting someone. We both knew that it was a handout. What the family needed most, of course, was money and specialist medical care that was available only in the West. Many were simply bewildered. 'I love my country. I love Iraq so much,' one woman shopkeeper in central Baghdad told me. 'But I am suffering a lot when I see the violence. The regime has gone and things should be much better and there should be a new beginning but I don't see that now. It hurts me to see Iraq as a battlefield. But what is my guilt? What is my family's guilt?' I had heard the question asked before.

And though no one expressed a wish to have Saddam back – such an idea seemed almost unthinkable – few could understand how things had gone so wrong. I was reminded of the Kabulis under the Taliban and all the stratagems they had evolved for coping. But it had taken the population of the Afghan capital a long time to learn how to live with the men from Kandahar and though life in Kabul had been far more arduous in terms of the bare necessities of life, it was certainly less violent. The Kabulis themselves recognized that, for all their faults, the Taliban had brought security. 'Will it get better? Will it get better in Iraq?' wondered Baghdadis when I asked them. They often repeated my questions to themselves several times, turning the words over carefully before giving their answer. Which was usually a self-conscious half-smile, an 'inshallah' and a shrug.

What was noticeable a year after the invasion was a hardening in the general atmosphere. The exposure to constant risk was steadily brutalizing people, forcing them back into themselves.

Thirty years of brutal dictatorial rule had already embedded violence as a natural part of everyday life and behaviour. The chaos of the new Iraq merely reinforced the tendency. As in Afghanistan and parts of Pakistan, the smallest dispute escalated rapidly. Violence was latent everywhere, a function of the general insecurity and absence of law. I once saw a man punch a stubborn horse in the head with his fist. On another occasion I saw a shopkeeper beating a child who had stolen an apple with a thick, knouted rope. He hit the child again and again, smashing him down into the dust of the road, in an extraordinary overreaction to a minor misdemeanour. The new wave of violence that was washing over the nation, so different in so many ways from the state violence that had characterized Saddam's rule, necessitated the creation of a whole range of new words to describe terrorists, firefights, bombings, mutilations, sabotage, kidnapping for ransom, kidnapping for propaganda, televised confessions and banditry.

And, inevitably, the foreign soldiers in Iraq became more brutalized too. On my return from Najaf, curious about what sort of men shot donkeys and their owners, I spent a morning interviewing the American snipers stationed in Sadr City. One, sitting outside his barracks in the sun smoking a menthol cigarette, described the feeling of power it gave him to watch a target through his sights. 'Don't think it's probably a very good thing,' he admitted laconically. He described how he had killed three men. 'I don't have no nightmares,' he said. 'Every one of them deserved it.' Even down in Basra, where a year previously I had accompanied British troops in soft berets in an open-topped Land-Rover on patrol, the atmosphere was noticeably nastier. Troops now moved around in armoured vehicles. On the lip of a bunker in a base that had been under constant attack for the best part of a month a soldier had scrawled: 'You'll be in a world of shit . . . I am already in a world of shit.' It was a line from *Full Metal Jacket*.

A constant problem was gauging support for the increasingly strong 'resistance'. First, any estimates depended on which militants you were talking about: al-Sadr and his militia, the so-called 'Sunni diehards' who were fighting in the west of the country or the militant Islamic factions, the jihadis, who were noisy but not particularly numerous. Immediately after the invasion of 2003 I had written that 10 per cent of the overall population was pro-coalition, 10 per cent were pro-'resistance' and 80 per cent were neither. Fifteen months later, my best guess was that only a tiny fraction remained favourable to the USA and its allies, a substantial proportion, perhaps 25 per cent, were not opposed to violent attacks against Western forces and a significant number, perhaps 5 per cent, were actually prepared to undertake such actions if given the resources, the opportunity or the right direction. The rest were just keeping their heads down. And though the actual total number of militants remained relatively small when considered in the context of an entire country, even a slight tendency towards general radicalization was a critical shift. Simple arithmetic meant that, even if only a tiny fraction of the angriest people actually picked up a gun, the more resentful people there were the more active militants there would be.

What I was most interested in, what would hold the key to the Iraqi debacle, I thought, was the process by which those Iraqis who had welcomed the US invasion, or at least had been ambivalent about it early on, had been led to active opposition. These were the people who were swelling the ranks of the resistance. Had they been brainwashed as some said? How organized were they? What role did religion play? Was there a connection to 'al-Qaeda'? All the issues I had been interested in for years seemed condensed into this one question.

I met 'Abu Mujahed' in a hotel just outside the centre of Baghdad. During the day, he told me, he worked behind a desk in a major ministry. At night, he fought for 'the resistance'. He was around 30 years old and had a shaven head, a pot belly, thick forearms and pudgy hands, and when I met him in a hotel in Baghdad he was wearing brown slacks, a sports shirt and a fake leather belt with a big brass buckle that said 'Miss Sixty' on it. He spoke fluently and intelligently and we talked for a long time. I do not think he lied to me.

First, Abu Mujahed, a Sunni born and raised in the big Baghdad quarter of Adhamiyah, had stressed that he had never been a member of the Ba'ath Party and that when he had heard that the Americans were coming to 'liberate Iraq' he was 'very happy'. American culture, to him, symbolized freedom, meritocracy and opportunity. 'Under Saddam, I liked listening to Bon Jovi,' he told me. 'The only way to breathe was to watch American film and songs and this gave me a glimpse of a better life, so I was happy when I heard that the US was coming. Our lives were just a straight line, with no left, no right, no deviation. I felt that I would be able to live well, travel and have freedom if the Americans came. I wanted to do sport, use modern appliances, get a new car and develop my life. The US or the UK were not my enemy and they are not now.' It was one of the most succinct expressions of the attraction of the West for hundreds of millions of people in the Islamic world that I had ever heard.

Two things had disillusioned him. The first was the images of civilian casualties – broadcast by Arabic-language satellite channels – that he watched on an illicit dish during the war itself and the second was the sight of American troops standing by and doing nothing to stop the looting of his home town. 'I saw the looters taking the marble from the Ministry of Higher Education in front of two American tanks!' he said. 'That convinced me that the Americans were not here to help us but to destroy us. If they came here as friends they would have protected what we had.'

For a while Abu Mujahed kept his faith in the invaders – 'I kept waiting for the situation to get better, just thinking it was the chaos of war' – but eventually decided that he had been wrong and that he had to act. The deciding moment, he said, was when the Americans started 'killing and arresting' his 'own people'.

Over a period of weeks, Abu Mujahed said, a group came together. There was no major effort at recruitment, certainly no direction from above or outside, just a band of like-minded people sharing a fairly indistinct goal and similar sentiments.

'My group, like many groups, contains one man fighting for his nation, another fighting for a principle, another who is an army officer who has been made jobless and is trying to get revenge. We have someone who is a religious man. There are six or seven of us and a few others who come and go.'

Nor was the process by which his group sourced the various basic elements that all militants and terrorists require – weapons, expertise and somewhere to train and rest and hide – any less amateurish or haphazard. Careful enquiries established that there was an underground network of arms suppliers already in existence. Finding people who had the specialist knowledge that the group needed to use the arms that were available took longer, but 'step by step' Abu Mujahed was able to locate experts in 'weapons, concealment and communications'. 'Former army people would help us out as a favour and did things like show us how to use a mortar in the front room of someone's house,' he said. 'Bit by bit, we learned what we needed to know.'

Yet Abu Mujahed and his friends were not entirely alone. Soon they came into contact with other similar groups. 'There is a network of links,' he said, switching unconsciously to the present tense. 'All the groups are made up of individuals but they are all linked to one man in the middle who is in charge, a [tribal] sheikh.'

And there was also Islam. Abu Mujahed admitted that he was 'not too religious' himself, only going to mosque on a Friday and rarely praying five times a day except during Ramadan, but he was clear that it was religion that unified his group and, crucially, legitimized their actions. 'Always we discuss what we are going to do in religious terms so we can say we are fighting for the sake of religion,' he said. 'We have formed our group to fight for religion and the main thing for our group is religion.'

Typically, their view of their faith was profoundly literal. 'For us religion is the Koran. If there is a verse in the Koran that says something then that is the truth. I am a believer. Sometimes after an operation we go to the mosque and pray.'

After three months the group launched their first major operation. 'We found three Americans walking in our area and we opened fire at random and ran away. The soldiers lay down so we couldn't tell if we hit them or not and we were confused and pretty scared but we had broken through the barrier and weren't frightened afterwards. Since then we have killed more.'

'How many?' I asked.

'I don't know because we can't check but maybe four or five, maybe as many as twenty.'

Abu Mujahed paused and looked around him. We were speaking in a room on the upper floors of the hotel. He went to the door, called to someone else, came back in, looked through a smeared window at the Tigris and the city beyond. I wondered if he was armed and decided he probably was. I was uncomfortably aware that, despite the various precautions I had taken, it would be very difficult for anyone to find me if Abu Mujahed had decided to add kidnapping to his group's activities.

'I have ordered some tea,' he said, guessing what I was thinking. 'Please be certain that I am not against any nationality. You are my guest now and there is no problem. You are my friend. It is only because the Americans are here. As a citizen I never did any crime or anything. I was never in any trouble. And kidnapping is a crime. And I like talking to you because you have a bald head like me.'

Since their first operation, Abu Mujahed told me, the group had learned rapidly. They started varying their tactics, sniping at the Americans from a distance one day, using makeshift roadside bombs the next, laying mines in the path of a patrol the day after that. 'We never got any orders from anybody. We were just told "today you have to do something" by the sheikhs but it was up to us to decide what was feasible and when to do it.'

Black American servicemen were a particular target. 'To be occupied by Negroes is a particular humiliation,' Abu Mujahed said, echoing the profound racism prevalent in much of the Middle East. 'Sometimes we aborted a mission because there were no Negroes that we could kill.'

Had the group suffered any casualties?

He shrugged.

'One of us was taken to Abu Ghraib. Other groups I know of had people killed. In my neighbourhood you can see at least five flags for the brave fallen martyrs of the resistance. They were killed because they made mistakes. We are making less now though.'

'And what about current activities?' I asked.

'Now we are eating and drinking mortars!' he answered with a big smile and slapped his broad thighs. 'Because it is very safe with mortars. We plan everything like the details and the ranges in advance so we just have to turn up and put the tubes up and then set them off and run away.'

Outside the sun was beginning to drop. I did not want to be driving around Baghdad after dark after a meeting with resistance fighters. One controversy among analysts was the degree to which the various resistance groups interacted. What, I asked, was Abu Mujahed's group's relation to the men I had just seen fighting in Najaf.

'The al-Mahdi army are fighting for one person, for Muqtada al-Sadr, not their country or their religion,' he said contemptuously. 'And most of the fighters are exactly the people who looted Baghdad.'

And what about the religious militants? The Wahhabis? The supposed 'al-Qaeda' members?

'We met some of them but we have refused to work with them because it is too dangerous,' Abu Mujahed said. 'Some are here for religion. Some have no allegiance to any group. Others I think are somehow linked with al-Qaeda because they have lots of money. But it is really not easy to work with them. They are really bloodthirsty people. They do not care if they kill honest Iraqi people. They are crazy, I tell you. They are terrorists, really; they are terrorists, I mean it.'

'Are you a terrorist?' I asked.

He looked horrified. 'No, no, we attack American soldiers,' he said. 'We are freedom fighters. We are the resistance.'

We had been speaking for nearly two hours. Samer, who had been translating, and I were tired, both slumped in the old foam chairs of the mouldy hotel room. I wondered what else to ask.

'Do you feel you have been humiliated?' I said.

Abu Mujahed leant forward, palms on his fat thighs. 'There is nothing worse, no greater shame than to see your country being occupied,' he said. 'The US has the ability to stop all these problems. If the Iraqis have full bellies and a good life then no one would fight. Iraqis' top priority is to provide a good living to their families. The US is a very rich country and it could build shopping centres and fill them with subsidized goods if it wanted to. My salary at the ministry is 240,000 Iraqi dinars. By the middle of the month I have no money because I have to pay the rent, I have three children, there are doctor's bills, my wife needs something, my house needs something. One kilo of chicken is 2,500 dinars.'

'One final question. Does your group have a name?'

'I am sure the day will come when we are known as a group, inshallah. But we have no need for a specific name, like "al-Qaeda" or anything. We are a local organization. It doesn't matter if we have a name or not.'

Back at the small house where I was staying, I sat down and wrote out my notes from the interview long into the night. Abu Mujahed's story had condensed many themes I had seen elsewhere. First, there was the simple confirmation of what was clear to anyone on the ground in Iraq: the large ideological rift between those motivated by what were effectively nationalist considerations, sometimes voiced in religious language, and those who were part of the broader, international modern 'jihadist' or 'al-Qaeda' current of thought and activism. Second, there was the amateurish, haphazard formation of Abu Mujahed's anonymous group. Abu Mujahed and his comrades were certainly a long way from the traditional 'terrorist' models of analysis favoured in London, Washington and elsewhere and were nothing like the organized, disciplined, hierarchically structured insurgents depicted in Coalition communiqués. Third, there was the obvious way religion had worked. Faith, or at least the language and ideological currency of faith, had proved enormously effective in drawing together disparate individuals, providing elements of a common identity, a shared purpose and a motivation and, crucially, a justification for violence. In this, Islam was fulfilling the role it had played countless times before, across the entire Muslim world, in the face of invasions, occupations, colonization, natural disasters or other threats, real and imagined.

But what interested me most was Abu Mujahed's initial, pre-war desire to be more Western, not less Western. His sense of humiliation, that crucial and recurrent factor in the spirits of so many in the Islamic world, had been doubled by his rejection by and his disappointment in the West when it had finally arrived, in armoured vehicles, at his front door. Abu Mujahed had been profoundly attracted to the whole package of Western values, as were hundreds of millions of others across the Islamic world, because it offered a way to fulfil so many basic human desires. Like anyone else, he wanted the security, wealth, health, freedom of speech, freedom of association, even, though he had not said it, sexual opportunity, that he saw as characteristic of life in the West. Yet the version of the West that he had encountered had fallen far short of his expectations, as it had for so many others in the Islamic world, and bitter and deeply disappointed, he had attacked what he had once sought.

14. A Centre of Gravity

The day after I interviewed Abu Mujahed, a middle-aged British engineer called Kenneth Bigley was seized from a house in a residential area of Baghdad by a group of Islamic militants. I immediately left my home in a similar residential area and moved back behind the concrete barricades of the al-Hamra hotel. Over the next three weeks, the group responsible for Bigley's abduction, led by the Jordanian-born militant Abu Musab al-Zarqawi, released a series of videos in a carefully choreographed operation designed to hook and hold the attention of the international media. The videos showed their captive, sometimes dressed in an orange Guantanamo Bay-style jumpsuit and behind bars, making a number of appeals to the British people and prime minister. All but the last film, which showed horrific scenes of Bigley's execution, were broadcast, in one form or another, by almost every major television network across the world and thus reached tens of millions of people. Though the video of Bigley's execution was not shown by any mainstream media it was posted on the internet and downloaded tens of thousands of times in just a few weeks.

The hostage-takers' manipulation of the images of violence and their dissemination struck me as the logical culmination of the process that over decades, if not centuries, had seen militants and activists of all kinds experimenting in different ways with the use of new media technologies. Though the aim of the militants' violence had always remained constant, none had ever before been able to communicate their message to such a large audience so easily, or had been able to control the spectacle quite so completely. In Kabul I had sat in a stadium to watch the execution of a woman with a few hundred others. I watched the last days of Kenneth Bigley with an audience of millions. Al-Zarqawi and the men behind the hostage videos kept a tight rein on every part of the creation of their spectacularly violent event. They were also aware of the controversy of their actions and so made strenuous efforts to convince sceptical audiences that their tactics were in fact legitimate, such as including a wide variety of religious and mythic references in the *mise en scène* and using stunts such as dressing their victims in Guantanamo Bay-style clothing.

What was unclear, however, was how al-Zarqawi's acts fitted into the more general pattern of Islamic militancy as it had evolved since September 11 and the subsequant war in Afghanistan. Since the spring of 2002 there had been Islamic militant bombs going off with monotonous regularity. The investigations into the successive attacks in Bali, Casablanca, Riyadh, Mombasa, Jakarta, Istanbul and then Madrid revealed that each involved a small cell of militants, almost all locally recruited, without much in the way of a connection to any central mastermind. Each appeared less connected with any central al-Qaeda command and control centre than its predecessor. It seemed obvious that, though exceptional circumstances in the 1990s had allowed bin Laden to concentrate many of the myriad strands of Islamic militancy in one place and exert a degree of strategic control over them all, the destruction of the training camps and the logistics infrastructure in Afghanistan had led contemporary Islamic militancy to mutate into, or indeed return to being, little more than a nebulous network of networks. Al-Qaeda was a successful ideology that bound itself to local grievances, articulating and expressing them wherever local cultural conditions meant that a radical Islamic package of ideas was accessible and comprehensible to substantial amounts of the population and wherever resentment and anger were sufficiently widespread for the arithmetic of militancy that I had seen working in Iraq to function. Just a small general tilt towards a greater political consciousness and anger in a given society would tip enough people into violent action to cause a substantial problem.

As a consequence, the crucial issue in the aftermath of the various attacks and al-Zarqawi's appalling videos was not what was said in Whitehall or the White House but what was said in the kebab houses, the souks, the homes, the mosques and the offices in the Islamic world. Did people see the violence as legitimate? Had they heeded the militants' call to arms or had they turned on them with disgust, hate and fear? What effect had the war in Iraq had? If the key to victory in the 'War on Terror' was winning the 'hearts and minds' of the world's Muslims, if this was militant Islam's 'centre of gravity', then this would determine how safe we would all be in the years to come. In late 2003 and 2004, between trips to Iraq, I had travelled to Kashmir, to Afghanistan and to the Far East looking for answers to these critical questions.

The conflict in Kashmir is one of the world's ugliest wars set in one of the planet's most beautiful places. Its roots lie in the chaos of the end of the British rule in south Asia when, forced to decide between accession to India or Pakistan, the Hindu maharajah of the mountain state, with Pakistani forces closing on his palace, chose the former. With a stroke of a pen, he made his largely Muslim subjects citizens of the secular but predominantly Hindu India. For the next five or so decades Islamabad and Delhi fought intermittently over the divided state, the most recent conflict being the one that I had witnessed at firsthand in 1999 as a guest of the Pakistani troops positioned on the other side of the high mountains that I could see along the western skyline out of my hotel window in Kashmir's capital Srinagar.

In 1988, following rigged elections, the Kashmiris had risen up against what they felt was discriminatory and heavy-handed rule from Delhi. Their anger had been voiced in a variety of ways, first in the language of Third World liberation movements, assorted leftists and the democracy movements of eastern Europe and then, when their claims were rejected and their activism brutally repressed, in the language of political Islam. Soon the spearhead of militant movement in Kashmir was ultra-radical religious groups, many of whose cadres were veterans of the war against the Soviets in Afghanistan and who were often funded and assisted by the secret services of neighbouring Pakistan. Their agenda was dogmatic, rigorous, extremely violent and utterly alien to the tolerant, moderate, Sufi-influenced Islam of most of the Kashmiris. Through the 1990s it was these groups who led a vicious guerrilla war against Delhi's security forces.

When I visited in the autumn of 2003, Kashmir was finely balanced between progress towards peace and plunging back into the horror of previous years. Around 700 civilians, 500 Indian security men and at least 1,000 militants had been killed in the first eight months of the year. Yet the late summer had brought a tentative truce, hints of political concessions from all parties and a small but noticeable increase in local economic activity. For the first time in a long while, some were hopeful.

For a week I drove around 'the valley', as the heartland of Indian Kashmir is known. It was as beautiful as everyone had said and the war was every bit as ugly. The horizon in every direction was a mass of sharp white-topped peaks which, etched against the clear blue autumnal sky, were reflected with astonishing clarity in the ponds and rivers and in the famous Lake Dal outside Srinagar itself. The main roads were full of traffic, bullock carts, overloaded trucks and buses and Indian army convoys, long series of blunt-nosed armoured personnel carriers in lines six feet apart like chains of oxen, crawling along the pitted and dusty tarmac and gravel. The war was not obvious. A beautiful glade of whip-thin trees with yellowing leaves would partially obscure a machine-gun post. The smoke damage around the windows of a burned-out house could easily be mistaken for traditional wooden carved decoration from a passing car. It was impossible to tell if the emptiness of Srinagar's streets in the evening was due to fear, the cold or the fact that it was Ramadan. When I arrived on the scene of a grenade attack on a post office just half an hour after it had taken place, traffic was already circulating normally and only the bloodstains on the ground indicated anything abnormal. The massive psychological trauma suffered by the population, described to me by a passionate young doctor working for an aid agency, was, of course, invisible.

Predictably nobody wanted to talk about 'the troubles'. Or if they did, they had clear agendas. To the Indian police chief who hosted dinner for me in his official residence, the insurgents were 99 per cent 'foreign'. The militants themselves claimed, equally predictably, that their fight was 99 per cent Kashmiri. 'We have been pushed to the wall and are fighting back against oppression,' an anodyne statement read to me over the telephone by one of the main groups said. As ever, half the war was being fought out in half- and quarter-truths, in tired platitudes and in the media.

But it was clear that September 11, the 'War on Terror' and the war in Iraq had had a significant impact locally. A doctor in the front-line town of Sopore spoke to me about the 'Crusader–Zionist–Hindu alliance', a good example of how the 'al-Qaeda' discourse could be bastardized to fit any local situation and a comment that he would have been very unlikely to have made before 2001. In the village of Bandipur I heard that seventy local young men had headed across the mountains into Pakistani Kashmir to get training and weapons over the summer, twice as many as the previous year. On the walls of one police station, after a long lecture from an Indian officer about the 'foreign' nature of the insurgency, I saw two dozen wanted posters, all of which were for locals, and though the official figures showing that 650 of the 1,000 militants killed that year were Pakistani or Afghan were probably accurate, they ignored the thousands of people who provided support for insurgents once they were inside 'the valley' but did not take part in combat operations. Then there were suicide attacks, unheard of among the Kashmiris themselves hitherto and evidence that the tactics as well as the language and ideas of 'al-Qaedaism' were spreading. In Afghanistan, Pakistan, Uzbekistan and elsewhere, young people were turning themselves into weapons, and often killing dozens of civilians too, in a way that was entirely new.

But it was too easy to jump to the conclusion that Kashmir was suddenly ablaze with a new radicalism. Despite a call for a boycott and the killing of political workers by the militants, more than 50 per cent of those eligible had voted in local elections in Kashmir a month or so before I arrived. In the aftermath of the grenade attack on the post office in Srinagar, the witnesses I interviewed were angry and bitter not at the security forces, but at those who carried out the attack. I spent an afternoon with a local lawyer who campaigned on behalf of victims of the brutality of the Indian security forces. He told me that there had been 119 'disappearances' in the previous three months. Sometimes the militants, who killed those they suspected of being insufficiently sympathetic to their cause, were to blame. In most cases, however, the Indian army and paramilitaries were the prime suspects. The lawyer led me through narrow streets behind a packed bazaar in Srinagar to a small brick house with basic furnishing and bad plumbing where a group of relatives of the 'disappeared' were meeting. The air was thick with the smell of sewage. Many of the women sitting on cushions on the floor, each in her best shalwar kameez, were 'half-widows', so called because their husbands had disappeared but had not been declared dead. As they could not remarry, they were caught in a social and legal limbo. Others knew exactly what had happened to their spouses or relatives, having seen them shot or battered to death in front of them. One had seen her brother bundled into a van by security men who then denied any knowledge of him. After ten years of campaigning, the Indian government had offered her compensation. 'I don't want money, I don't want vengeance, I don't want any more violence,' she told me, pulling her white veil closer around her face with one hand while plucking at the emerald green hem of her long shirt with the other. 'I want my brother back.'

On my last day in Srinagar I went to see a veteran politician and campaigner who, despite indirect links to armed groups, was apparently a key proponent of a moderate Islamist strategy in Kashmir. He believed, he told me, that 'if secular ideas and all other systems fail to provide peace, prosperity and respect for human values and morals and all the other expectations that all people everywhere have of life then people will be bound to search for another system', and that 'as Islam is the only system that can give you these things, they will turn to Islam'. I had heard such words many times before and what interested me more was an argument between two of his party officials. Earlier I had noticed one, who wore a shalwar kameez and a beard, shake his head violently when his leader had denounced bin Laden as a 'terrorist' whose actions were 'un-Islamic'. 'Anyone fighting secularism, communism, capitalism and these -isms is a freedom fighter, a mujahed,' the official told me. But a colleague, clean shaven and wearing a suit, disagreed. 'Muslims have lost a lot because of extremism,' he said. 'We need education, not extremism. The Americans have education and because of that they are ruling the world. The West is superior to the Muslim world because of its hard work and effort. That effort is not being made in the Islamic world. I think that if Osama bin Laden had invested all his money in technical institutions and universities and colleges it would have been better for the ummah.' Near by was the extensive 'martyrs' graveyard' where the mujahideen were buried. It was unmarked but well maintained and, though empty of mourners, the two small joined cemeteries were crowded with graves. I counted sixty-two headstones. Most marked the tombs of Pakistanis but, working my way down the haphazard lines, I found the names of a Sudanese fighter, several Afghans, a dozen or so Kashmiris and the grave of 'Abdullah Bhai, also known as Aruf Bilal, from Birmingham, UK'. An inscription on the grave read: 'Those who died on the path of Allah are not dead so do not call them such. They are martyrs and so alive.' Bilal had apparently been killed on 30 December 2000, 'in a blast when fighting security forces'. I wondered for a moment what had taken a young British man from the Midlands to an ambush in midwinter in the foothills of the Himalaya.

From Kashmir I headed, via Delhi, to Afghanistan. On the way I visited a prison where the Indian authorities kept captured militants and I spent a couple of days listening to their life stories. Most were familiar. Abdul Latif, a 37-year-old Pakistani from Karachi, was typical. He had become involved in radical Islam when at university studying sciences. It was at the time when Benazir Bhutto's government was in charge of Pakistan. 'Secular politics were corrupt,' he told me, not inaccurately. His story was similar to many, many others that I had heard. After joining a moderate Islamic group he had been targeted by a more radical organization; the extremists' propaganda had convinced him and he had subsequently fought in Afghanistan and Kashmir. He had been captured a few years previously. Surprisingly, he too stressed the importance of education to 'catch up' with a West committed to 'the impoverishment and repression of Muslims'. 'A good Muslim should be an Islamic scholar, a mujahed and, simultaneously, a computer engineer or a doctor.' The triumph of Islam was inevitable as the communist system had failed and now the capitalist system was failing too, he said. Of course, the Jews ran the world and the Americans were Crusaders committed to global domination. He had been in prison for years and was likely to be locked up for the rest of his life. 'I regret nothing and will do it all again if they let me out.'

Though much of what he told me was fairly predictable, two things that Abdul Latif had said intrigued me. First, though he saw modernization, globalization, Westernization and 'neo-imperialism' as virtually synonymous, he insisted on the importance of modern technology and of education to 'catch up' with 'the West'. This seemed to me to confirm that he and his like were not usually pure reactionaries but were trying to reconcile 'modernity' with their own cultures and values and interests. They did not want to turn the clock back but wanted to be in control as the clock went forward and it was abundantly clear that this process was somehow intimately linked to the generation of violence. Second, I was struck by the many similarities between Abdul Latif's thought and radical secular left-wing ideologies. The standard profile of leaders of Islamic radical movements – usually men between the ages of 18 and 35, often from middle-class families and often educated to graduate level – was very close to that of many left-wing radical activists. So was their interest in 'propaganda by deed' and the radicalization of the masses through spectacular violence. The very concept of a small number of enlightened men struggling to raise the people against a tyrannical power, though very much a part of Islamic religious thinking and culture over centuries, also clearly shared much with the Leninist concept of the revolutionary 'avant-garde'. Marxism and its offshoots offered, like radical Islam, a dogmatic explanation of the evils of the world and an equally dogmatic programme that would lead to their apparent solution. Marxists saw history in terms of an inevitable dialectic, consulted and selectively cited key and immutable texts and so, of course, did men like bin Laden. Left-wing groups and systems of government had their rituals, their languages, their semi-godlike individual leaders, their mythologized history, their hierarchies, their globally applicable identities that ignored national boundaries and, of course, their martyrs. So, plainly, did the Islamic militants. Then there were the more obvious direct links. Many of the radical Muslim groups set up in the 1970s and 1980s made no secret of the fact that they had learned their tactics and organization from the left and a surprising number of Islamic militants had actually flirted with left-wing activism before becoming involved in religious radical movements. There was also the anti-Semitism that marked much left-wing and all radical Islamic thought. Notwithstanding the many differences – such as attitudes to women – the coincidences were striking and clearly suggested similarities in the function that such packages of ideas performed for individuals and groups. I wondered how many of the militants I had interviewed might have been radical left-wing activists if the collapse of the Soviet bloc and the triumph of Western, liberal, democratic free-market capitalism had not discredited communism, leaving them with no other ideology or language of opposition to the West beyond that of radical Islam.

There was much too that radical Islamic militants, though they would undoubtedly have denied it, shared with ultra-right-wing ideologies, particularly those that had gripped half of the population of Europe in the middle of the twentieth century. There were parallels in terms of the social groups from which the leaders were drawn, there was the common anti-Semitism and the similar traditions of martyrdom. Then there was also the snarling association of modernity with mediocrity or degeneracy, an insistence on morality and racial or religious purity, an appeal to a mythic past imagined as a perfect era of stability and firm values. In addition, Islamic and radical right-wingers shared a strong sense of being rooted in a real or imagined space and territory, a distrust of urban environments coupled with a glorification of rural ones and a powerful radicalizing quasi-millenarian sense of threat and impending doom. There was also the obvious common appeal to a higher authority, whether that be God, Hitler, 'the Party' or a mixture of all three, and the shared emphasis on demagogic, charismatic leaders drawn from outside the standard political and elite classes. All contributed, in secular right-wing and in radical Islamic activism (and indeed in many of the other fundamentalisms that were attracting so many in the late twentieth and early twenty-first century), to a powerful and convincing argument that it was the responsibility of every individual (or at least every adult male) to act and act quickly in defence of his community and way of life.

One element common to both left- and right-wing ideologies seemed to me to be particularly important. Left-wing ideologies had taken hold in western and central Europe and then, slightly later, in eastern Europe, at times of massive social change when everything that was certain and reassuring was dissolving in the face of massive industrialization – and a wave of globalization – coupled with very rapid technological advance. Right-wing ideologies had been particularly popular, a few decades later, among the swathes of people who felt themselves as suffering in, or at least not benefiting from, the new order of 'the modern world'. This all seemed to suggest that contemporary radical 'Islamic' militancy might share more than just structure and language with more secular ideologies. Rather than being rooted in 'Islam' it might, at least in part, be a product of very major shifts on a worldwide scale that had provoked a sense of alienation and insecurity and a consequent yearning for certainty and clarity among hundreds of millions of people as well as, crucially, a simultaneous sense of grievance and anger at what was perceived to be the 'unjust' nature of the distribution of power and economic resources in the contemporary world. The violence was an attempt to assert control. If radical left-wing thought was a product of the massive changes in the late nineteenth century and right-wing extremism a consequence of the political, social and cultural instability of the early and middle decades of the twentieth, then radical

Islam, as well as the resurgent fundamentalisms elsewhere across the globe, might thus be a function of the inherent instability, both creative and destructive, of our own era.

This was an interesting but not particularly consoling line of thought. It had taken the best part of a century, significant concessions and the eventual collapse of the Soviet Union to reduce all the various strains of radical left-wing violence to the relatively minimal nuisance they were by the last decade of the millennium, and even then no one could be certain they had gone for ever. The hard right, ranging from radical conservatism through to outright neo-Nazism, still had the potential to cause very real problems despite the horrors of the past. What, I wondered, would be the timeline on the demise of radical Islam?

I flew from Delhi to Kabul on an Afghan Airways plane. The fact that there was a national carrier providing air links to the outside world was a mark of how far Afghanistan had come since my last visit a year or so previously. I had dinner with Ekram in a new kebab restaurant and though he complained about the cost of living and moaned about how 'the Tajiks' were dominating the government, I knew that he was actually very happy with how things were going. So were most people, it seemed. A new constitution was being drafted, the currency was stable and though the president, Hamid Karzai, might have been derisorily referred to as 'the mayor of Kabul', so limited was his apparent authority, he was generally popular. The biggest problem facing the new government appeared to be opium cultivation. The claims one minister's aide made to me regarding the risk of Afghanistan turning into a 'narco-state' were not exaggerated. There was also a continuing low-level insurgency concentrated where the drugs were in the east and southeast of the country but its impact on Kabul was minimal. The insurgents were sufficiently active, however, to render the newly resurfaced road to Kandahar too dangerous to drive. So I booked a seat on the first public and commercial flight from the capital to the city for over a decade instead.

A lot had changed in Kandahar and simultaneously almost

nothing. The roads were covered with slick new black tar; there were several internet cafés and a functioning mobile phone network; the TV in my hotel room received CNN, BBC World, Star Sports, the National Geographic channel and a panoply of Indian films and music videos; there were no checkpoints and, especially given that I had arrived on a Friday lunchtime, a lot of activity. There were people moving in the streets, the bazaars of the old town were busy, there was plenty of traffic and the torpor that had characterized the city on my previous visits had gone. Around the outskirts, big new private villas were being built with the profits of the trade, licit and illicit, that now centred on the city. There was even a woman policeman who, for a minuscule salary, had the thankless task of trying to resolve what she called 'family clashes'. These usually involved, she said, 'a boy and a girl becoming friends and then running away together'. Since the end of the Taliban rule, such problems had apparently become very common. In the city's hospital I found a ward full of starving children. On one peeling wall someone had taped a badly handwritten sign reading, with unconscious pathos, 'Therapoetic Feeding Centre'.

I spent several days interviewing local officials, talking to captured militants, visiting people I had met several years earlier. It rapidly became clear that the rough remnant of the Taliban who were still active were restricted to hit-and-run strikes on remote government offices, laying mines for American convoys and the occasionally more ambitious bomb or assassination attempt. Though that was enough to render many roads risky for foreigners, the ability of the 'neo-Taliban' genuinely to destabilize the country seemed limited. Much of their support came from across the border in the tribal lands of Pakistan where bin Laden and al-Zawahiri were hiding – though there was apparently little contact between 'the Arabs' and their erstwhile hosts. I interviewed one militant in Kandahar prison. He was a pitiful figure who had joined up to fight 'the occupation by the Crusader–Zionist alliance' and because he had been told it was his religious duty. He had also needed the money he had heard he might earn from the Taliban commanders.

Badly trained and badly equipped, he had been captured on his first operation.

Sangesar, the village where the Taliban had started in 1994, lay twenty miles southwest of Kandahar. I reasoned that if people there were not supportive of the movement then nobody would be. I contacted the warlord who ran the area, who assured me that it was safe, so with a translator, a young local student called Mansoor, I drove out of the city along the pitted concrete road that led west towards Herat before turning off south into the desert. We drove along sand roads between empty dry fields that were little more than squares of dust edged by low stunted trees. Opium, I remembered, needed only a fraction of the water of other crops and soon I could see the distinctive poppy stems in several plots set back a little from the track. After twenty minutes we came to the outskirts of the village itself, where we stopped by a house that had been destroyed by an American rocket during the war. It had belonged to Mullah Omar, the Taliban's still fugitive leader. He had last been spotted on a motorbike in the badlands to the south. I got out and walked with Mansoor through the empty streets.

The village mosque was a small single-storey building with a minaret consisting of a metal pole with a loudspeaker tied to the top, set in a small compound about fifty-feet square with low walls and a twisted tree in one corner. Half a dozen men were sitting in the tree's paltry shade. One was the local mullah. It was time for the call to prayer and the priest, a very young man with a wide mouth in a round, dark brown face who wore a filthy shalwar kameez and a very large creased black turban, fiddled with an old amplifier powered by a car battery before clearing his throat with an emphysemic cough and tunelessly singing out the first words of the *adhan*: '*Allahu akbar*, God is great, I bear witness that there is no God but Allah . . .' His harsh Arabic clattered out over the village, each syllable like a ladle rattled in a saucepan. I thought of my impromptu lesson in Muslim theology more than five years earlier, sitting by the broken-down car on the road from Kabul to Kandahar a hundred or so miles north, listening to my translator explaining the basics of Islam. In those days, the incumbent cleric at the mosque in Sangesar had been the nominal leader of Afghanistan. After prayers I asked the mullah where the rest of the villagers were. 'In the fields, in the city, in Pakistan, at home,' he said and shrugged.

'Is it all right if I ask some political questions?' I asked.

'Like what?'

'Like what the problems are here?'

A pause.

'Water is the biggest problem here and there are roads to be built.'

Another man, squatting near by with a brown blanket over his shoulders and huge, callused hands like spades, nodded. 'It is OK with the new government but there are still problems,' he said.

'Every day people are killed by criminals and bad people. The Taliban brought a lot of peace here. When we see the present circumstances we think it was better then. The US said they would come and stabilize us but they haven't done.'

Another worshipper quickly broke in and I could not tell if he was trying to stop the other telling the truth or merely wanted to add something. 'But we are grateful for the Americans for coming with their forces, otherwise there would have been a civil war here,' he said. 'The real problem is the price of oil. It has trebled. We need oil for the water pumps for the fields. If we don't cultivate opium we could not survive.'

'Isn't opium *haram*, forbidden in Islam?' I asked.

They shrugged and looked at the mullah. He shrugged.

'What else can we do?'

'What about bin Laden?' I asked.

An older man spoke.

'According to Islam, bin Laden is a mujahed. But I think he has brought big problems to Afghanistan. If he had stayed in his own country to do what he has done it would have been better.'

'And Mullah Omar and the Taliban?'

'Mullah Omar was a just a simple student of Islam who acted because of the problems at the time as a good Muslim should. Then people convinced him to be their leader because of the problems we were facing here. We still have problems but I don't think the Taliban can solve them.'

The speaker said his name was Mera Ahmed Torchi and that he was 40 years old.

'We are poor here because we have had thirty years of war, drought and lack of education. The Soviets destroyed all the orchards and the irrigation and no one has rebuilt anything,' he added.

'What about Iraq?'

'It is bad that there are some in the West who want to oppress all Muslims and take their oil but Iraq is a very long way from here.'

'What did the villagers want more than anything else?' I asked. The question prompted a long discussion. Then Torchi turned to me.

'A well,' he said. 'We want a well. Can you get us one?'

I got back from my trip to Kashmir and Afghanistan in early December 2003 and covered events in Iraq for most of the next six months. Then, in July 2004, I set off again, this time to Thailand to investigate a suddenly resurgent militancy in the Buddhist state's southern Muslim provinces. Working amid the emerald green rubber plantations and hills and the stunning beaches in the Far East was a welcome change after the arid landscapes where I had spent much of the previous years, even if the subject matter was as grim as ever. It was the rainy season and the paddy fields were full to overflowing and the sight of the mosques among the palm trees and the creepers and the herds of broad-headed oxen with ridged horns was a useful reminder that the conflation of 'the Muslim world' with the Arab world or even the Middle East was a mistake. The biggest single Islamic country was, after all, Indonesia with a population of 230 million, ten times that of Iraq. In fact, considering the size of the Muslim community in the Far East, the classic signifiers of the ummah should have been minarets not above the desert but above a rice plantation.

From the scruffy local capital of Pattani I drove up to a village in the hills called Suso. It was a scattering of wooden and concrete shacks set back from a good road lined by very tall coconut palms.

There was a large concrete government school and a smallish mosque in brick and wood that was being renovated. Most of Suso's thousand or so inhabitants worked on the local rubber plantations and a government-run programme provided a small income for those women with the time and energy to do some needlework in the evenings. There was a small district headquarters staffed by Buddhist Thais from Bangkok. When I visited, there was one empty desk. The local functionary who had worked at it had been shot by militants a few days earlier and his pencils and pens and papers still lay neatly arranged on its surface.

There was little out of the ordinary about Suso and the people who lived there except for one salient fact. The village's football team had been almost entirely wiped out in an attack on a police post a few weeks before. Armed only with knives, the players, some of whom had joined the side only a few months before, had charged security forces armed with M16 automatic rifles. Nineteen young men, the youngest 17, the oldest 32, had died. In a small bamboo hut opposite the village's dusty playing field which had served as the team's club room, their coach showed me a picture of the players posing in neat strip, lined up in two rows and with balls at their feet. His brother, killed in the attack, was among them. All the men were smiling. The coach could not explain what had happened. A few of the players had gone to a Saudi-funded religious school near by, he said, but none of the others had been particularly religious. He shook his head, shrugged, rubbed his eyes. 'It was bad people who came from outside,' he said finally. 'They were brainwashed.'

The situation in southern Thailand was extraordinarily complex. A whole range of subtle local ethnic, religious, cultural and political factors underlay the violence and a huge number of different actors were involved in various ways. Very few people really knew what was at the root of the trouble and even fewer were prepared to say. When a series of bombs exploded outside a row of nightclubs, authorities blamed gangs of racketeers, then groups of Islamic militants, then groups of the latter hired by the former. Even when it was clear that the attacks were indeed the work of young religiously inspired men, it was difficult to see where the influence of local customs stopped and that of faith, let alone new international jihadi ideologies, began. The Suso football team had apparently sprinkled dust blessed by a cleric over roads in the belief that it would stop pursuit, a tactic that was hardly standard 'al-Qaeda' modus operandi. It was also hard to separate the ethnic from the religious. Thailand's Muslims were predominantly of Malay descent and in many ways should have been part of neighbouring Muslim-majority Malaysia. I was shown two notes that had been pinned to the body of a slaughtered monk. 'Stop the oppression of Muslims', said one. 'Stop the oppression of Malays', said the other. In the mind of the killers at least, the two slogans appeared interchangeable.

Yet, despite the opacity of the conflict, the week or so I spent in southern Thailand helped crystallize my thinking on several important points. I found that the insurgency which had suddenly flared up after September 11 in the predominantly Buddhist state's three southernmost provinces, like so many in southwest Asia or the core Middle Eastern Arab states, actually had long historical roots. It had started around a century before as an 'Islamic resistance' movement fighting the Thai annexation of what had once been the independent and wealthy Muslim sultanate of Pattani. It had then mutated into a left-wing liberation movement with a quasi-Marxist ideology. The return to a more Islamic ideology in recent years was thus just the latest in a series of manifestations of a long-running violent activism. There were parallels here with a variety of other insurgencies in the region, such as in the Philippines, and further afield in southwest and central Asia and the core countries of the Middle East. This seemed to confirm my idea that it is the grievance that comes first and is voiced within whatever discourse is available and makes sense at the time. Where Islam is not available, as the Maoist rebels in Hindu and Buddhist Nepal showed, an alternative is often found.

One interesting ingredient in the complex soup that was the insurgency in southern Thailand was that very few people had satellite televisions so the local population were not exposed to images from Israel–Palestine, bin Laden's statements or the pictures coming out of Iraq, and though I spoke to one Saudi Arabian-educated cleric who spouted the normal bile about Jews and the West's designs on the 'lands of Islam', the new globalized radical language of militants elsewhere was not yet a part of general conversation. This meant there was no 'al-Jazeera effect' and may have explained why the insurgents' activity and rare communications seemed so parochial and local. It certainly seemed very unlikely that any international super-terrorist organization, or even some kind of local 'subsidiary' or 'franchised' group, was somehow invisibly orchestrating the violence. What there were, however, were familiar factors from many other places where there had been or continued to be Muslim insurgencies – such as a long-standing local tradition of resistance and independence, an easily mythologized 'glorious past' and a profound resentment of rule by a distant ethnically and religiously different government as well as a lack of confidence in the local judiciary or in fairly shaky democratic structures. The Thai government's almost deliberately brutal and repressive counter-terrorism policy and close relations with America did not help either. All this had undoubtedly helped a few individuals to sell the protean, dynamic and changing package that was radical Islamic militancy to a small minority of young men.

Travelling in southern Thailand also reminded me of the degree to which religion is only one component in the messy reality of living people's identities. Though 80 per cent of the local population were indeed Muslims they had far more in common with local non-Muslims than they had with any of the people I had spent so much time with in Iraq, Pakistan, Afghanistan or the Maghreb. One evening I sat in a cheap café with a book I was reviewing that spoke repeatedly of 'Muslims' as a single homogeneous bloc who 'loved Allah'. I looked around me. In the café there were Buddhist Thais and Muslim Thais. They shared the same taste for very hot curried soups, the same relatively conservative customs and, excepting a headscarf for some of the women and a small cap for some of the men, the same clothes. They could also communicate easily and, judging by the conversation and the posters on the wall, shared a common affection for Manchester United Football Club. All my various friends from Algeria to Afghanistan would have found the strongest spiced curries as hard to eat as I did, the local clothes as alien and the local tongue as difficult to understand. They would have been as unenthusiastic about Manchester United as I was as well.

Then, of course, there was the variety within the Muslim community. As in Malaysia just to the south and, of course, in Indonesia, which I had visited on a number of occasions, in Thailand I had seen a huge and complex range of ways of 'being a Muslim'. In Indonesia, local Islamic practice was heavily influenced by Hinduism and animism and was often so moderate as to be barely recognizable to even a less than observant Saudi Arabian. There, some of those labelled 'Muslims' were deeply devout, others saw their faith more as part of their cultural heritage and some saw it as part of their ethnicity; most gave it little thought unless they were pressed somehow to consider what that particular element of their identity meant. Only in Aceh, on the northern tip of Sumatra, where local people felt themselves to be exploited by a quasi-colonial Javanese-based elite and had experienced centuries of trade with and influence of the Middle East, were practices more conservative. There was an equal diversity in Thailand, as there was in every Muslim country heading west from Bangladesh to Morocco. How anyone, particularly a Western author, could have the temerity to generalize in entirely unqualified terms about 1.3 billion people across half the planet of a dozen different racial and several score different national backgrounds in a way that would have been utterly laughable, and indeed quite offensive, if they had been referring to 'Christians' or even the world's relatively small Jewish population, escaped me.

I got back from Thailand and set off for Iraq and Najaf almost immediately. Then came the abduction of Bigley and al-Zarqawi's video and the crucial questions of who was winning the 'battle for hearts and minds' in the Islamic world moved to centre stage once again. This time, unlike two years before, I felt I had some possible answers.

While travelling over the previous eighteen months I had undoubtedly found evidence of an enhanced level of political awareness, anger and resentment throughout 'the Islamic world'. Much of this was expressed in radical and sometimes violent language rooted in a relatively new globalized vision of Islamic identity that was based, at least in part, in an idea of an epic and eternal struggle against the West. An integral part of the construction of this new identity was the broad sense that it was time for believers to 'think global, act local'. Modern communications, exploited by militant groups and hardline preachers, had made the ummah a more practically realistic idea than ever before and deaths in the Gaza Strip or in Iraq were thus felt personally in an unprecedented way. In addition, as the successive bomb attacks showed, there were many more active militants than there had been five years, or certainly a decade, previously. Hundreds, for example, were heading to Iraq to fight and, though the role of such volunteers was far more limited than the British and the American governments claimed, their presence was evidence of a significant and new radicalization. In addition, though many insurgencies around the world had been active one way or another since the days of the first wave of Western colonial expansion into the Islamic world in the eighteenth and nineteenth centuries, a significant number had become more bitter and more violent since 2001. In addition, 'martyrdom' had been embedded in everyday language and, increasingly, in acts and words in many Muslim communities across the world in a very new and very worrying way. In broad terms, even among moderates, the political atmosphere almost everywhere in the Islamic world was more febrile and agitated than at any time since the early seventies. All of this was very bad news.

Yet – and this was absolutely critical – my travels had shown me that none of these developments should be mistaken for evidence of a broader trend towards a mass uprising among the world's Muslims. The videos of Bigley and, a few weeks later, of an abducted aid worker from Britain called Margaret Hassan, provoked a significant and noticeable backlash in the Islamic world, the opposite of the effect intended by the hostage takers. Polls in the spring of 2005 confirmed my perceptions showing that, though anti-Americanism, anti-Zionism and anti-Semitism remained as strong as ever, support for bin Laden and al-Zarqawi and such men was actually dropping around the Middle East, especially in countries that had been exposed to the brutality of the militants or suffered the impact of the conflicts they had provoked. In places where Islamic parties offered hope of replacing corrupt regimes with a competent and honest alternative, such as in Egypt and Palestine, Islamist ideologies remained strong, but where governments were more or less democratic and more or less capable of providing basic services, such as in Indonesia and Malaysia, they completely failed to win mass support. There, hundreds of millions of people had taken a long look at the hardline radicals' policies, programmes and tactics and rejected them. The cumulative importance of all these events could be exaggerated but I felt they pointed towards a powerful underlying truth.

In Algeria, militant violence in the early 1990s had provoked a reaction from the authorities that had led into a spiral of increasing brutality, decreasing popular support, increasingly effective security action, significant concessions from the state and the eventual end of the insurgency. Something similar had happened in Egypt in the mid-1990s. Though the angry, disaffected, alienated, scared, frustrated or simply disillusioned might have gravitated to the Islamic militant camp, the crucial broad popular support necessary to sustain any insurgency had disappeared rapidly when the reality of what conservative religious rule would actually entail – and the extent of the violence that a genuine attempt to impose it would involve – became clear. It looked to me that the contemporary Islamic militant movement was following or might soon follow the same trajectory but merely on a global rather than a national scale. There had been the initial success of the attacks of September 11. The core leadership of the 'global jihadi movement' had certainly been subsequently degraded by military and security action. The violence of men like al-Zarqawi and the Madrid bombers was evidence of an increasing fragmentation strategically and tactically. There was certainly an increasing number of 'indiscriminate' attacks on targets that had little symbolic or real value which were apparently provoking a nascent reaction against the militants. Yet how long the global, contemporary Islamic militancy would take to follow the trajectory outlined by so many previous, more local insurgencies was unclear. Much depended on the reaction of 'the West' and much, of course, on the world's Muslims. And, given that 100,000 or more had died in Algeria and tens of thousands in Egypt and elsewhere, it was hard to say how many would die along the way either.

Yet I did know that no matter where I had travelled in the years following the 9/11 attacks, from Indonesia to the Maghreb via Malaysia, Thailand, India (the 140-million-strong Muslim population of which remained resolutely moderate), Pakistan, Afghanistan, Qatar, Iraq, Jordan, Syria, Israel–Palestine, Lebanon and Turkey, I had never met with any direct, personal hostility. Even in Iraq I was still always confident that the vast majority of people would not harm me. The truth was that, despite the terrible abuses at Abu Ghraib and Guantanamo Bay, despite the constant disappointments of everyday life, despite the deaths of 30,000 civilians in Iraq, despite the frustration of so many aspirations and hopes, despite the best efforts of men like bin Laden and al-Zawahiri and al-Zarqawi, despite the incompetent, corrupt, sclerotic dynastic rulers still clinging to power everywhere, despite the aggressive, warmongering rhetoric on every side, despite the massive broadcasting of a message of hate, prejudice and violence, despite it all, the ordinary people of the Islamic world, those caught in the crossfire, those whose voices were so often drowned out by shouting and gunfire, those in the middle, had not been won over by the radicals. The centre had held. Yes, some were angry; yes, others were resentful; yes, a few had turned to militancy and, without doubt, many more would turn to militancy in the coming years. But when bin Laden had said 'the awakening had started' he had believed that his spectacular acts of violence would spark a vast surge of support throughout the Islamic world. And he had been wrong.

Conclusion: London and Pakistan

And then, on 7 July 2005, four bombs exploded in central London, three on underground trains and a fourth on a bus. Fifty-two people were killed and over 700 injured. The scenes that I had so often watched unfolding somewhere else were now taking place on my own doorstep. The sirens, the crowds, the injured, the exhausted rescue workers, the TV satellite trucks, the scorch marks on the walls, the blast patterns in the road, the reports of casualties with the typically low early count, the sudden surge in the numbers and then the settling back to a single blank black statistic were all horribly familiar. But then there were the patient queues at the red telephone boxes, the crowds outside the pubs in the sunshine, the instant dark humour and the blue and white police tape outside Tube stations that I had used all my life. Like many, I walked a lot in London in the first days after the attack, partly because much of the Tube network was shut, partly because the weather was beautiful, partly because I did not like being underground in the tunnels and partly because I wanted to reassure myself that everything was actually the same as it had always been.

The nascent optimism I had been feeling vanished the instant I heard about the blasts. I was profoundly saddened too. And, of course, extremely angry. I was angry at the ridiculous statement, repeated again and again by politicians and 'community leaders' alike, that 'Islam is a religion of peace'. In fact, as I had learned on the ground, any faith is what its believers make of it and Islam had resources that could be utilized to justify appalling brutality as well as to encourage mercy and tolerance. Something terrible had happened and slogans were not going to help make sense of it or stop it happening again. I was also angry at the British government's stubborn and utterly unjustified pretence that there was no link between the attack and their policy in Iraq. Britain had indeed been a target for terrorism before the war in Iraq, as the government claimed, but the UK had become a far more likely target as a result of its close support for the United States and the policy of the Bush administration. Scores of interviews with militants, as well as plain common sense, had taught me this and to see supposedly responsible cabinet ministers stating otherwise was extremely depressing. But most of all I was angry at the bombers. I was angry at them because of what they had done, because they would never see the pictures that no newspaper printed of dismembered corpses in Tavistock Square, because they would never hear a fireman describing working amid the shredded limbs and scorched skin in the subterranean charnel house that was the wreckage of the trains, and I was angry at them because they would never realize what it actually meant to kill and maim and leave hundreds of grieving parents and spouses and children. And finally, I was angry because the bombings seemed, even after years of studying modern Muslim radicalism, completely incomprehensible. Of course I knew the arguments, the ones that I had heard on the Gaza Strip and in the Khyber Pass and dozens of times since, and I knew the twisted logic which might have convinced someone that a city's transport network was a legitimate target but, when I was confronted with the reality of an attack in the place where I had grown up and lived, I found it almost impossible to understand what had been going through the minds of the bombers when they had detonated their devices.

Those behind the attacks turned out to be four young men, all British citizens, three born in the UK of Pakistani parents, the fourth born in Jamaica and recently converted to Islam. There did not appear to be a mastermind who had recruited the bombers, run the cell and then fled the country, nor was there evidence of any connection to Osama bin Laden or anyone close to him. It was one of the first examples of a group of citizens born in a Western country launching an attack on their homeland in the name of Islam. The cell was, apparently, entirely 'home grown', vindicating my theory that the radical ideology that had been spreading since the late 1990s did not need organizations, camps or leaders to move people to action, that if there was any threat from Islamic militancy to the UK it came from within. I knew from Iraq and elsewhere that the arithmetic of terrorism meant that only a small shift in general radicalization would create a sufficient number of people prepared to commit enough violence to cause serious harm. That shift, as I and others had predicted, had happened.

Yet I had little reason to be pleased with my analysis. During the year preceding the London attack I had become increasingly convinced that the menace from radical Islam within the UK, notwithstanding the radicalizing effect of the war in Iraq, had been exaggerated. This conclusion owed a lot to the series of sensational claims of terrorist activity made by the British police and government, many of which had proved completely unfounded, and to my own concern that the general scaremongering risked promoting an extremely dangerous general anxiety. Also, being publicly committed to a particular argument, I naturally wanted to be proved right. Though I still felt that the climate of acute fear that had prevailed before the attack was unjustified, and though I had always said that an attack of some sort was inevitable, I had certainly misjudged the level of the threat.

The investigation into the bombings quickly established that at least two of the bombers had visited Pakistan in the year before the bombing. The leader of the group, a 30-year-old special-needs teacher from near Leeds called Mohammed Sidique Khan, had apparently spent time in or around the city of Lahore, fifteen miles from the Indian border. So, exactly seven days after the bombings, I found myself standing, slightly bewildered, in an immigration queue at Islamabad airport at 5 a.m. watching, through the dirty windows of the terminal, men with shotguns cycling down the runways looking for stray birds to shoot. I had watched the same scene, I remembered, when I had arrived in the country to live there seven years before.

It was bizarre to be back in Pakistan. I had not visited the country for several years and, in the aftermath of the London attack, was wary of my own reactions as much of those of the people around me. The anger I had felt in the immediate aftermath of the bombings was still there and I was unsure whether I could, should or even wanted to fight it. I checked in with some old contacts in Islamabad, learned very little, made a few calls, learned less, hired a car and headed east towards Lahore. Pakistan did not appear to have changed very much. The streets of the roadside towns were still crowded with men wearing white, blue or grey shalwar kameez. The carriageway itself was still choked with packed buses covered in mirrors and multicoloured reflective plastic and shiny tinsel and foil. By the roadside, schoolboys in shorts with satchels over their shoulders crowded around stalls selling old-fashioned ice cream. A line of women in white headscarves with papers in their hands stood patiently in the sun outside some kind of administrative office with small, grubby infants pressed to the tails of their long skirts. Groups of policemen in blue short-sleeved shirts sat on rickety chairs outside their station house drinking sweet *masala* tea beside squatting prisoners in irons. Beside the whitewashed gates of a barrack block, soldiers in starched khaki stood beside an old cannon and a hand-painted regimental crest. The army, of course, was still in power, though no one seemed particularly bothered. There was little evidence of any profound unrest but then there was little indication of any greater general prosperity either. Between the towns the road ran through open fields, past wasteland, quarries, brick kilns served by children in rags and tracks that led nowhere or to small villages or to both. Smoke rose from the flat roofs of the houses set back from the highway and old tractors spluttered through the mud followed by docile oxen. The scenery alternated the green and brown of the countryside with the choked chaos of the cities until the fields disappeared and the buildings all merged into one long chain of concrete and painted hoardings and traffic and then I recognized Lahore and the magnificent red Mughal fort and mosque rising above the jumbled alleys and narrow houses of the old city and the kites flying above the scruffy parks and the broad belts of middle-class suburbs with their villas and gardens and canals in which children of the servants swam and played among the garbage.

It was wet season and there was no dust at all but puddles in the road and great bands of warm, grey rain sweeping in every afternoon.

Though when I had lived there Pakistan had not been much of a story, since 9/11 the country had lurched in and out of the fairly narrow focus of the international news media. A huge investigation had recently revealed that rogue Pakistani scientists had been selling nuclear technology – thus incidentally confirming the rumoured reasons for the amateurish surveillance of the North Korean embassy and my flat a decade earlier – and there were repeated if intermittent surges of interest in Pakistan's efforts to help capture bin Laden and al-Zawahiri, both probably hiding in the tribal badlands along the country's northwestern border. In the aftermath of the London bombings it was the religious schools in Pakistan, the medressas, that suddenly interested everybody. By the time I reached Lahore a dozen Western reporters had already visited two such 'terrorist training schools' where the bombers had allegedly stayed. One was a small, very conservative medressa in the centre of the city. The other was a large, more modern complex at Muridke, which I knew was the headquarters of one of the most violent Pakistani militant groups. Both schools, predictably, denied any link with the London plot and there was little hard evidence, beyond dubious leaks from Pakistani intelligence organizations, that proved otherwise. One of the bombers appeared to have spent the winter with relatives not far from Chak 100P, the village where I had once investigated the murder of Muradam Mai, the supposed witch. There was a picture of another passing through Karachi airport and reports of a meeting in a mosque in the industrial city of Faisalabad but details were unclear. Before a fortnight was out, the world's interest in Pakistan rapidly began to ebb once again.

There was one man I wanted to see, Javed Parachar, the conservative tribal chief, cleric and lawyer who ran a number of medressas up in North-West Frontier Province and who had spoken to me years earlier about 'justice' and 'moral corruption'. I rang him from Lahore and he boomed a welcome down the crackling line, telling me to visit him at his home in the town of

Kohat after he had led Friday prayers in his local mosque. I drove back to Islamabad and then took the long straight road southwest across a high plateau of fertile fields, a continuation of the rich agricultural lands of the Punjab region, and down to the river Indus, swollen with meltwater from the Karakoram mountains to the north and turned to the colour of caramel by silt. Beyond an old British-built bridge was the thin band of the North-West Frontier Province, the thinner band of tribal territory where Pakistani troops were sweeping for bin Laden and then the mountains and Afghanistan.

We crossed the river and I realized immediately that I had forgotten quite how raw and bleak the province was. The dust in the air meant the hills were barely distinguishable in the haze on the horizon. We passed a man with no legs sitting beside the road in the sun. He was watching a child fill in potholes with gravel in the hope that a few rupees might be dropped by way of reward from the occasional passing car. Along either side of the road were cracked rocks, tough-looking sharp-leaved cacti and straight eucalyptus with papery bark peeling away to reveal smooth wood underneath, yellowed like old candle wax. Every other tree had been hacked at or burned down for wood. Goats, some of them going up on hind legs to reach the lower leaves of trees and spiny bushes, were tethered to stakes. We passed through a short and narrow gorge blasted through a ridge made up of bands of white, yellow and red rock and came out beside a small mosque, little more than a whitewashed baked-mud hut, with a man lying on a rope bed outside holding a green shiny nylon flag. He was collecting alms. Then there were the high-walled houses of the frontier with turrets and gunslits and cakes of manure with handprints on them stuck to their walls to dry and cut thorny branches laid over small haystacks to protect them against goats. The cakes of manure were for use as fuel. We passed a graveyard with silver tinsel decorating lopsided but carefully carved headstones and a herd of thin cows grazing in a sudden bright green patch of maize planted in irrigated soil. The road surface disappeared, washed away, my taxi driver said, by a flood two years ago and not repaired since. Near a deserted, rusting petrol station whose sign improbably offered 'phone/fax/email', a dozen men were sitting in the shade of a tree around a small radio on a chair.

Kohat itself had more life than its hinterland. Parachar's directions – 'ask anyone where I live, they all know me' – proved optimistic and we were quickly snarled up in traffic in the middle of the main bazaar. I got out and walked through the butchers' stalls with their hanging sides of beef and offal, lungs and kidneys and tripe, laid out like an anatomical display on slabs of wood, and through the vegetable sellers' barrows of mangoes, peaches, yellow pumpkins and ginger roots still covered in earth. The alleys of the market were hung over by sackcloth awnings full of holes through which shone straight shafts of light full of dust. There were a few women in full head-to-toe burkas. I went on, tripping over hooped wooden cages on the ground containing chickens and fighting cocks, and through the stalls selling huge earthenware pots and finally out into a small courtyard and then down a passageway to Parachar's rambling house.

The electricity was down and Parachar was sprawled bulkily on a rope bed. He greeted me in his heavily accented English and asked if I had any children yet and made a joke about the virility-inducing water in Kohat. We spoke for a while about his work on the 'international jihad co-ordination council' which, he said, worked for 'unity between Sunni groups, resolved problems with local Shias, took care of welfare, health, scholarships for children, grants for poor ladies so they could be married'. And fighting the Americans in Afghanistan too? I asked. Parachar smiled. 'Is it possible if you are sleeping with your wife and children in a room and someone comes in with a gun you are not telling them to go and defending yourself?'

The conversation followed a predictable course. Yes, Parachar had worked to free 'hundreds' of prisoners, including a dozen or so British 'mujahideen' held in Pakistan. Yes, the 9/11 attacks were 'a good action' and so were those in London. Why? Because 'they are killing our wives, our children, ourselves'. Parachar was a lawyer and it showed. 'Is there any law in Abu Ghraib?' he said,

pausing dramatically between sentences and waving a finger at me.
'Is there any law in Fallujah? Is there any law in Bosnia, Kashmir,
Bethlehem, Chechnya? Is not Tony Blair killing thousands of
people in Iraq? Is there not a clash of civilizations?'

'Is there a clash of civilizations?' I asked.

'Of course, there is a clash of civilizations,' he replied. 'It has all
been engineered by the Jews. Islam is a religion of peace but the
Jews manipulate everything. They are creating differences between
people. Jews are the enemies of humans and the enemy of all
religious people.'

'Have you ever met a Jew?'

Parachar laughed. 'No,' he replied.

'In Afghanistan, it doesn't look like the Taliban have much
support,' I said.

'The Taliban are totally alive and very active. They are supported
by all the Afghans,' he answered, hawking sputum into a copper
pot. 'They are the best of Muslims. The best Muslims ever. I have
500 students in the schools I run who all support the Taliban.'

'Can I visit the schools?'

'No. There would be a problem with your security. They do
not like foreigners.'

'But I used to get on very well with the Taliban. They looked
after me once in Kandahar. And I visited your medressas when I
was last here.'

'Times have changed.'

'Last time I was here, you spoke to me of moral corruption,' I
said.

'Yes, yes,' Parachar nodded. 'It is coming everywhere. We are
fighting against it. It is coming by satellite TV and internet where
there are programmes made by the Jews and America to destroy
the ummah and the nations of Muslims.'

'What about honour killings?'

'It is a problem in the more modern areas that are exposed to
vices. When the moral corruption comes we have the problems.
But our punishments control the crime.'

Two boys in their early teens joined us. They were Parachar's sons. A servant brought sweet mixed tea and sponge cakes coated in pink icing and flakes of coconut.

'What do you think of these "moderate" Muslims?' I asked.

'Islam is peace, Islam is justice. Islam is the Taliban and nothing else.'

I had had enough. I felt a wash of the anger I had felt in London rising in me once again. Once I had thought Parachar an interesting exotic; now he sickened me. I very much wanted to leave. I stood up to go and noticed a little girl in a red shalwar kameez embroidered with sequins who was watching me and the cakes shyly from the doorway. It was Parachar's daughter. He called her over and she skipped to him, held his hand and rested her head on his shoulder.

In Urdu, I asked her what her name was.

'Khadija,' she said. The name of the prophet Mohammed's first strong, independent and capable wife and the first person to convert to Islam.

'How old are you?'

'Don't know. Four.'

'I am called Jason.'

'Shayshen.'

Khadija looked at her father, who nodded encouragement, and then walked quickly over to me and held my hand very tightly with a look of great concentration and then smiled.

On the way back from Kohat I thought about how my reaction to Parachar had changed. It was hardly difficult to work out why I felt so differently about him. Five or so years earlier his views had been repellent but had not seemed any personal threat to me. Parachar, high in the hills of the North-West Frontier Province, had seemed very, very distant. It was now evident that to have considered Parachar no concern of mine had been a mistake. The London bombings had made it abundantly clear that in the first decade of the twenty-first century the world was simply too small a place for ideas and acts anywhere to be safely ignored. The planet was simply too closely connected for anywhere to be 'distant'. The rhetoric and activities of Parachar and those like him, as well as the poverty, the frustration, the sense of injustice and humiliation, the corruption and the myriad local problems that fuelled the spread of his violent and hate-filled ideology, was as much my problem as anyone else's and to pretend otherwise was wrong and dangerous. It was no longer possible for anyone to be just an observer.

Almost paradoxically, however, it was that growing closeness that lay at the root of much of what Parachar thought and said. Everything he did, it occurred to me as I bounced back over the rutted road, across the bridge over the surging brown river, past the sleepy guards and up on to the plateau, was aimed at maintaining distance, at blocking the growing cohesion and interconnectivity of the modern world. This, he clearly felt, was essential if he was to keep things unchanged, or at least ensure that any change would be on his terms. For him, like so many other conservatives and militants in the Islamic world, modernity defined as the package of values and systems that together composed 'the West' meant 'moral corruption' and a personal threat. It meant uncertainty and chaos and an end to his power and his way of life. Decreasing distance between people and communities meant that ideas could penetrate societies, influence huge numbers of people and bring change in a way that could not be controlled. If there were to be change, he clearly felt, then it should not be imposed by someone else but be managed carefully and selectively by him or men like him. This was not a conclusion that Parachar had arrived at after careful consideration, it was something he knew instinctively. And it was something that the hundreds of children in his schools, too poor to go anywhere else, were learning.

And then I saw that the key to the London bombings lay in this increasingly interconnected nature of the contemporary world too. I had seen them as incomprehensible because they had targeted exactly what I considered most likely to be of most benefit to most people both in the Islamic world and to Muslim communities in the West, and was something I myself valued most highly: tolerance and an absence of prejudice and an absence of distance. The London attacks had been at King's Cross, Edgware Road, Aldgate

East and in Tavistock Square, each among the most cosmopolitan places in one of the most cosmopolitan cities on earth. Tavistock Square, full of tourists and students at the major universities near by; Edgware Road, the heterogeneous heart of the city's Arab population; Aldgate East, one of the biggest Pakistani and Bangladeshi areas, and King's Cross, one of the greatest melting pots in the world. And as they had detonated their bombs, the last sight that the young men would have seen would have been a train carriage or a bus full of individuals, all of different races and religions, all, through the myriad tiny compromises demanded by an open, modern, successful society, getting on together and, through their coexistence, thriving. And that, I realized, was, for the bombers, not a hopeful vision of something good and worthwhile and positive but a nightmare. For them too, as for Parachar, Western society did not mean freedom, opportunity and progress but had come to mean the dissolution of identity, chaos, incertitude and loss. And their violence had an aim beyond mere destruction. What motivated the London bombers was what had motivated al-Zarqawi and his brutal videos and bin Laden and all the other militants, whether they knew it or said it explicitly or not. By sowing fear and anger among victims, by forcing witnesses to choose between support and opposition, by creating complicity among perpetrators and their sympathizers, by creating solidarity among those who have been attacked, the militants' violence aimed to build walls where they were breaking down, create difference where difference was disappearing, maintain distance where people were coming together. The aim was to hold back, stall or otherwise manage change and the mixing of people and races and religions by polarizing the world into antagonistic blocks.

Back in Islamabad I wrote and filed my story and walked down to one of the markets to find something to eat. It was a Friday night. Back home friends were out celebrating a birthday. I made a few phone calls, left a few messages and had a not very good dinner at what once had been a good restaurant. It had been a profoundly depressing day. I suddenly felt very tired, tired of the bigotry, the small-minded narrowness, the myths, the ignorance, the casual recourse to violence, the hate and the prejudice, tired of the flicker of anxiety I now found I felt despite myself when I heard the call to prayer. I bought some dried fruit from a stall and chewed on gritty fibrous figs as I walked back to the guesthouse where I was staying. The wind that always followed the afternoon's monsoon downpour picked up as I walked and whipped dirt into my eyes.

At the guesthouse there was a message waiting for me. It was from Ershad Mahmud, a Pakistani journalist, academic and friend who had called to ask if I wanted to go to the Bari Imam shrine on the outskirts of the city the next evening. I had seen Ershad a few days earlier at his office in central Islamabad and had told him that I not been to the shrine since the *urs*, the festival that I had seen seven years previously, and was curious to see what had changed. He had remembered and was offering to drive me over to it the next evening.

Ershad picked me up in his battered tiny car late the next afternoon. Security barriers now blocked access to the diplomatic quarter so we took a long detour on a narrow road through the gorse bushes and scrubby trees around the outskirts of Islamabad. Ershad had once been a very devout young man but marriage, children and a friendship with a Western academic who had helped him in his career had changed his views. Though he now slightly self-consciously described himself as 'liberal', he was still a man of deep faith for whom religion was important in a very profound way. 'I suddenly found that the religious books I was reading all said the same thing,' he explained to me as we drove, 'and as I got older I learned a little more about the world.' Ershad brought me up to date on what had been happening at the Bari Imam shrine. There was little good news. Drug traffickers had finally killed the cleric at the shrine a few weeks before, putting an end to his long campaign to end the sale of heroin in the local villages. Worse still, a suicide bomber in the middle of the shrine in the spring had killed dozens of worshippers. The bomber was linked to one of the groups that Javed Parachar was suspected of being involved with. I told Ershad about my interview the day before. He shook his head and said nothing.

We parked and walked up the track past Nurpur, the village adjacent to the shrine. It was still a jumble of single-storey brick and concrete houses with tin roofs divided by muddy paths. Tangled electrical cables and dozens of television aerials hung from rusting poles. There were oxen in the big pond and children diving from their backs into the muddy water. Behind the village the dark wooded slopes of the Margalla hills rose up as steeply as I remembered and I could hear the monkeys hooting in the trees.

Ershad wrote a weekly column in his newspaper and, when we had spoken earlier in the week, he had asked me about the causes of the London bombing. I had explained some of my ideas, pointing out how the war in Iraq had crystallized so many disparate resentments, speaking of the problems between older generations of immigrants in Britain and their children. The bombers had placed a globalized Islamic identity above any kind of British identity, I said, and that that must have been one of the critical factors in how they had managed to get to the point of seeing a trainload of commuters as an enemy. We had spoken for several hours and I asked him what he had eventually written.

'I wrote that an English journalist friend had come to see me who had lived in Pakistan and who was a friend of this country and I said that this time I had seen him he was a bit changed,' Ershad said. 'He was a bit sad and a bit angry because of the 7/7 tragedy and because he had seen death in his own town. And I said that he had asked me one question which I could not answer. He asked why millions of people demonstrated against the war in Iraq but you did not see one demonstration in a Muslim country against terrorism. I had no answer.'

I smiled. The comment about the demonstrations had been an off-the-cuff remark that I had completely forgotten. It was not entirely fair but I had evidently said it with some heat. Just before meeting Ershad that day I had been reading letters in Pakistani newspapers which had said that the London bombings were the work of the British government, the Israelis or the CIA and they had revived my anger at the moral evasion and intellectual cowardice of those everywhere, particularly those in the UK who did not have the excuse of ignorance, who sought refuge in such dangerous conspiracy theories.

'You really wrote that?' I said, slapping at a mosquito. An old woman on her way to the shrine jostled me out of the way. We walked slowly towards the shrine and stood under the huge banyan tree watching the steady flow of worshippers around the small chamber, glittering with mirrors, where the tomb of Bari Imam lay.

'Yes,' said Ershad, 'and I said that I knew that Muslims might say that I was naive or stupid and that the West are imperialists and coming to get the oil only and Muslim peoples' resources and I know that partly they were right but I said that, just because there are a few bad apples, the whole barrel is not bad.

'Actually, Jason,' Ershad continued, his slim hands suddenly animated, bunching into fists and then opening and carving the air in front of him. 'There is a very interesting argument among Muslims now about what to do so I wanted to make a point. So I also said that whenever I read the life of the prophet I am drawn to different conclusions and that I have met many Christians and they are as good religious people as any Muslims. I said too that I have read the Koran and the Bible and they both say the same thing. And I said that we Muslims have a mixed history. A bad history and a good history and we should follow the good history. It is our responsibility and not enough Muslim people are saying that. And I said that the Christians and the secular people and the Jews should recognize that they too have a bad history and a good history too.'

Ershad noticed that I was scribbling in my notebook and laughed and carried on talking.

'I tried to propose that Muslims should form an alliance with these people in the West who oppose injustice and that there were many of them and that we need to have a discourse and a dialogue with Christians and Jews and all people who are against violence, but that there are some people who do not want that dialogue to happen at all and they will go all out to stop it however they can,' he said. 'So now I will wait and see what sort of response there is from the readers.'

So we stood there talking and then walked on through the compound of the shrine, circling through the broad dirt yard where the tents were pitched during the *urs* itself, back past the gate where I noticed the scars in the uneven tarmac of the road from where the suicide bomber had killed himself, past where free rice was being distributed to the poor. I thought back over all the militants I had known or interviewed – the Taliban, the people I had known in Pakistan, Didar the football-loving suicide bomber in Suleimaniyah, Abu Mujahed in Baghdad, the Shia militiamen of Najaf, the men in the prisons in Kashmir and in Kandahar, all the others. There was no single rule governing why the various strands of 'Islamic' radical ideology had worked for them. The path each one had followed had been different. Some had sought a solution to what they saw as social and economic injustices, some wanted revenge for a perceived or real injury or humiliation, some merely wanted friends or self-respect or adventure. Others wanted to fight what they saw as the occupation of their homeland. Some had clearly been brutal, hardened and angry men from the start, people who just enjoyed the sense of power that harming others brought. Others merely wanted to demonstrate their faith in the most extreme way possible. Some understood that their acts were part of a carefully calibrated political programme. Most believed that they would be lauded by their communities as heroes. A few did not care what their peers thought. For a long time I had been trying to find some kind of general theory that would unlock the secret of 'Islamic militancy' and I suddenly realized that it was impossible to do so. There was no single answer. Indeed the point was that there was no single answer.

And I thought about all those others, the thousands of people I had spoken to, sat next to, eaten with and travelled with over the previous years. I thought about the Kurds back in 1991, of Majid Khan, the young Yorkshireman who was exactly the same age as the leader of the London bombers and who had spoken of his pride at the sight of the Bari Imam shrine and then hidden his prayers from me seven years before; I thought of Ekram laughing at a bad joke I had just made as we drove through a bad bit of country near Kabul and I thought of all those in Afghanistan striving to eke a living out of a harsh land, of the refugees dying of cold in their school that evening in 2001, the Therapoetic Feeding Centre in Kandahar, the schoolgirls in the playground in Jalalabad and their proud teachers, the fighters on all the various front lines, most of whom were just infantrymen like infantrymen have always been in all armies in all ages; I thought again of Mohammed Sekkoum and his family in north London and in Algiers, and of Iraqis like the old man who had sheltered us in Najaf or the woman with her two disabled children in Baghdad and the man who ripped the flyleaf from the dictionary he sold me in the book market which I still had on my shelves at home in London and of all the people simply caught in the middle of bombs and war and politics whose voices are drowned out by the fighters and the shouting of those on every side who are full of fire and righteousness and rage and intolerance. And I realized that not only was there no general theory about militancy but there was no general theory that could explain 'the Islamic world' and that to search for one was not only futile but in fact counter-productive. It was doing exactly what the men of violence wanted. It was drawing lines around people, designating them as part of one bloc or another, deciding that instead of being tall, small, fat, thin, old, young, literate, illiterate, a man, a woman, childless, with children, employed, unemployed, healthy, ill, they were Muslims or non-Muslims and that this almost entirely arbitrary distinction was how people could be divided and subdivided and divided once again and communities defined. By its very nature the only things that could define 'violent Muslim radicalism' were 'Islam' and 'violence'. The definition was a circular argument that would lead inevitably to the simple conclusion that the two are inherently connected. In fact the violence that confronted us was a profoundly complicated contemporary phenomenon with roots in cultural, political and economic developments and the interaction between individuals, groups, nations and societies around the world over centuries. And, as it was meant to do, the violence confronted us with a choice of great importance. In the aftermath of the bombs, as in the wake of the executions and the honour killings and the videotaped murders, we could seek to emphasize division or its opposite. And if the London bombings had taught me anything it was that to gather people together, whether hundreds of millions of people across huge swathes of the planet or fifty people in a Tube carriage, and demarcate and label them and designate them simply as one thing or another, as enemies or friends, as Western or Eastern, as Muslims or non-Muslims, as believers or non-believers, is something no one should ever do. And if my travels during the previous years had taught me anything, it was that to emphasize the differences when there is so much that binds, to emphasize the divisions when so much is the same, to emphasize the distance when there is so much that is increasingly close, is not just dangerous but is wrong.

Ershad and I spoke for a long time. As we talked I sensed that the optimism I had felt before the London attack would return, perhaps not immediately, but soon. Around us the crowd at the shrine began to thin a little and only a couple of pairs of shoes were left in the dust outside the marble steps leading down to the saint's tomb. The shutters were coming down on the stalls around the car park that sold fried curried potatoes wrapped in newspaper and pink and green bangles for a rupee each and a small boy in ragged clothes tugged at my shirtsleeve and then ran off laughing. There was a smell of old cooking oil and wood smoke from the village and of the recent rain. The lights came on first in the distance over the city and then closer in the village and then long looping strings of multicoloured bulbs flickered into life above the gates of the shrine and very soon it was almost dark and we walked away.

A Guide to Further Reading

This list is in no way comprehensive. Its aim, not unlike that of the book, is to suggest and to provoke, not to offer a single 'off the shelf' conclusion. So what follows is simply a list of books that might be useful, interesting and enjoyable. It is partial, in every sense of the word.

I have avoided a classic bibliography for various reasons. First, it would have been out of keeping with the rest of the book, in which I have tried to avoid the academic and the inaccessible. Second, compiling a comprehensive list of all the books, articles or other works that I have read, skimmed or otherwise consulted over a period of several years of interest in Islam, militancy and foreign affairs would be impossible, as I have left half of them in hotels, on planes or in cars, or I have given them away. Third, even if it were possible, such a list would be of little practical value, as most readers simply do not have the time to work their way through piles of specialized books. And, finally, to recommend books that have given pleasure is in itself one of the joys of life, so to reduce the exercise to one of purely practical value is a great shame.

Instead, I have picked a number of books which have particularly influenced my own analysis, which I have particularly enjoyed or which I think might provide an interesting insight for anyone who wants to pursue some of the ideas that I have sketched out over previous pages in more depth.

One such idea, for which sadly I appear to have been unable to find space in the preceding 110,000 words, is the influence of myth – and longstanding traditions of representation – in constructing identities and the framing of policy. I hope therefore that Karen Armstrong's *Holy War: The Crusades and their Impact on the Modern World* (Random House, 2001) and Andrew Wheatcroft's *Infidels*

(Viking, 2003) will, to some extent, fill the gap for me. Armstrong's analysis of the extent to which European identities were formed by the Crusades as well as her profound knowledge and her broad vision (her books on Mohammed and Islam are both excellent general introductions) makes what is sometimes a fairly heavy read very much worthwhile. Wheatcroft's book is erudite, exciting and astonishingly perceptive. Rashid Khalidi's *Resurrecting Empire* (IB Tauris, 2004) takes as its basic premise the important idea that the West has an infinitesimally small memory span especially concerning the Middle East and explores the consequences of that failure rapidly and intelligently. Fred Halliday's *100 Myths about the Middle East* (Saqi Books, 2005) brilliantly deconstructs many of the so-called 'givens' about the region.

Malise Ruthven is one of the most original and intelligent writers about modern radical Islam, and his *A Fury for God* (Granta, 2002) is a highly readable and profoundly informed cultural and intellectual history of radical Islam that is packed with brilliant ideas. Ruthven's more recent work, *Fundamentalisms* (OUP, 2004), is a magnificent, scholarly comparative analysis of various fundamentalisms around the world and is particularly good on the common elements shared by such movements.

And, remaining in the realm of the broad historical and conceptual contexts of radical Islam, *Occidentalism*, by Ian Buruma and Avishai Margalit (Penguin, 2005), draws on an astonishing range of references (from Japan in the 1930s to the pre-biblical Middle East) to explore the reaction to the arrival of 'Western modernity' around the world over the last two centuries. As this is a personal list of books I will include two books by European critical theorists, Jean Baudrillard's *The Spirit of Terrorism* (Verso, 2002) and Slavoj Zizek's *Welcome to the Desert of the Real* (Verso, 2002). Do not read them expecting a coherent analysis of radical Islam, Islam or in fact a coherent analysis of anything much, but do expect some amazing ideas.

There are now of course many hundred works on 'al-Qaeda' and Osama bin Laden, including my own. These range from the atrocious, full of unsourced, plagiarized, ideologically tilted, fabricated rubbish, often written by people who have no experience whatsoever of the people or countries about which they are writing, to the extremely good. As most readers now have basic working knowledge of 'al-Qaeda' and 'radical Islam' I would suggest going straight to the primary sources themselves. Sayyid Qutb's *Milestones* (American Trust Publications, 1990), the ur-text of modern militant Islam, is available and is short and easily digested. To give it some modern context, Montassar al-Zayat's *The road to al-Qaeda* (Pluto Press, 2003), the personal history of a radical Egyptian lawyer involved in activism, is useful. The words of bin Laden himself have now been helpfully compiled in *Messages to the World*, edited by Bruce Lawrence (Verso, 2005). Peter Bergen's *The Osama bin Laden I know* (Simon and Schuster, 2005) is a very useful oral history put together by an excellent American journalist. *Voices of Terror*, edited by Walter Laqueur (Sourcebooks Inc., 2004) places modern Islamic militancy in its historic context, as merely another of the various waves of such activism over centuries, and is full of interesting original documents ranging from the statements of Jewish sectarians fighting the Romans to tracts by Russian anarchists. Also useful for a general perspective is the concise and beautifully executed *Terrorism: A Very Short Introduction*, by Charles Townshend (OUP, 2003).

There are of course a huge number of publications on Islam generally and Islamism more specifically. Concentrating on the latter, Gilles Keppel's magisterial *Jihad: The Trail of Political Islam* (IB Tauris, 2002) provides a very useful overview. *Knowing the Enemy*, by Mary Habeck (Yale University Press, 2005) is an excellent concise guide to the ideology of radical Islam. There is also the analysis of Olivier Roy, a French political scientist who is reasoned, undogmatic and intelligent, and always worth reading, even if in English his recent work is marred by poor translation. I'm not even going to start recommending books on Israel–Palestine or individual works on Iraq, Afghanistan, Pakistan or elsewhere. There are simply too many and they are too varied. There are travel books or journalistic memoirs which are astonishingly knowledgeable and there are academic treatises that are exciting and well-written. There are many works that are neither.

I have also found that reading around the topic of Islam and radical militancy has provided useful historical perspectives. Eric Hobsbawm's classic *Primitive Rebels* (Manchester University Press, 1959) is interesting; a number of books on nineteenth-century anarchists have been helpful; *The Coming of the Third Reich* by Richard J. Evans (Allen Lane, 2004), on the appeal of Nazism, and Philip Knightley's *The First Casualty* (André Deutsch, 2003), on the uses and abuses of propaganda in war, are both relevant. I found Robert Harvey's *Comrades*, on the rise and fall of world communism (John Murray, 2003), to be a useful, if somewhat slanted, overview of left-wing ideologies and their appeal.

Finally, there is a huge amount of fiction that is of enormous relevance and importance and often ignored. Among recent works my favourite is Amin Maalouf's *Balthasar's Odyssey* (Vintage, 2003), which I read in Baghdad in the summer of 2004. It is a superbly written, wry, amusing, intelligent story about tolerance, intolerance, religious fanaticism, violence and love 500 years ago, which has a message that is clearly and deliberately contemporary. Writing in late 2005 Amos Oz, the Israeli author, spoke of how literature, and the ability to imagine other cultures, people and sensibilities, helped him understand his world and contemporary history. The imaginative effort of reading fiction, as much as the knowledge of others that books can bring, helped, Oz wrote, bridge gaps in perception that otherwise yawn wide. He was right.

Paris, February 2006

Glossary

Al-Haramain: the holy places of Mecca and Medina.

Al-Qaeda: an Arabic word with a number of meanings, including 'the base', 'the methodology', 'the support', 'the law', 'the maxim'. Most famously, the name, or the function, of a group set up by Osama bin Laden and a small number of associates in 1988 or 1989 in Pakistan.

Amir (or **emir**): one who commands, a prince or a military commander, one who has authority in any given situation. Often used to refer to the leader of an Islamic group.

Amir-ul-Momineen: 'commander of the faithful'. Title of the caliph. Used by Mullah Omar, leader of the Taliban.

Ayatollah: 'sign of god'. Title of high-ranking Shia religious leader.

Ba'athism: a radical, secular, quasi-socialist Arab nationalist ideology. Origins in the late 1930s and early 1940s. The name comes from the Arabic word for 'renaissance'. Iraq, until the fall of Saddam Hussein, was nominally a Ba'athist regime.

Barelvi: school of Islam dominant in Pakistan, relatively tolerant and mystic.

Caliph: from Arabic 'khalifa', successor or viceroy, refers to political and spiritual leader of the world community of Muslims, the successor of the prophet Mohammed, God's viceroy on earth.

Caliphate: lands ruled by a caliph, originally from Medina. Later from Baghdad and Cairo. The Ottoman caliphate, the most recent, was ended in 1924 through the creation of Turkey.

Da'wa: literally 'call' or 'invitation'; effort by pious Muslims to convince non-Muslims to accept Islam and Muslims to live more religiously.

Deobandi: conservative school of Islam. founded in India but subsequently split into Indian and Afghan-Pakistani strands.

Fatwa (plural **fatawa**): a legal opinion given on a religious question by a recognized scholastic authority that is binding.

Fitna: strife, sedition, literally 'ordeal'; infighting among political factions with ideological differences, such as in the time after the death of the prophet.

Hadith: the traditions of the prophet, including his habits and the sayings attributed to him. Not revealed but very important in establishing the shari'a, especially for Sunni Muslims.

Haj: the pilgrimage to Mecca, one of the five 'pillars of Islam', which all Muslims should perform within their lifetime.

Halal: permitted under Islamic law.

Haram: forbidden by Islamic law.

Hijra: literally 'migration'; refers most often to the journey of the prophet Mohammed to Medina with the early Muslims in 622 BC to escape persecution in Mecca. A similar migration is a duty for all Muslims who are unable to practise their faith freely. A key concept for militants.

Ijtihad: the process of interpretive reasoning as applied to the core Islamic texts. Comes from the same root as 'jihad', thus the implication that it is the 'effort' to understand.

Islamists: Muslims who aim to establish a pure (i.e. reformed) Islamic society through the appropriation through activism of modern state structures.

Jahilliyya: barbarism and ignorance that preceded the coming of Islam in Arabia.

Jihad: effort, struggle, a legitimate war. A much-debated term with many different meanings at different times. Not one of the five pillars of the Islamic faith. 'The Jihad' usually refers to the war against the Soviets in Afghanistan. There are two forms of jihad. There is the greater jihad, the personal struggle to resist temptation and to live life according to the shariat, and the lesser jihad, a violent struggle against unbelievers or aggressors. The latter is divided into two further categories, the offensive and the defensive jihad. The latter is an obligation on all believers.

Jihadi/Jihadist: preferring the violence of jihad as a tactic to the non-violence of dawa, social or political activism

Kafir, kufr: unbeliever, unbelief; one who rejects the truth despite being shown it.

The Maghreb: literally 'Western' in Arabic; means land west of the Nile and north of the Sahara.

Mecca: city in current Saudi Arabia where the shrine of the Kaaba is located, where Mohammed the prophet was born and where the haj pilgrimage takes place. Holiest site in islam.

Medina: literally 'the city'. Specifically, the city to which Mohammed fled when persecuted in Mecca.

Medressa: religious school, college.

Mullah: a local religious leader or functionary, usually in southwest Asia. In some parts of the Middle East a term of respect for a religious scholar.

Munafiq (Plural **munafiqeen**): hypocrites. Those who perform the outward signs of Islam but do not have faith. Originally those in Medina who recognized the prophet Mohammed's authority but worked against him. Used by militants to describe Muslim rulers such as Hosni Mubarak of Egypt, the house of al-Saud, etc.

Muslim: one who submits to God; from the Arabic *alama*, 'to surrender', 'to seek peace'.

Muhajiroun: literally 'the migrants'. Those who followed the prophet on his migration from Mecca to Medina.

Mujahideen: those who struggle or fight.

Salaf: 'the righteous ancestors', the first generations of the Muslim community. In the modern sense, those activists (salafists) who believe that Muslims should strive to return, in a very literal sense, society to the state it was at the time of the Salaf. Wahhabis are salafist.

Salat: ritual compulsory prayer.

Shahadah: the testament of faith. 'There is no god but Allah and Mohammed is His prophet'.

Shahid (plural **shahuda**): martyr, witness.

Sharia: the right path, the behavioural guidelines that all Muslims should live by, the Holy law of Islam, as compiled and codified by the great Muslim jurists of the eighth and ninth centuries.

Sheikh: head of a tribe or religious order, especially Sufi.

Shia: party or faction, those Muslims who believe Mohammed designated his son–in–law Ali and his rightful descendants to be the true leaders of the umma. Between 10 and 15 per cent of world Muslims.

Sufi: a mystic tradition within Islam. Name thought to derive from rough woolclothing (*suf*) worn by early ascetics. Individuals commit to their own path to enlightenment under the tutelage of a master but have historically been grouped into 'associations'. Sufism is often described as an 'inward' journey complementing the shariat or 'outward' law. A chief vector of the expansion of early Islam.

Sunni: majority of Muslims, often called 'orthodox'.

Talib (plural **taliban**): student, literally 'seeker (of knowledge)'.

Ummah: the Islamic nation or community of all believers.

Wahhabism: rigorous and conservative doctrine of the followers of ibn Abdul al-Wahhab, a puritanical eighteenth-century Arabian preacher.

Zakat: gift of a percentage of all wealth donated by Muslims for distribution to the poor. One of the five pillars of Islam.

Acknowledgements

Happily, I have many, many people to thank. Sadly, there are far too many to mention each individually by name. There are, of course, my colleagues at the *Observer*: the editor, Roger Alton; executives such as Paul Webster, John Mulholland, Allan Jenkins, Tracy McVeigh and many reporters too. I am also grateful to many other senior people on Fleet Street who have helped me and taught me an enormous amount. Then there are also dozens of colleagues, both in the British media and overseas, who have been such good company so often in so many different places. To those who have read the drafts of this book I owe a special debt. And of course there are the scores of people, drivers, translators and fixers who have worked with me, so patiently and so competently so often.

I must mention my agent, Toby Eady, and my editor, Simon Winder (and his team at Penguin). Without their knowledge, professionalism and energy, this book simply would not exist.

My first book was dedicated to Sam and Sidney, my grandparents. This one is dedicated to my parents, Jeffrey and Tessa. It is a very small measure of appreciation for everything they have given me over the years. For their love, and that shown to me by all my friends, by my grandmother and by my brothers and sisters, I am more grateful than words can ever express.

Paris, January 2006

Index of Places

Abu Ghraib, Iraq 222, 271
Aceh, Indonesia 259
Adhamiyah, Baghdad 237
Afghanistan 41–77, 116–52, 154, 165, 174–5, 249–57, 272, 280
al-Mouradiya, Algiers 107–8
Algeria 106–15, 122, 153, 174, 263
Algiers, Algeria 106–9, 113
Amu Darya river 43
Arbil, Iraq 157, 164, 169, 179, 190, 194–6, 200–202
Ariana Square, Kabul 150

Baghdad, Iraq 39, 64, 81–4, 89, 93–4, 196–224, 233–43
Bagram air base, Afghanistan 140–48, 218
Balad, Iraq 218
Baluchistan, Pakistan 35
Bamiyan, Afghanistan 149
Bandipur, Kashmir 247
Bangkok, Thailand 258
Bari Imam, Islamabad 23–8, 34, 276–8
Basra, Iraq 89–92, 149, 235
Bazarak, Afghanistan 72–3

Camp Victory, Baghdad 217
Cappadocia 2

Chak 100P, India 28–34, 77, 115, 269
Chamchamal, Iraq 167, 196
Cholistan desert, Punjab 29

Damascus, Syria 156
Darunta, Afghanistan 126
Delhi, India 245–6
Dohuk, Iraq 4, 162
Dushanbe, Tajikistan 69–71

Egypt 263–4

Fallujah, Iraq 208, 209, 214, 222
Farm Hadda, Afghanistan 68, 126–7

Gardez, Afghanistan 130, 132, 149–50
Gaza Strip 95–9, 101–2, 105, 106, 122, 262
Ghazni, Afghanistan 47, 149
Great Zab river 158

Hadda, Afghanistan 137
Hakkari, Turkey 2
Halabjah, Iraq 8, 17, 174–8, 199–200
Handpur Kaloney, Pakistan 25

Herat, Afghanistan 53–4, 165
Hindu Kush, Pakistan 43, 116–28

India 14, 23, 36–7, 245
Indonesia 257, 261, 263
Indus River 270
Iran 2, 86–7, 180–81, 212
Iraq 1–12, 17–19, 79–94,
   156–241, 261–2, 265, 277
Ishkashim, Afghanistan 73
Islamabad, Pakistan 21–3, 26,
   37–9, 123, 267–76
Israel 88, 96–8, 102, 104–5, 120
Istanbul, Turkey 193

Jalalabad, Afghanistan 61–7,
   123–7, 132, 136–7, 150
Jerusalem, Israel 96, 98–9
Jordan 206, 209

Kabul, Afghanistan 41–6, 53–6,
   73–6, 128–37, 149–51, 243,
   253
Kabylie, Algeria 112
Kandahar, Afghanistan 46–57,
   127, 137, 146, 180–82, 253–4
Karakoram mountains 35, 270
Karbala, Iraq 209, 214, 222
Kashmir 35–6, 40, 245–9
Khazer, Iraq 200
Khost, Afghanistan 132–4, 150
Khyber Pass, Pakistan 61–2,
   116–17, 122, 124–5
Kirkuk, Iraq 166–7, 196, 201–2,
   205
Kohat, Pakistan 38, 270, 271

Kurdistan (Iraq) 3–12, 17–19, 85,
   156–88, 195
Kuwait 1, 92

Lahore, Pakistan 27, 169, 268–9
Lake Dal, India 244
Lake Dokan, Iraq 7, 158, 166
Landi Kotal, Pakistan 124
Lesser Zab river, Iraq 6
London, United Kingdom 265–7,
   273–5, 281

Machmur, Iraq 201
Mahmudiyah, Iraq 222–3, 231
Maidan Shah, Afghanistan 44
Malaysia 259, 263
Margalla Hills, Pakistan 277
Masada, Israel 102
Mazar-e-Sharif, Afghanistan
   122–3
Mecca, Saudi Arabia 26, 36, 49,
   64, 66
Medina, Saudi Arabia 64
Milawa valley, Afghanistan 137
Mosul, Iraq 163, 202, 205
Muridke, Pakistan 269

Najaf, Iraq 209, 214, 222–31,
   235, 240, 261
Nepal 259
Netzarim Junction, Gaza Strip 97,
   99
New Delhi, India 33
North-West Frontier, Pakistan 3,
   165, 269–70, 273
Nurpur, Pakistan 277

Occupied Territories (Israel)
95–105
Oxus river 43

Pakistan 21–40, 58–65, 77–9, 109,
116–25, 165–74, 249, 267–77
Paktia, Afghanistan 131
Paktika, Afghanistan 131
Pamir mountains 70
Panjshir valley, Afghanistan 69,
71–2
Pattani, Thailand 257, 259
Peshawar, Pakistan 38, 58–62, 68,
116–31, 169
Philippines 153, 259
Punjab, India 28–9, 270

Qala Diza, Iraq 7–8, 156–63
Qalat, Afghanistan 48

Rafah, Gaza strip 99, 100
Rahim Yar Khan, Pakistan 29
Ramallah, West Bank 96–8
Russia 153

Sadr City, Baghdad 208–9, 214,
235
Salahadin, Iraq 161
Samarkand, Uzbekistan 69
Sangesar, Afghanistan 255–6, 257
Saudi Arabia 16, 59, 64, 120,
167–70
Shatt al-Arab waterway 91
Shlef, Algeria 112–13
Shomali plains, Afghanistan 43,
123, 140

Silopi, Turkey 193–4
Sopore, Kashmir 247
Spin Ghar mountains 63, 136
Srinagar, Kashmir 245–8
Suleimaniyah, Iraq 8–10, 157,
160, 165–72, 179, 184, 195,
202
Suso, Thailand 257–9
Syria 156, 212

Tajikistan 43, 69
Tashkent, Uzbekistan 69
Tel Aviv, Israel 99
Thailand 255–9
Tigris river 82, 157, 203, 207,
216, 218
Tikrit, Iraq 87, 202–5, 215,
216–20
Tora Bora, Afghanistan 136–8,
151
Torkham, Pakistan 62, 124
Turkey 2–4, 10, 19, 135–6, 167

United Kingdom 184–5
United States of America 14–16,
118–27, 135, 142, 185, 266
Uzbekistan 43, 69, 153

Van, Turkey 2
Vietnam 143–4

West Bank 96, 98, 101, 102

Zagros mountains 166
Zakho, Iraq 10–11, 19
Zamangar Square, Kabul 75